Dear Reader:

The book you are about to read is the latest bestseller from the St. Martin's True Crime Library, the imprint the *New York Times* calls "the leader in true crime!" Each month, we offer you a fascinating account of the latest, most sensational crime that has captured the national attention. St. Martin's is the publisher of perennial bestselling true crime author Jack Olsen (SON and DOC) whose SALT OF THE EARTH is the true story of how one woman fought and triumphed over life-shattering violence; Joseph Wambaugh called it "powerful and absorbing." DEATH OF A LITTLE PRINCESS recounts the investigation into the horrifying murder of child beauty queen JonBenét Ramsey; the author is Carlton Smith. Peter Meyer tells how a teenage love pact turned deadly in BLIND LOVE: *The True Story of the Texas Cadet Murders*. Fannie Weinstein and Melinda Wilson tell the story of a beautiful honors student who was lured into the dark world of sex for hire in THE COED CALL GIRL MURDER.

St. Martin's True Crime Library gives you the stories *behind* the headlines. Our authors take you right to the scene of the crime and into the minds of the most notorious murderers to show you what really makes them tick. St. Martin's True Crime Library paperbacks are better than the most terrifying thriller, because it's all true! The next time you want a crackling good read, make sure it's got the St. Martin's True Crime Library logo on the spine—you'll be up all night!

Charles E. Spicer, Jr.
Senior Editor, St. Martin's True Crime Library

A GRUESOME DISCOVERY

As she walked past the family room she noticed her father's feet on the couch. The television was on, and she figured he had fallen asleep. Later, retracing her steps for homicide detectives, she said that after phoning her boyfriend she went into the kitchen to get a snack when she noticed a trail of blood on the floor.

"And then, that's when I saw my mom. I saw my mom. She was lying there and then I . . . I ran into the living room to see what my dad was doing," she said.

"He wasn't asleep. . . . "

St. Martin's Paperbacks Titles by Clifford L. Linedecker

THE MAN WHO KILLED BOYS

NIGHT STALKER

KILLER KIDS

MASSACRE AT WACO, TEXAS

DEADLY WHITE FEMALE

POISONED VOWS

DEATH OF A MODEL

SMOOTH OPERATOR

THE VAMPIRE KILLERS

THE
VAMPIRE KILLERS

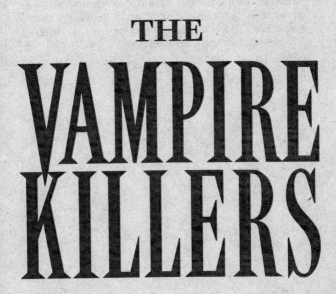

CLIFFORD L. LINEDECKER

St. Martin's Paperbacks

THE VAMPIRE KILLERS

Copyright © 1998 by Clifford L. Linedecker.

Cover photographs of people courtesy Sygma. Background cover photograph by Clifford L. Linedecker.

ISBN: 0-312-96672-5

Printed in the United States of America

St. Martin's Paperbacks edition / October 1998

St. Martin's Paperbacks are published by St. Martin's Press, 175 Fifth Avenue, New York, N.Y. 10010.

10 9 8 7 6 5 4 3 2

In fond memory of my friend, the late Dr. Stephen Kaplan, founder and director of the Vampire Research Center.

ACKNOWLEDGMENTS

Books do not write themselves, and they are not produced without the help and cooperation of many people working in concert with the individual finally credited as the author. Some of the people and organizations or agencies who gave of their time to help make this book a reality and to whom I owe a debt of gratitude include:

Jim Mahanes, lead singer for "Trippin' Lizard," and reporter for the *Ledger & Times* in Murray, Kentucky; the friendly folks at the State Library of Louisiana in Baton Rouge; the staff of the Eustis Library for their courtesy and ready assistance to a stranger; Sheriff's Captain Christopher Drinan of the Lake County Detention Center; and to all the other people in Lake County, Florida, and Calloway County, Kentucky, who were so helpful to me in compiling information for this book.

Special thanks are due to my agent, Tony Seidl of T. D. Media; and to my editor, Charles Spicer at St. Martin's Press.

CONTENTS

INTRODUCTION

Vampires have become hauntingly fashionable.

They're the superheroes of the 1990s; sensual lovers surrounded with a romantic aura of danger, and mysterious beings with superhuman powers. For the most part, based on contemporary depictions in literature and film, they long ago lost the ugly, rotting corpse–like appearance and grave stink of Max Schreck's portrayal of a vampire in the 1922 silent film, *Nosferatu*. Today's fictional vampires are more likely to have the urbane romanticism and darkly erotic glamour of a George Hamilton or a Tom Cruise.

For the most part they are creatures who are irresistible to women or attractive to men; the kind of lover many people wouldn't mind sharing a passionate interlude with—or a little blood.

One of the nicest things about them is that despite the aura of erotic danger, they're perfectly safe because everyone knows they don't really exist. They're no more real than gnomes, or trolls or the scary giant who lived at the top of Jack's magical beanstalk and ate little boys. Or are they?

To many Americans today, and to other people around the world, vampires are as real as a timber rattler or a black widow spider. A few years ago, Dr. Stephen Kaplan of the Vampire Research Center in Elmhurst, New York, launched the first vampire census of North America. Then, and in succeeding years, he interviewed scores of men and women who were convinced that they were real vampires who were dependent on blood for survival. The first census turned up twenty-one people, most of them married with children and regular jobs. But some of them slept in coffins and drank human or animal blood. He talked to one beautiful blonde who appeared to be in her twenties, but was actually in her sixties and traded sex for blood, which she collected by making tiny incisions in the flesh of her donors with a scalpel. Blood, the researcher concluded, greatly slowed the aging processes.

Kaplan and others learned that a thriving vampire underground exists in America. They have their own support networks, publications, Internet contacts and E-mail addresses which they use to keep in touch, swap information and set up meetings between blood drinkers and voluntary blood donors. Hundreds of women contacted Kaplan to sign on as volunteer donors in return for meetings or dates with vampires.

Vampires can be very sensual, very sexual. And they can be very dangerous, indeed, even when they're not the real thing. Many of the people Kaplan talked to and corresponded with during his activities as founder and director of the VRC he later described as "kooks, crazies, oddballs and blood cultists," who sought blood as a psychological manifestation. But they were not true vampires who drank blood as part of a physiological need.

The kooks, cultists and other pseudo-vampires are the most dangerous, and they can be every bit as sinister, depraved and ruthlessly savage as their fictional counterparts while prowling city streets, trolling highways and lurking in the darkened byways of college campuses to seek out prey for ghastly blood feasts. They're a ghastly mix of Satanists, whacked-out druggies, twisted loners and counterfeit vampires turned on by fantasies of power, kinky sex, or both.

Ironically, "the Sunshine State" seems to attract more than its fair share of vampires—both real and imagined. One of Dr. Kaplan's yearly enumerations disclosed that Florida and Illinois were tied for sixth place for the most vampires counted, with fourteen each. For awhile, Miami was said to have a clandestine vampire bar where blood was mixed in with the vodka and tomato juice for Bloody Marys with a real bite to them. More ominously, a Winter Park lawyer from a prominent family of attorneys was arrested a few years ago after two beautiful young women filed separate complaints that he lured them to his room at a local Holiday Inn, drugged them, then filled syringes with his own blood and squirted it on them. The vampire lawyer was a heavy cocaine user, and eventually entered into a plea agreement on drug charges. He was sentenced to a four-and-a-half-year prison term.

The area near the central Florida city that is internationally famous as the home of the Orlando Magic and Disney World has more trouble with vampires than with giant mice. John Crutchley was a math genius with a master's degree in engineering who developed a computer language for the Navy and once held security clearance at the Pentagon before he earned a nickname among law enforcement agencies and the press as Florida's vampire rapist. He was sentenced to prison for abducting a nineteen-year-old hitch-hiker from California and holding her prisoner at his home in Malabar, near the Kennedy Space Center, while raping her and guzzling nearly half her blood. She escaped through a window while he was at work, and staggered down a road, handcuffed and naked until she was rescued. He told her, "I'm drinking your blood; I'm a vampire," she reported to police.

When Crutchley was released on parole in 1996 after serving nearly eleven years of a twenty-five-year sentence for sexual battery and kidnapping, he was accepted at an Orlando halfway house. Residents of the Malabar and Melbourne area, and of his former hometown in Clarksburg, West Virginia, rejected efforts to settle him in either of those communities. But he didn't stay very long in Orlando. Shortly after protests by outraged neighbors and the Orange County sheriff, he was ordered to spend the rest of his life in prison for parole violation. He had tested positive for marijuana during a urinalysis, and told police he had inhaled it at a going-away party the night before he was released from the Union Correctional Institute in Raiford.

A few weeks after Crutchley was paroled to the halfway house, a band of teenagers who were fascinated with blood and the so-called "undead" made international headlines when they became the object of a multi-state dragnet as suspects in the ghastly murder of a quiet, hard-working middle-aged couple in central Florida, only a few minutes' drive northwest of Orlando. The fugitives were four teenagers from western Kentucky said to have banded together as the nucleus of a vampire clan—and the fifteen-year-old daughter of the murder victims.

This is their story, recounted as faithfully as I can tell it. There are no made-up names, and all conversation and quotes are taken from interviews, court records or published news accounts. The only license the author has taken is presentation of some of the courtroom activity slightly out of chronological order. That was done in order to smooth out the narrative and make the story more readable.

"Listen to them—
the children of the night.
What music they make."
—Bram Stoker
Dracula

"If they're bossy enough to take two people's lives,
then they could've just as easily taken my little
old life. . . . I would have had no defense against a
crowbar or whatever it was."
—Jennifer Wendorf
statement to homicide investigators
December 9, 1996

PROLOGUE

Murray, Kentucky
Wednesday, October 16, 1996

Darla Speed knew something was seriously wrong the moment she stopped her car to open the chain-link gate at the Murray–Calloway County Animal Shelter and was greeted by about thirty dogs running loose.

It was a typical, crisp mid-October morning, but it wasn't the low sixty-degree temperatures that chilled the shelter director. Overnight, someone had cut a hole in the chain-link fence on the east side of the compound, and tried unsuccessfully to break into the building by removing a window panel. The intruder failed to get inside the building, but had propped open the kennel doors, releasing forty dogs into the enclosure surrounding the compound and allowing them to escape through the hole in the fence. Only two dogs were still locked up inside their individual kennels, and ten of those freed were either carried away or had wandered into nearby woods or residential Murray neighborhoods. The shelter was at the end of a gravel road known as Sycamore Street Extended, and was quiet and isolated.

The dogs were milling around the shelter, many of them frightened, their tails tucked between their legs. Several of the dogs were bruised and showed signs of having been beaten. A couple of mixed-breed black Labrador retriever puppies from a litter dropped off at the shelter a few days earlier had suffered a much more gruesome fate.

Deputies from the Calloway County Sheriff's Department in Murray, dispatched to investigate the vandalism at the shelter just outside the southern city limits, discovered the broken bodies of the fifteen-pound puppies in a field a short distance east of the enclosure. One of the puppies had been stomped to death and its crushed body was lying at the center of a circle of tall grass that was flattened as if some strange ritualistic dance had been performed there. The legs were ripped off of the other dog and, along with other body parts, were apparently carried away by the killers.

Mutilation and killing of the puppies was a gruesome, frightening act, and one of the most disturbing aspects of the perplexing atrocity was the possibility that the abuse and loss of life might have been even worse. "After seeing what they did to these puppies, I'm grateful they weren't able to get inside where the cats are kept," the shaken shelter director told a local newspaper reporter.

While the county dog catcher began looking for the missing animals, news spread through the southwestern Kentucky community about the horror at the shelter. Local residents were appalled and frightened. It seemed that anyone who was vicious enough to focus such a savage attack on a pair of defenseless puppies might not be satisfied with mutilating animals the next time they were driven to satisfy their bloodlust. The next time the victims might be human, possibly children.

Sheriff Stan Scott, a lawman with twelve years' experience on the department, was one of those who was concerned by the perplexing crime and the possibility that it might be the precursor of more serious violations. Calloway County was a fine place to live but, like other American communities, it wasn't untouched by crime. Most of the problems that Scott and his small force of seven full-time deputies and four part-timers were called on to deal with involved traffic violations, domestic quarrels, assaults, burglaries or minor thefts. On a few occasions, sheriff's officers and their colleagues with the Murray Police Department were even called on to investigate armed robberies and homicides.

The shelter break-in and mutilation of the puppies was altogether different from the types of crimes Murray law enforcement agencies were used to dealing with, however, and it raised troubling implications that there were some kind of ritualistic killers or blood cult at work in Calloway County. "We're dealing with some sick individuals and I want them caught," the sheriff declared. He theorized that as many as four people were involved, and the puppy killings might be "related to some kind of cult activity."

Then Scott and his deputies began talking to people, trying to figure out what was going on. Most of the people they talked with were local teenagers.

1. JENNIFER

A few minutes before 8 p.m., Jennifer Lynn Wendorf began preparing to wind up her shift as a cashier at the Publix Supermarket in Mount Dora, balancing out her cash register and turning over the cash drawer to the night supervisor.

It was a typically comfortable, cool mid-autumn central Florida evening when the pretty teenager walked to the parking lot, slid gratefully into the driver's seat inside her shiny 1996 candy-apple-red Saturn convertible and backed out of the space. The car the high school senior drove was an early graduation gift from her parents, Richard and Naoma Ruth Wendorf. They were planning to present a similar gift to their younger daughter, Heather Ann, when she celebrated her sixteenth birthday early the following year.

The Wendorfs were proud of both their girls. Their vivacious oldest daughter was a good student who played a prominent role in extracurricular activities at her high school and had already been accepted for enrollment at Florida State University in Tallahassee. Their fifteen-year-old was a high school sophomore, and although she seemed to be experiencing the throes of some teenage rebellion, she was already showing promise as an artist and had proven to possess diverse musical skills. She played piano, oboe and the xylophone—all exceptionally well.

It had been a long day but before returning to her home in rural northeastern Lake County, Jennifer had one more stop to make. She drove to the apartment of her boyfriend, Tony Stoothoff, on Northland Road in Mount Dora a few blocks from the supermarket. The seemingly casual decision to visit her boyfriend would later acquire alarming significance.

Some time later, after promising to telephone and let Stoothoff know she had arrived safely at home, Jennifer finally scooted back into the driver's seat of her convertible and began the twenty-minute drive. There was still plenty of time for a chat with her parents before turning in and getting some sleep so she could arise early and prepare for school Tuesday morning. Jennifer was one of the most popular girls at Eustis High School, where she was a senior, a pep rally leader and co-captain of the varsity cheerleading team that supported "the Panthers" when they played football or basketball against teams from Mount Dora, Leesburg, Tavares and other area schools.

The cheerleaders were close friends on and off the sidelines where they leaped and tumbled during games, and they often teamed up to shop, hang out, and attend frequent slumber parties. More than half the time Jennifer was the party organizer and they were held at her house.

Although she worked in Mount Dora, a quaintly bucolic community of about seven thousand people, one of a scattering of small towns clustered so close together that they share common borders, or are separated by no more than a five- or ten-minute drive, she and her sister attended school in Eustis. With a population of about ten thousand, Eustis was only slightly larger than Mount Dora and was a couple of miles' drive north along State Road 437, then seven or eight miles west on State Road 44, from the Wendorf home on Greentree Lane. Conveniently for the sisters, Eustis High was just a couple of blocks off Orange Avenue (SR 44) on the east edge of town.

One of the main reasons the senior Wendorfs scrimped and saved until they were able to buy the five-acre plot of land, then build their home in the development of new brick and wood houses eight years earlier, was because of their concern for the welfare of their daughters. Space, privacy and the opportunity to insulate the girls from the rapidly expanding metropolitan sprawl that surrounded their previous home in Orlando, about thirty miles to the southeast, were important factors in the decision to relocate the family in the quiet little residential development, where they could avoid all the urban problems and social ills that went along with living in or near a major population center.

Richard and Naoma Wendorf also liked plenty of walking-around room and the house was constructed with 3,129 square feet of floor space, including a screened-in porch area and an outdoor pool. The single-story "L"-shaped brick house was designed with separate bedrooms in the northwest wing for each of the girls. Jennifer's bedroom was on the northwest corner and Heather's was next to it, to the east. Heather's name was prominently displayed on the door of her room. The rooms of the two sisters were joined by a hallway that led to the rear bathroom and the family room on the west side of the house. The master bedroom was at the opposite end of the house, separated from the girls' rooms by the family room, breakfast nook, kitchen, dining room and living room. The arrangements afforded maximum privacy for the teenagers, and for their parents.

Richard and Naoma Wendorf enjoyed indulging their daughters, and each of the sisters had her own telephone, and a television set with a videocassette recorder. The main reason Naoma worked as a volunteer at the school was because she wanted to be closer to her daughters.

Jennifer's thoughts may have flickered briefly toward concern for her younger sister when she pulled her convertible to a stop, climbed outside and walked into the garage, then moved into the house through the laundry room entrance. Heather was creating serious problems within the family, and during a chat with her mother earlier in the day, Jennifer had suggested calling a family conference that night to discuss how the trouble should be handled.

The mother and daughter had talked earlier that afternoon after Mrs. Wendorf drove from the school to Stoothoff's home in the Eudora Apartments. Mrs. Wendorf worked from 7:30 a.m. to 1 p.m. as a volunteer in the high school office during school days, and she had wanted to talk to Jennifer about her reasons for skipping Monday classes to spend the day with Tony. The discussion soon turned to Heather. Jennifer suggested during the mother–daughter chat that her little sister might merely be going through a phase. "I don't think it's a phase," Mrs. Wendorf replied. "She's been up in my face lately."

But Jennifer also had other things on her mind when she walked into the house. She had promised to telephone Tony to let him know she was safely home and say goodnight. As she walked past the family room she noticed her father's feet on the couch. The television was on, and she figured he had fallen asleep. Later, retracing her steps for homicide detectives, she said that after phoning her boyfriend she went into the kitchen to get a snack when she noticed a trail of blood on the floor.

"And then, that's when I saw my mom. I saw my mom. She was lying there and then I . . . I ran to the living room to see what my dad was doing," she said.

"He wasn't asleep."

Belinda North was working the late shift at the Florida Regional Medical Emergency Service in Mount Dora when she logged a call at almost exactly 10:30. Ms. North was an experienced professional, who was trained to handle emergencies and to keep her cool under pressure—even when fielding a call from someone like the agitated young woman who was on the other end of the line.

911: Where is your emergency?

CALLER: My emergency is in Eustis, Florida, 24135 Greentree Lane. I need two ambulances. My mother and my father have just been killed. I just walked in the door. I don't know what happened. They are dead.

911: Both of them, ma'am?

CALLER: Excuse me?

911: Both your mother and your father? They are not breathing at all?

CALLER: I don't know. I didn't check. I can't get that close; they're my parents.

911: Is anybody there with you, ma'am?

CALLER: I have no idea. I don't know who is in the house. I have no . . . I, I . . . hang on, there's somebody on the other line.

911: Hello, ma'am?

CALLER: Hello.

911: Yes, ma'am.

CALLER: OK.

911: All right, ma'am, what's your first name?

CALLER: My name is Jennifer. My last name is Wendorf.

911: What makes you think that they have been killed?

JENNIFER: There is blood everywhere. Please, as fast as you can . . .

911: OK, we're on the way. We have law enforcement on the way also. Are you there alone?

JENNIFER: I have no idea. There could be somebody in the house.

911: I mean, nobody came there with you?

JENNIFER: Who?

911: Nobody is there with you?

JENNIFER: My sister is gone, though. I don't know where my sister is. She's gone.

911: What do you mean? She lives there with your parents?

JENNIFER: She should be here. She's only fifteen years old. And she's gone.
(Jennifer gives the dispatcher directions to the house.)

911: All right, ma'am, what I would like you to do is get out of the house and sit outside in your car, OK?

JENNIFER: OK.

911: If you're not sure if anybody is still in the house. You can't tell anything's going . . . When you tell me there's blood everywhere, you mean like on the floor, on the walls?

JENNIFER: Yes, yes.

911: The floor?

JENNIFER: My mom is [garbled]. I can't go in there. I'm just afraid to leave my room, to leave my sister's room.

911: OK, that's when you came in the front door and went straight into your sister's room?

JENNIFER: I walked in the front door and I didn't really pay attention, but I thought my dad was sleeping. Then I went and called my boyfriend to tell him I was home. Then I came back in and I saw blood. Then I ran into the kitchen. My mom was in there. Then I ran to the couch and my dad was there. There was blood everywhere.

911: So your mother's in the kitchen and your father's in the living room? OK, we're on the other line with the law enforcement. We're going to make sure law enforcement is en route out there, OK?

JENNIFER: OK. And my sister's gone, and the Explorer's gone.
(Pause)

911: I want you to stay on the phone with me, OK? You don't have a portable phone, do you?

JENNIFER: No.

911: You're in your sister's bedroom?

JENNIFER: Yes.

911: OK. Is there a way you can lock your door, your bedroom door?

JENNIFER: They won't, they won't lock.

911: OK, you can't lock the bedroom door? OK.

JENNIFER: Would it be all right if I called somebody, like my grandparents?

911: No, no, you stay on the phone with me. I don't want to tie up the line, OK?

JENNIFER: OK.

911: In case there's somebody else in the house, I want you to be in contact with me. . . . Have you touched anything in the house?

JENNIFER: No. Just the phone.

911: OK. Just bear with me. . . . What's your sister's name, Hon?

JENNIFER: Heather.

911: Your sister's name is Heather?

JENNIFER: Yes.

911: And what's her last name?

JENNIFER: Wendorf.

911: You don't happen to know the tag number on your father's Explorer, do you?

JENNIFER: I know the first three letters are P-U-U. And it's an electric-blue Explorer, a 1994 model.

911: Your last name is Wendorf, also? We're giving this information to law enforcement on the other line. . . . And what was the first letters on the tag?

JENNIFER: P-U-U.

911: What was the last time you heard from your parents and your sister?

JENNIFER: Last time I heard from my dad was last night. The last time I heard from my mom was today at my boyfriend's house, and that was around 3 p.m., and then I haven't heard from my sister since this morning.

911: So the last time you talked to your mom was about 3 o'clock this afternoon?

JENNIFER: Yes.

911: Is the front door to the house open?

JENNIFER: I have no idea. I . . .

911: Well, when you came in, did you lock it behind you?

JENNIFER: No. I came in through the laundry door, and it is unlocked.

911: OK. And where is the laundry door? Is that a rear door to the house?

JENNIFER: It's kind of off to the side and it goes to the garage.

911: Do you have to go into the garage to get through there?

JENNIFER: Yes.

911: And is the garage door up?

JENNIFER: Yes.

911: OK.

JENNIFER: No, no, no, the garage door is not up. My mom's van is outside. The garage door is not up. There's a main door right to the left of the garage door.

911: I'll tell them to go to that door. That's a side door off the garage?

JENNIFER: Yes.

911: I'm going to stay here with you. OK, Jennifer?

JENNIFER: Yes.

911: OK, I don't want you to feel like you're here by yourself.

JENNIFER: Yes. . . . (near whisper) Can I go check to see if my parents are even alive?

911: Pardon?

JENNIFER: Can I go check to see if my parents are even alive?

911: Do you feel comfortable going up there to do that?

JENNIFER: I don't know. I worry for them, but I don't know how long it's going to be until . . .

911: Well, it shouldn't be too long before we get there.

JENNIFER: (Unintelligible) OK, I'll try to stay calm.

911: That's all right, you're going great. You're doing great.

JENNIFER: I don't, ma'am, I don't even know your name, but I . . .

911: My name is Belinda.

JENNIFER: Belinda, I've seen these things on TV, and I know the things that can happen. But, I can't believe . . . Oh, my gosh. . . . Do you know about how long when they're going to get here?

911: Well, let me see. Hold on just a second. . . .

JENNIFER: I'm so sorry. I'm sorry, I . . .

911: Well, you're doing fine, Jennifer, you're doing fine. OK, the sheriff's department is right in front of the ambulance, and they are just a few minutes away. So I'm going to let you know when they're there so you can . . . (To a dispatcher:) Tell them, tell me, what's the notes . . . where to go to enter, because she don't know the front door's unlocked. I think my notes tell them to go to the side door . . . (To Jennifer:) OK, I have an ambulance on the scene. Now, they're going to wait for law enforcement to go in. That's our procedure.

JENNIFER: Can I go outside now?

911: Well, I want you to wait and make sure law enforcement's there, then I want you to go out and I want you to let them know where you're going to be coming through at. (To a dispatcher:) See if law enforcement's on-scene and she'll step out. (To Jennifer:) We don't want you to be going through any . . .

JENNIFER: Well, the ambulance is out there, aren't they? Someone needs to get in here.

911: They're on-scene. . . . OK, if you want to step out the side door. I told them to go to the side door.

JENNIFER: I'm just going to lay the phone down.

911: (To a dispatcher:) She's going to go step out to the side door. Tell them not to be startled by her. No, she doesn't see them, but she hears them out there.

Nine-and-a-half minutes after the dispatcher answered the teenager's desperate call, Lake County sheriff's deputies and an ambulance crew pulled their vehicles to a stop in front of the house. Then they stepped into a scene of grisly horror.

2. HEATHER

"Lizzie Borden took an axe
And gave her mother forty whacks.
When she saw what she had done,
She gave her father forty-one."
          —*Children's ditty*

Fears for the safety of Jennifer's missing younger sister, Heather, were uppermost in the minds of friends and family members as word of the gruesome discovery at the Wendorf home began to filter through the neighborhood and the larger community.

Heather was missing from the home, along with her father's trusty 1994 powder-blue Ford Explorer. Lake County Sheriff's Department homicide investigators didn't know if Heather had been kidnapped or become a third murder victim of the mystery killer, or if there was some other explanation for her ominous disappearance.

Jennifer met the emergency rescue team and police officers near the back door of the house and she was safe—but it was too late for her parents.

The body of forty-nine-year-old Richard James Wendorf was sprawled face-up on the family room couch in front of a television set, exactly where his distraught older daughter had told the dispatcher it was. His face and head had been battered into a mass of shattered bone, tissue and blood.

Naoma Wendorf's body, clothed in a blue bathrobe, was face-down on the floor of the kitchen, with her head just inside the entrance to the dining room. The head and upper

body of the fifty-three-year-old homemaker were surrounded
by blood. Two separate sets of bloody footprints were
starkly visible on the floor of the kitchen, a hallway and a
bathroom.

The family's white poodle crouched protectively on a
throw rug next to Mrs. Wendorf's body, nervously growling
whenever anyone tried to get too close. It was several
minutes before investigators were able to lure the agitated
pet away from the corpse of its mistress. The Wendorfs'
other dog, a handsome golden retriever, was also seriously
spooked, and roaming around outside the house, alternately
whining and barking at the rapidly growing clutter of men
and vehicles. Eventually the confused animal lay down between a couple of parked LCSD squad cars, continuing to
whine and nervously lifting its head whenever police officers
walked in or out of the house.

Preliminary inspection of the bodies indicated that both
husband and wife were killed by blows to the head with a
heavy, hard, sharp instrument such as a tire tool, hatchet,
claw-hammer or crowbar—and possibly also struck with "a
sharp, chopping kitchen utensil." Investigators couldn't immediately identify the exact murder weapons. A more
closely accurate description of the type of tool used by the
killer would be determined later after further investigation,
including a more thorough inspection of the injuries. No
bloodstained implements likely to have inflicted the injuries
were found near either of the bodies.

Whatever the instruments were, they were as brutally effective as a Viking battleaxe or a fourteenth-century mace.
Areas of the neatly kept home were so splattered with blood
that it looked like a slaughterhouse. Richard Wendorf's forehead was caved in by a blow that had crashed through tissue
and bone, and ripped into the frontal lobes of his brain.
Naoma Wendorf's skull was also battered, but most of her
injuries were to the top and back of her head, indicating that
she had been struck from behind. Her head and hair were
smeared and matted with clots of blood, chunks of torn pink
brain tissue and shredded bone. The floor and nearby walls

were splattered and crimson with gore. There was a disturbing aura of insanity about the murders. It was a case of overkill, of unnecessary viciousness. The savagery, and sheer rage or glee by a killer who gloried in the pain, fear and power of the act hung over the scene.

The pattern of the bloody footprints, the location of Mrs. Wendorf's injuries and the position of her body indicated that she may have been chased from the family room by someone who caught up with her in the kitchen after her husband's murder. Investigators found additional footprints outside the south side of the house. Both sets of the outdoor prints matched those found on the inside. One set of footprints was marked by a heavy lug-boot pattern, and the other with a familiar zig-zag design common to tennis shoes. Each of the shoe prints, inside and outside the house, was photographed after rulers or metal tapes were laid nearby to provide a reliable reference of the size.

The Wendorfs weren't dead for very long before their bodies were discovered, probably about an hour or a little more, based on the temperature of their skin, the lividity and the absence of rigor mortis.

The moment their hearts stopped beating and their systems shut down, blood began settling into the lower levels of their bodies. After the breakdown of the hemoglobin, the blood vessel walls and surrounding tissue were stained, leaving the outer flesh mottled with an ugly purple and an overall pink flush. Their eyes were blank, appearing as dry and gritty in their sockets as if they'd been sandpapered; at the moment of death, the tissues had begun to lose their moisture, to harden and flatten. If eyes are truly mirrors to the soul, the mirrors were broken. They were devoid of the spark and shock that might have revealed the images of horror they had seen. The initial stages of rigor mortis wouldn't become noticeable for a few hours, however, when the process would begin with the freezing of small muscles, including those in the face, as a result of the cessation of blood flow, the interruption of their energy supply and the coagulation of protein.

For the time being the bodies were allowed to lie where they were, silent, cold and slowly stiffening while strangers traipsed through the couple's house, poking through the accumulations and detritus of their lives. Sober-faced men with handguns strapped to their waists or carried in shoulder holsters opened doors, peered into closets and looked through medicine cabinets, meticulously examining every room while recording their observations with notepads and cameras. Outside the house, other officers stretched yellow crime-scene tape and erected floodlights.

Inspection of the front door turned up indications that it may have been forced open. The three bedrooms in the house also showed signs of having been ransacked. Some drawers were open, and two drawers in a nightstand in the master bedroom had been pulled out and dumped.

Except for the slight disarray in the bedrooms, the two dead bodies and the blood, the interior of the rest of the house was surprisingly neat. It was as orderly as a household could be that included two adults, a couple of active, healthy teenagers and two dogs. Furnishings weren't lavish, but it was obvious that the home had been decorated with an eye for taste and comfort. Naoma Wendorf had created a home for her family that was less a showpiece than an inviting refuge to be lived in and enjoyed. Rooms were filled with knickknacks, keepsakes and photographs collected over the nearly twenty years the couple had lived together as husband and wife. Pictures or other mementos of their girls were in nearly every room.

The reminders of middle-class American family life and respectability that existed throughout the home provided a pathetic contrast to the dreadful carnage that had occurred there. The house the couple had worked so hard and faithfully to make into a comfortable home and sanctuary for their family had been invaded and forever soiled. Concerns of investigators, however, were on matters other than the decor.

Lake County sheriff's detectives and crime scene technicians had barely begun their investigation, and before they

were finished, few, if any, Wendorf family secrets would be
left undisturbed. Rigor mortis would come and go long before the strangers were finished sifting through their lives.
The stiffness goes away about twelve to thirty-six hours after
it sets in, when the proteins in the muscles begin to decom-
pose. The intruders working to unravel the mystery of the
twin murders were likely to continue their necessary snoop-
ing into the lives of the victims for weeks or months, perhaps
longer than that.

Even the privacy of Richard and Naoma's bodies would
be invaded. Bone saws and razor-sharp scalpels would be
used to slice open their skulls to permit close-up examinations of the terrible damage done to their brains. Scalpels
would also slice through tissue to permit pathologists to peel
apart the flesh and muscle of their abdomens and chests, then
reach inside to remove samples of partially digested food,
and blood, tissue, bile and urine. It was all part of the effort
that would be made to solve the mystery surrounding their
violent deaths.

Before anything inside the house was moved, a forensics
photographer recorded everything on videotape. The bodies
were photographed from different angles, with long-range
shots taken to show their position in relationship to other
features of the rooms, and with close-ups that zoomed in to
focus on the blood and bone and mangled flesh.

Careful measurements were also taken by crime scene
technicians to show the exact position of the bodies. Blood
spots were marked, and samples were carefully stored in
vials, tagged and labeled with the date and the exact location
in the house where they were collected. There was a lot of
blood to work with. The floor and walls of the kitchen were
pooled and splattered with gore, and more blood, ranging
from thick smears to tiny specks, was found in the family
room, the dining room, Heather's room and in one of the
bathrooms. Furniture, including an end table, was also
blood-smeared.

As early as it was in the investigation, there was every
reason to believe that blood and the secrets it could reveal

would play a key role in the murder trial that might occur
in the future. Blood was everywhere, some of it already
dried or drying. It didn't matter if the blood was dry, con-
gealing or still fresh and viscous. Forensic scientists can
work with dried blood as well as with fresh blood, and with
a glassful or a drop barely big enough to cover the tip of a
fingernail.

O.J. Simpson prosecutor Marcia Clark once won a murder
case when she and other investigators didn't even have a
body to work with. The only physical evidence they had
was a single spot of blood found under the rear passenger
seat of a car driven by the defendant. Collecting blood samples from relatives of the presumed victim, she used DNA
comparisons to prove that the spot of blood found in the car
came from the missing man. It was almost a certain bet that
the revolutionary genetic fingerprinting technique utilizing
DNA (deoxyribonucleic acid) and its complex molecular
patterns would also play an important role in the Wendorf
case if and when the suspected killer(s) came to trial.

DNA typing and its use as a forensics tool to help solve
crimes and convict or clear suspects was first used successfully by police to solve a serial rape–murder case in England, but its first use in a criminal trial in this country
occurred in Orange County, Florida, a few minutes' drive
from Eustis. A man suspected of being a serial rapist who
terrorized women in the Orlando area during a crime spree
that began in the spring of 1986 and continued into the next
year was convicted and sentenced to a long prison term,
largely on the strength of DNA evidence. In that case, semen
samples taken from the victims were compared with blood
extracted from the suspect, and he was convicted of raping
two women in separate incidents. DNA samples can be taken
from blood, semen, hair or tissue, then broken down in a
laboratory to make comparisons and pinpoint the unique genetic pattern of each individual.

Most of the investigators called to the Wendorf home had
been around violent death before, and their work was me-
thodical and coldly professional. Before they completed their

inspection of the interior of the house, they collected swabs from fifty-six separate blood stains. They also found a tooth knocked out of Richard Wendorf's mouth, and bone fragments in the dining room.

Lake County is no more violent than most semi-rural communities of its size, but murder and other forms of violent death are no strangers to local law enforcement agencies. It wasn't that blood had never been shed by deliberate violence during the area's near–110-year history as a county, or before. But few crimes had occurred in modern times to rival the horror worked on Greentree Lane. And none had become so notorious.

Initially, the Wendorf case, as it would become known when it wasn't being referred to in more dramatic, tabloid-sounding terms, stood out because of the brutality. There were other factors that made the crime stand out, as well. The Wendorfs weren't like so many people who become murder statistics because of a dangerous lifestyle or other behavior that puts them at special risk. They had nothing to do with drug trafficking or the sex business, and they didn't live in a tough, inner-city neighborhood where violence is as common as food stamps and pint bottles of "Mad Dog." Richard and Naoma Wendorf were as quietly middle-class as Ward and June Cleaver, and about as unlikely to become murder victims as anyone could be. Or so it had seemed, until something went dreadfully wrong.

Now, a virtual platoon of investigators was trying to sort out the complicated forces and events that led to the blood-bath. The seasoned investigators who spread through the house didn't carry up-to-date homicide statistics in their shirt pockets or inside their heads, but they were aware that most murder victims are killed by someone they are closely related to or associated with. That was especially true for people who were killed in their own homes.

The location of the Wendorfs' home, more than eight miles east of the nearest town, and well off heavily traveled highways such as the Florida Turnpike and Interstate Highways 75 and 95, virtually ruled out the possibility of a chance encounter. The house on Greentree Lane was too isolated for some homicidal hitch-hiker or murderous transient merely to stumble across and decide on the spur of the moment that it might be a good idea to force his way in and kill the occupants.

It was also unlikely that a professional or part-time burglar would scout out the semi-isolated home and pinpoint it for a break-in. The closest neighbors were no more than a few minutes' walk away, and several of the homes in the area—including the Wendorfs'—had dogs that were sure to raise a ruckus if strangers were lurking around. Furthermore, most professional burglars take great care to avoid breaking into houses or other buildings that are occupied, and early Monday evening the Wendorfs' home was well-lighted and there was every indication that people were moving around inside. Equally important, although the Wendorfs lived comfortable lives, there were far juicier pickings for professional burglars a few minutes' drive to the south. Several senior executives whose jobs were tied to Disney World, Universal Studios, Sea World of Florida and other tourist attractions in and around Orlando had moved into Lake County and constructed palatial multi-million-dollar homes with carports and garages that sheltered sleek Cadillacs, Lincolns, BMWs and Jaguars.

The brutal murders didn't have the imprint of casual killings. It's not easy for most people deliberately to take the life of another human being. Military leaders know that, and even during some of this country's most devastating wars, only a fraction of the soldiers on the front line actually aimed their rifles at their enemies when they fired. The rate of American soldiers who shot to kill climbed significantly when the round concentric circular targets were changed to targets resembling men. It was a matter of conditioning, and it seemed that whoever murdered the Wendorfs had conditioned himself to bloodletting.

Killing up-close by choking, stabbing or bludgeoning is even more personal and satisfying for certain killers than shooting. Those are the kind of methods favored by most serial killers, people who commit murder for pleasure, because they enjoy the feeling of power they experience by inflicting pain and fear—or because murder is part of some kind of grotesque ritual.

Nevertheless, at that stage of the investigation it was easier to rule out unlikely suspects than it was to focus on a solid candidate. It wasn't because of a lack of intriguing clues and potential evidence. The killer, or killers, left signs of their presence all over the house and in the neatly kept yard outside. The bloody footprints were the most obvious clues, but they were not the only calling cards left behind by the killers. Evidence technicians collected 133 latent fingerprints from door handles, walls, bureau drawers and other locations inside the Wendorf home, by dusting them with a special powder, then transferring them onto transparent tape to be photographed.

Several butts from different brands of cigarettes were picked up and bagged. The butts would be compared later with any cigarettes that might be collected from other sources further along in the investigation, and saliva would be submitted to laboratory analysis. Hair and other trace evidence was also collected by technicians combing the house for clues. Each item was photographed before it was moved or picked up for collection. Then investigators and evidence technicians recorded a description of the item, its condition, location, the date and time of collection.

All evidence was carefully marked to identify it, if it was possible to do so without damaging it, and/or placed in bags and other containers, which were then sealed and marked for transport to the sheriff's department headquarters in Tavares. Every step of the evidence-gathering process was systematic, and carried out according to long-standing regulations. Enormous care was taken by detectives and evidence technicians to protect the chain-of-custody, and to keep the number of people involved to a minimum. Every person who has handled any piece of evidence in an investigation may be called to testify at a trial.

The evidence technicians worked from a mobile crime lab

parked a few feet from the house. The green-and-white van was marked with the logo "SHERIFF'S OFFICE LAKE COUNTY" in big block letters, and technicians and detectives loaded evidence through the open rear doors. Some of the officers walking back and forth between the laboratory and the house were dressed the way many traditional police detectives dress in Florida while they're working outside, in dark pants and white short-sleeved shirts open at the neck. Others were dressed from head-to-toe in special white one-piece hooded suits to avoid contaminating evidence. The suits gave them the look of astronauts from the Kennedy Space Center a hundred miles or so east.

Impressions from two very different shoe prints, neither of them matching foot-sizes or shoes owned by Naoma or Richard Wendorf, or their daughters, were preserved from the bloody tracks inside the house. One of the prints was made by a lug-sole boot; the other by a tennis shoe. It would be weeks before the presence of the intriguing clues was disclosed in court documents, and even then it wasn't immediately revealed whether the shoe prints were left in dirt, mud or blood. Police also found a pair of high-top shoes on the lawn near a row of decorative bushes along the front of the house that looked as if someone had casually stepped out of them and walked away. They were marked with evidence tags stuck into the ground, to be photographed and collected by technicians—and eventually examined for traces of blood and matched against the bloody prints left inside the house.

Inside Jennifer's bedroom, the telephone had been ripped from the wall, but there was no sign there of the dreadful human carnage that had occurred in the family room and in the kitchen of the house.

When investigators moved their search into the master bedroom, it was also found to be mostly devoid of any signs of the violence that had erupted in the home. The bedroom formerly occupied by the couple was orderly, with the bed still made-up and everything in its proper place. A small porcelain figurine and a card were on the top of Richard

Wendorf's dresser. The words "Dad, Friends Forever" were etched along the base of the figurine. The card read:

> To my dad, the best father any daughter ever had.
> Love, Heather.

The loving message was poignant, but investigators were more interested in another note written by Heather that they discovered in a hall bathroom.

"I don't have much time but I must say that I love you all so very much," the note read in part. "I will be fine. Please don't try to find us." The words, "I love you all so very much," were underlined. She also wrote in the note that she had to run away so that she could look after another girl, Jeanine Monique LeClaire, who had been her best friend since the seventh grade.

There was no indication whether Heather's parents had seen the goodbye note before they were bludgeoned to death. But the neatly handwritten message left in the bathroom clearly seemed to indicate that Heather had run away from home. At that stage of the investigation, however, detectives couldn't firmly rule out the troubling possibility that someone may have coerced her into writing the note before forcibly taking her away. Worse yet, she could have been forced to write the note before becoming the third victim of the killer—or killers. The mystery of the girl's absence from the home wasn't yet totally solved, and locating her remained a top-priority matter for the sheriff's department investigators.

It was 7 p.m. Tuesday before crime scene technicians finished their initial work in the home and the last earthly remains of the couple were finally released to the Lake County Medical Examiner. The bodies had already passed into the process of rigor mortis, and the muscles and limbs were stiff, chill and sticky with their own coagulated blood, when they were at last lifted onto gurneys. The cold, inert bodies had that curious characteristic of corpses that makes them seem heavier than they really are, or would appear to be if the cold, empty husks were still occupied by a living being who was only sick or injured and able to help the lifter in subtle ways. The corpses were covered head-to-toe with sheets, and secured to the gurneys with heavy straps.

The Wendorfs left their country home for the last time as they were wheeled outside and loaded into a waiting ambulance that was parked amid a clutter of LCSD cruisers and plain cars assigned to homicide detectives and evidence technicians. Naoma Wendorf's Chevy Blazer was still parked a few feet from the house, exactly where she'd left it when she returned home for the last time the previous afternoon. The bodies were driven to the Lake County Medical Examiner's Office in nearby Tavares. Autopsies were scheduled to begin at 8 a.m. Wednesday, before the bodies were transferred to a funeral home, and family members could move on to the vitally important step in the grieving process of saying their final goodbyes. Closure, of course, was still a long way off. There was a killer, or killers, to be found. And the mystery of Heather's ominous absence was still to be cleared up.

Shortly after daylight Tuesday morning, a squad of sheriff's deputies formed a line and walked ten abreast across the front and side lawns that Richard Wendorf had tended with such meticulous care. Lake County Sheriff George E. Knupp, Jr., also ordered a helicopter to assist in the search. Here and there around the quiet neighborhood, porch lights were still burning, and at one home a woman wearing a bathrobe and hair-curlers peered curiously from behind her half-closed front door for a few moments at the activity surrounding the Wendorf home. Unconsciously, she raised one hand to her mouth, then eased the door shut.

Small, bright orange cones were posted next to a throw rug and a pair of shoes lying on the grass near the house. When the deputies completed their inspection of the five-acre property, they continued their sweep along several hundred yards of nearby Lake County Roads 437 and 439, State Road 44A and Greentree Lane. Some members of the search team rode golf carts borrowed from a nearby golf course.

The law officers were as thorough and careful, perhaps more so, as any squad of military recruits policing the yard around a barracks. Cigarette butts, minute scraps of paper or a tiny torn swatch of cloth could all be possible clues, and anything that was observed that was out of place was carefully marked and left for later attention by evidence technicians and homicide detectives.

Officers spread through the neighborhood, knocking on doors to interview residents, asking about the night of the murder, about strangers who may have been seen lurking around the neighborhood, and any other information that might help piece together the puzzle.

Gary Parker, who lived behind the Wendorf house, was working on his computer Monday night when he heard a dog barking ''like crazy'' between 9 and 10 o'clock. The barking was so agitated and prolonged that Parker asked his daughter to look outside to see if she could tell what was bothering the dog. She didn't notice anything especially alarming; just the neighbors' dog barking and looking over a hill. No one, however, reported hearing shouts, screaming or other sounds of the furious life-and-death struggle that had occurred inside their neighbors' home.

While officers were canvassing the neighborhood, some of their colleagues began interviewing acquaintances who knew members of the Wendorf family through shared work, school, church or social activities. No one knew of any enemies who might have harbored a grudge serious enough to lead to the killing of the couple. There were no indications of any quarrels with business associates, and there were no hints of any back-alley romances that might have gone astray and led to the slaughter. If there were troubles within the Wendorf union, the couple kept it to themselves.

Richard Wendorf loved the outdoors. When he was not on the job in middle management at Crown Cork & Seal, or sitting at the kitchen breakfast table studying the stock market, he was on a golf course, or mowing the lawn, trimming hedges and generally spiffing up the area. He was an organized, orderly man.

He was also a hard worker and responsible employee, who remained with the same company for twenty-three years, climbing his way up the ladder of success in the business of manufacturing metal cans and plastic containers. A few weeks before his death, he was one of the local executives who survived a corporate-management downsizing and closure of the company's plant in Plymouth, a lickspittle town of a few hundred people a half-hour drive south from his home. Wendorf was reassigned to a job as a storeroom manager and purchasing agent in the town of Winter Garden twenty miles south of Eustis at the edge of Lake Apopka. The new location added another twenty minutes to the daily commute between the family home and his job.

Richard Wendorf's twin brother, William, lived with his family in the suburban Orlando town of Winter Park, another, similar, name tied to the Sunshine State's reputation as a haven for snowbirds. The siblings, along with a younger brother, Robert, moved to Florida with their mother from Galveston, Texas, when Richard and William were thirteen years old. Robert also lived in Winter Park. The brothers were close and the twins had played golf on Monday afternoon, only a few hours before the horror of the double murder intruded into their lives with such devastating consequences. The previous Saturday Richard had played eighteen holes of golf with his father, James F. Wendorf, at the Mount Dora Golf Association. During the hours the father and son shared on the links they chatted and brought each other up to date on news about the close-knit family. About a year earlier, almost everyone in the family had attended grandfather Wendorf's wedding.

The senior Wendorf later recalled during an interview with a reporter for *The Orlando Sentinel*'s Lake County edition that he was relaxing with his son on the couch in the family room after the golf game when Jennifer burst inside after returning from work. "Did you tell him?" she asked her father. When Richard Wendorf shook his head and told her she could break the news, she proudly announced to her grandfather that she had been accepted at FSU.

The elder Wendorf was awakened late Monday night by a telephone call from a relative with the dreadful news about the murders. He drove to the house on Greentree Lane early the next day and talked with police and family members. Jennifer was eventually driven to Winter Park to stay at the home of her uncle, William, and her aunt, Gloria. The couple helped her sign up for classes at a new school, but declined to disclose the location to the press. Gloria Wendorf explained that she and her husband wanted to shield their niece from the glare of further unnecessary publicity, so that she could get on with her life and prepare for her freshman year at FSU.

Both the victims were surrounded by close relatives in central or south Florida, in addition to their daughters. Naoma was born in the tiny rural Lincoln County town of Harts, West Virginia, near the Mountain State's westernmost tip, and moved to Florida from the larger city of Logan in 1966. A sister, a brother and her mother all lived in Florida within an easy drive from Eustis of a few hours or less. Richard Wendorf was born in Oshkosh, Wisconsin, but most of his closest relatives also lived in Florida, including his mother, Betsy M. Wendorf, in Winter Park.

Monday night and early Tuesday, while neighbors stood in their neatly clipped front yards or peered curiously from behind half-shuttered windows at the rapidly growing collection of green-and-white cruisers and unmarked cars, investigators were already delving into the relationships within the family. Plainclothes detectives and uniformed officers explored every nook and cranny of the lives of the four people who had lived at 24135 Greentree Lane.

Interviews with Jennifer and other work by investigators began developing a disturbing picture of a family disrupted and torn by seemingly normal dissensions that might exist within most homes with two active teenage daughters: the natural competition, resentments, the first stirrings of independence and clashes over parental control. The Wendorf sisters were not latchkey kids. Both their father and mother took parenting seriously, and played active roles in shaping the character of their girls. They established household rules, sometimes discussed problems at family conferences, did their best to keep track of the friends of their daughters, and tried to teach discipline through example by behaving with fairness and consistency. Like most parents, they were more successful with some aspects of the effort than with others.

Approximately two full years older than her sister, and with an after-school job, a steady boyfriend and a goal of beginning pre-med studies in Tallahassee shortly after turning eighteen, Jennifer appeared to have her head on her shoulders and her feet firmly set on the ground.

Heather was a different story, and was struggling with the trying growing pains and difficulties common to many fifteen-year-olds. It was a difficult age when she was neither a little girl anymore, nor yet a grown-up woman. She was rebellious and resented her mother's efforts to exert authority by enforcing curfews and other household rules. The mother and daughter quarreled furiously over trivialities. Moving from childhood dependence to the freedom, confidence and self-reliance of adulthood is a rite of passage all adolescents must negotiate. It's a process that is more difficult and painful for some than for others.

At times, according to Jennifer, when Heather was ordered to clean up her room, she would lose her temper, and snap that she would clean her room when she felt like it. Other emotional blow-ups occurred over use of the telephone, or when Mrs. Wendorf forbade Heather to go out at night with her friends. She was a stubborn, willful girl who was likely to explode in anger and fight back whenever she didn't get her way.

Heather fretted about her isolation and complained about being left with nothing to do except "staring at the trees." Not only was she stuck among the small towns of Lake County but her home was almost ten miles from Eustis where most of her friends lived and she attended high school. As a fifteen-year-old, she was still too young to drive and had to depend on family or friends for transportation. Everyone in the family except Heather had his or her own car. Jennifer had the Saturn; the girls' mother had the Chevy Blazer, and their father drove the Explorer.

As testimony to the sense of security the family felt living in their isolated rural home, both parents sometimes left the keys to their cars in the ignitions when they parked them in front of the house for the night. Except for periods when the family was away on vacations or for entire weekends, the doors to the house were left unlocked. The Wendorfs didn't even bother to close the gate to the driveway. Jennifer once recalled that about the most troubling problem the family experienced on Greentree Lane occurred when a dog killed and ate their chicken.

Heather apparently didn't share her parents' pleasure in the sense of security and relative isolation offered by their location in the quiet street of homes constructed on large lots, with neighbors who were courteous but for the most part minded their own business. George and Ruth Pawliczak lived across Greentree Lane, but during the approximately eight years that the two families were close neighbors, they didn't socialize. Their contact with each other was confined to a wave of the hand or an occasional spoken greeting. It was that kind of neighborhood.

Heather also apparently didn't share the attitude of her parents and many of her neighbors and schoolmates, who believed that the county, named for its more than 1,400 freshwater lakes, with their fine bass, perch, crappie, catfish and shellcracker fishing, was a good place to live.

Most of the lakes, with names including Dicie, Dot, Gracie, Ida, Irma, Joanna, Louise, Minerva, Myrtle and Nettie, were named after the wives and daughters of early settlers. One of the most scenically beautiful is Lake Dora, which also provided the inspiration for Mount Dora, the name of the charming little town of historical New England–style homes, antique shops and art galleries where Jennifer worked. Bait and tackle shops, small marinas and boat landings dot the shores of placid lakes, ringed by stately live oaks draped with soft, thick, cooling cushions of Spanish moss, palmetto and Florida's official state tree, the distinctive sabal palms that look like large upended green, brown or gray dustmops—the color depends on the recent heat index and rainfall.

Heather was apparently unimpressed with local history, or by the stark, sunbaked beauty, gritty yellow sand and red clay of the terrain which, during the Spanish explorations of the sixteenth century, was roamed by a branch of the Timuca Indian tribe known as the Acueras, and later by Seminoles. The gently rolling hills have been referred to by historians as "the Florida Mountains," and are the nearest topographical features the flat peninsula has to the real thing.

Heather's high school, the town and the seven-mile-long lake it borders on the east shore were all named after a stern, bearded U. S. Army Colonel, Abraham Eustis. Old Abe led the local militia and skirmished with Indians during the Second Seminole War, then was promoted to Brevette Brigadier General.

Formed from a portion of northernmost Orange County and a big chunk of eastern Sumter County in 1887, Lake County was first known for its lakes and its herds of cattle, but soon became famous as "the Citrus Capital of the World." But like most teenagers, Heather was more concerned with the present than with the distant past or with the drybone history of Lake County. She was impatient and anxious to get on with her life, to explore and see what was on the other side of the mountain. Other teens in Eustis and nearby towns complained and groused about the same things as teenagers in small towns all around the country. They belly-ached about being tired of cruising through the tiny downtown business districts, hanging out at local malls and fast-food outlets, and generally being stuck with nothing to do and no place to go. Stranded out in the country, Heather was even more isolated than most of her friends in town, who at least lived within walking distance of schoolmates.

Sometimes when she was especially depressed she would slash one of her arms with a razor blade, her sister later told law enforcement authorities. She also passed through a stage when she stopped eating. Jennifer added that Heather was envious of her, believing that her older sister got all their parents' attention, but according to Jennifer, that simply wasn't true.

Richard and Naoma were proud of Heather's obvious talent in art and music. Heather once taught one of her close friends and classmates to play the "Moonlight Sonata" on the piano. Heather had taught herself to play the piece after picking it up by ear, her friend later recalled. Heather also played oboe and the xylophone in the Eustis High School band.

The accomplished, intelligent schoolgirl also maintained a position near the top of her class, academically. She belonged to the National Junior Honor Society, and was one of only three girls who were members of Eustis High School's "gifted and talented" program. Heather had a vivid, creative imagination and designed and sewed some of her own outfits for school and other activities. One time she fashioned a pair of tights with one leg black and the other red. She was so good at composing her own words to describe friends and other people that one of her chums recorded some of them on index cards so she could use them herself.

"They were very proud of Heather," Jennifer said of her parents. Despite all the schoolgirl's accomplishments, however, there were times when her behavior led to serious clashes with other family members.

A considerable amount of the tension and discord in the household revolved around a troubling relationship Heather developed with a boy who was a student at Eustis High School before he dropped out in May of the previous year and moved to Murray, Kentucky. Roderick Justin Ferrell and his mother, Sondra Gibson, were originally from western Kentucky but relocated to Eustis in the spring of 1993 to be near her parents, who had moved to Florida after retirement. While Sondra lived in Eustis, she worked at a few part-time jobs, including a few months at a supermarket. But most of the time she was unemployed and drew food stamps and welfare benefits. She attended a computer course at a local business school for awhile, but dropped out before completing her studies.

Heather dropped by the house to say goodbye to Rod the day he and his mother left in December 1995, a few days before Christmas. It was the only time that Heather and Sondra Gibson saw each other, even though Rod and the girl were close friends. The elder Gibsons, Harrell and Rosetta, followed their daughter and grandson back to Kentucky a short time later.

Rod Ferrell was bad news: a scruffy, bony youth with a dirty fall of stringy dark hair that slumped over his shoulders and ran down his back, and a ring that dangled from a pierced eyebrow. He was a poor student and didn't show much interest in schoolroom studies in the final months before dropping out of Eustis High and moving to Murray. In class he spent much of his time doodling or writing poems about death and suicide that were as morbid as the grave. His doodles were uniformly gruesome: drawings of severed heads, or other body parts that were pierced with knives or dripping blood. He boasted to some of his classmates that he was a vampire, and killed small animals and drank their blood. He blamed his morbid interests on the Devil, whom he said had taken him over.

Rod was directionless and couldn't even seem to settle on a name that permanently suited him. Sometimes he used his middle name and the last name of his mother, and identified himself as Justin Gibson. To his closest friends, however, he was "Vassago," a name lifted from a Satanic character played by Jeremy Sisto in the horror film, *Hideaway*, starring Jeff Goldblum and Alicia Silverstone. Rod did his best to dress the part, and wandered around in the Florida sunshine wearing black pants, a loose black shirt, a black trenchcoat, black combat boots and an inverted cross swinging from a cheap metal chain around his neck, and carrying a sturdy wooden walking stick that was so long it reached to his shoulders. Inverted crosses are common symbols of Satanism, black magic or other forms of diabolism.

According to Rod, he wasn't just some run-of-the-mill

vampire, but a powerful revenant lord who was centuries old. He seemed always to have some new darkly imaginative prattle about the undead. Rod was already smoking marijuana, according to later statements by his mother, Sondra J. Gibson. He was also a heavy tobacco smoker.

Heather and Rod met each other through her longtime school chum, Jeanine LeClaire, who dated Rod when he was attending Eustis High. For awhile the teenagers were quite an item—Rod in his usual all-black get-up, and Jeanine in costumes that were often composed of layered, baggy clothes that, if not up-to-date Paris-stylish, were certainly eye-catching. The first time Sondra saw Jeanine, the girl came to the house with a boy named ''Matt,'' talked with Rod awhile, then left. At first, Rod didn't appear to be all that impressed with the slender girl, but when she returned about a half-hour later ''all of a sudden he was madly in love with her,'' according to his mother's later recollections.

Sondra didn't share her son's enthusiasm for the girl. Jeanine dropped by their home on a Sunday after attending services at a Lutheran Church. Sondra recalled that she was wearing cloth tennis shoes, a pair of torn leotards, two or three skirts layered on top of each other and a couple of shirts and a sweater. Her skirts were long, her sleeves were long, she had a high neckline and hair hanging over her face. It wasn't a typical Florida outfit.

After meeting Jeanine, Rod began getting lots of calls from youngsters his mother didn't know. Rod was secretive about his new friends, and when they telephoned with messages for him they usually left only their first names. She didn't know their telephone numbers, last names or who their parents were. He had an active social life that she wasn't a part of, and she was beginning to worry about what he was up to. Some of his behavior was downright bizarre. One evening when she returned home and walked into the house, her son was sitting on the living room floor with a girl, and they were lapping up each other's blood from slashes in their arms.

Even though Rod developed a romantic relationship with

another girl after moving to Murray, and Heather had a boy-friend in Eustis, he continued to stay in close touch by mail and telephone with her and with Jeanine. Heather was never his girlfriend, but she confided some of her most closely guarded secrets to him, and looked up to him as a father figure who some day would return to Florida for her so they could live together like a family, friends later recalled.

The preferred form of communication between the two teenagers was long-distance telephone calls, and their chats, which could last an hour or more, became an expensive indulgence that exacerbated tensions in the Wendorf home. If Mrs. Wendorf happened to pick up the telephone while Heather was talking with Rod, the girl would order her mother to get off the line, Jennifer later told the police.

She told investigators that telephone bills sometimes ran as high as $60 to $80 for the calls her younger sister placed to Rod and his friends in Murray and for the collect calls she accepted from Kentucky. The older sister said that when her father complained about the mystery calls, instead of telling him who she was chatting with in Kentucky, Heather snapped that she would take care of the bill. Despite his habit of indulging his daughters, there were limits to Richard Wendorf's patience. He put his foot down, and forbade Heather to accept any more collect calls from Kentucky.

Like many teenage girls, Heather not only loved long talks on the telephone, but she was also a spirited letter writer. In a letter she wrote on March 11, 1996, to another boy in Murray, she complained about her humdrum life in Lake County and talked about two sides to her personality. "My soul feels split in two, like two different people," she wrote. One side was the "non-resistant, passive, non-aggressive" personality she showed to other people, she said. The other side was darker, more sinister.

"Then [side] two is the essence of vengeance, hate and destruction," she wrote. "Purely chaos molded into a hideous monster, writhing and tearing the inside of me to ribbons. She wants out. She wants to show herself and to do what she sees fit to do. I do well to trap her inside and not yet free her. Not yet at least!''

Heather wrote to a couple of Rod's friends but her most consistent Kentucky pen-pal was identified in some of the letters by the vampire name, Damion. The name was spelled with the letter ''o'' as the last vowel, rather than the more commonly used letter ''e.'' Damien, when it is correctly spelled, was the name of Satan's son, the anti-Christ, in the hugely popular 1970s horror movie classics, *The Omen*, *Damien—Omen II*, and two other sequels. In her letters, Heather indicated that Rod had decided that she would be Damion's queen and he her sire. For awhile Rod had planned to become Jeanine's sire—but that apparently changed after he found a new girlfriend in Murray. Damion's birth name was John Goodman, and he had been a friend of Rod's since they were in the fourth grade together in Murray. After Rod returned to Kentucky, the boys resumed their close friendship.

James W. Elkins was another of Heather's correspondents in Murray, and she also talked to him a few times by telephone. The letters to Elkins were as gloomy and darkly menacing as those to Goodman.

The March 11 note, and others, later became part of the public record after court authorities released several letters to defense attorneys as part of a legal process known as ''discovery,'' through which potential evidence is shared prior to trials. The letters, some of them six and eight pages long, were seized by investigators who traveled to Murray and talked with Damion. Additional correspondence, found in Heather's bedroom along with some morbid drawings depicting bats, blood, and tears dripping from eyes, was also seized by investigators. The letters written by Heather disclosed an obsession with an eerie, ominous world of blood, vampires and violence.

''Blood would taste really good about now,'' she wrote in one of the notes. ''Or maybe ice-cream. Hey! What am I saying? Blood is good all the time.'' Another time she wrote about dreaming that she grew fangs and sucked the blood from a prowler.

A dismal tone of loneliness, desperation and menace ran throughout much of the correspondence, and at times she referred to conflicting emotions over her thoughts of running away. When she talked of the home she shared with her family on Greentree Lane, she referred to it as "hell." The gloomy teenager wrote: "I really want to cry aloud all the time but I keep it in, or try to kill it with drugs or alcohol. And if I'm not passed out from crying, I want to run and run until I collapse or die."

In another letter she wrote about grotesquely sinister dreams of sucking the blood from a baby, and still tasting the blood and smelling the child's scent after awakening. Expanding on her reaction to the dream, she wrote: "It makes me ask questions about myself. Is this what real evil is like? Did I enjoy it? Does this make me a monster? Do I care anymore?" Another time she described dreaming that she, Rod and Damion killed two people, then sucked their blood. After awakening, she said she could feel her fangs tingle. Once, when the subject turned to her longtime school chum, she wrote: "As long as Jeanine and I have been friends, we've always dreamed of a vampiric life . . ."

Were the scribbled words Heather wrote nothing more than the innocent ramblings and adolescent soul-searching of a bored fifteen-year-old eager to spread her wings and move beyond the limits of family, school and hometown, who was caught up in dark but harmless fantasies? It may have seemed so at the time, but the letters later took on an air of ominous significance in light of the tragedy that ripped apart and destroyed the Wendorf household.

Jennifer further aroused the suspicions of local law officers that a sinister dark side of her little sister's personality may have contributed to the tragedy by recounting a chilling conversation one night when Heather asked her if she ever thought about killing their parents. If Jennifer ever needed anyone killed, the younger girl reportedly added, ". . . next time Rod's down he can do it." Jennifer dismissed the bizarre conversation as just more of her little sister's idle talk or musings. But she wasn't the only person the younger girl made similar shocking remarks to. Some of her friends, and a former boyfriend of Jennifer, witnessed behavior by Heather that in hindsight was chillingly disturbing.

She once told teenager Mandy Renee Jones that she wished her parents were dead. By that time, Heather had developed her own attention-getting persona. She called herself "Zoe," and according to some later reports, claimed to have talked with spirits and participated in foul rituals that involved the drinking of human blood. "Zoe" was also the name of a character in "Hideaway," who made a play for Vassago in a bar and was murdered by him. Heather also developed a grotesque personal costume for school and other activities that was as darkly riveting as Rod's. Like him, she dressed in black, but highlighted the basic colors with dramatic accessories that included black fishnet stockings, a dog chain around her neck, upside-down crucifixes worn as necklaces and natural blonde hair that she dyed bright purple, shocking pink, or other inappropriate colors that seemed designed to elicit a "tut-tut" from a parent or school teacher. As a macabre final touch, she carried a dismembered Barbie doll dangling from a miniature noose tied to her mesh school backpack. During her freshman year of high school she was featured in the "Rave" section of *The Orlando Sentinel* with her hair dyed blue and pink.

At home she kept a copy of *The Witches' Bible* in her room, and also became absorbed in reading books with vampire themes. Jennifer said her little sister filled her room with "dark and dreary" things. Heather tried unsuccessfully to convince Jennifer to change her cat's name to "Vassago," like Rod's.

Heather was a teenager who behaved as if she was desperate for attention, but she turned in an adequate performance as a student. Once in a while she cut a class or two, and she was late a few times, but never stood out as a discipline problem. She didn't cause any more trouble for her teachers than most of her peers. Later recalling her bizarre get-ups for a newspaper reporter, a Eustis High School senior who knew both sisters said that even though Heather dressed differently from other teens, she had "the same outgoing personality as everyone else." Principal Jim Hollins added: "She did the new wave thing, but you can't fault her for that at all."

Her garb and behavior were curious nevertheless, for the granddaughter of a man who was as firmly tied to strong Christian ideals as seventy-five-year-old James Wendorf. The elder Wendorf was retired after a gratifying career as a lawyer for the Billy Graham Evangelistic Association and was a recently remarried snowbird who spent winters in Florida and frequently visited with his sons and their families at other times during the year. He kept a winter home in Umatilla, a flyspeck town of about a thousand people a ten-minute drive north of Eustis at the south edge of the Ocala National Forest.

Amateur psychoanalysts, had they wondered about the quirky girl's oddball behavior, may likely have written it off as nothing more than evidence of a teenager's striving to show her individuality and independence. The pressures to stand out can be especially strong on a younger child who has an older sibling as popular and proven an achiever as Jennifer was at Eustis High.

The mother of one of Heather's closest friends later recalled her daughter and Heather behaving like normal teenagers when they were together, playing music and giggling over shared confidences. The mother, who didn't want to be identified, said Heather was bright, creative and a talented artist.

Another of the teen's closest girlfriends, who had been a classmate since the sixth grade, confided to Heather that she envied her because her life was so perfect. Yet another girl, who had only recently moved into the area, thought at first that she was a little bit overly sweet. Heather was always bragging about her mother and the way she shared confidences with her. She didn't believe in fooling around with drugs, and apparently didn't use alcohol, the newcomer said.

Heather's seventy-five-year-old grandfather also dwelt on evidence of wholesome teenage behavior when he talked about her. "Heather's so quiet. She's a demure little girl. I never saw evidence of anything like that," the Associated Press quoted him saying, in response to the horrid stories circulating about his granddaughter's reputedly morbid behavior. In other statements he said family members joked with the sisters that they had their parents wrapped around their fingers. His son and daughter-in-law loved the girls, he said.

It was true that Heather wore eccentric costumes and was a bit of a nonconformist, but that didn't shut her off from other kids at Eustis High. And although she may not have been as popular as her buoyant and white bread–wholesome older sister, she had lots of friends. She watched movies at the theater and on VCRs with male and female friends, and on homecoming night, when the Panthers played their last home game of the season on their home field, she hosted a big party at her house.

Jeremy Scott Hueber, Heather's boyfriend, didn't dress any more outrageously than any other average teenage boy at Eustis High School. His shock of wavy light hair curled over his ears in a style that wasn't much different from that worn by other high school boys. And he didn't imagine that he was a vampire, or prattle to friends about a need to drink blood and achieve immortality.

Heather's school friends were teenagers, like she was, and they were dealing with their own particular growing pains. Heather appeared to be experiencing more self-doubts and insecurities than most of her chums, however. And she seemed to have learned as well that, even if she hadn't equaled her bubbly sister's popularity and accomplishments, there were other ways to get attention. There were times when Heather behaved like a headstrong, spoiled brat. Early in the new school year her father confided to a friend at Crown Cork & Seal that he was worried his younger daughter was involved with the wrong crowd. Max Hargrove had been a friend of the family for eleven years and he didn't get the impression that a crisis existed in the Wendorf household. Every parent has problems with his or her children at some time or another, and Wendorf didn't behave as if he were in over his head and caught up in a family predicament that he couldn't sort out.

During the last few days leading up to the murders, however, the dissension and strains within the Wendorf household were veering rapidly out of control and darkling forces were gathering that would shatter the family and forever alter the lives of the two teenage daughters whose parents loved them so passionately.

While evidence technicians and other officers were combing the inside and outside of the home on Greentree Lane for clues, colleagues were announcing their search for Heather and four other teenagers from southwestern Kentucky who were wanted for questioning. The Kentucky youths were identified as sixteen-year-old Roderick Justin Ferrell; sixteen-year-old Howard Scott Anderson; nineteen-year-old Dana Lynn Cooper, and fifteen-year-old Sarah "Shea" Remington. The younger girl was also known as Charity Lynn Keesee, according to the announcement.

Early Tuesday morning Seminole County sheriff's deputies discovered a nine-year-old Buick Skylark with faded red paint abandoned along U.S. Highway 17–92, between Eustis and Orlando. The car was at the side of the road on the outskirts of the town of Sanford near Lake Monroe and the Central Florida Zoo. A check of the license number showed the plates were issued to Richard Wendorf for a 1994 Ford Explorer. After the Skylark's vehicle identification number was fed into a police computer, it was traced to Howard and Martha Anderson in Mayfield, Kentucky. They had reported to law enforcement authorities that the car and their oldest son, Howard Scott Anderson, were missing. The boy and the car had been gone from the home since Saturday.

Scott, who preferred his middle name, had run away before, but his parents were worried sick nevertheless. They feared that he might be wandering the streets somewhere, hungry and broke, or that he could be dead. They were also concerned about the car. Except for the clothes they wore and a few sticks of furniture, the old Skylark was about the only thing they owned.

The license plates on the Skylark and the sports utility vehicle had been switched and police said they were looking for a blue Explorer carrying Kentucky tag number DTB-836. Color photographs were taken of the old Skylark and it was loaded onto a flatbed truck, then hauled to the Lake County Sheriff's Department auto pound in Tavares to be held as evidence in the homicide investigation. A few days later, members of the Lake County sheriff's underwater search and rescue team pulled on their rubber suits, goggles and oxygen tanks, then slipped into the tepid waters of Lake Monroe. They were sweeping the muddy lake bottom for the murder weapon but eventually ended the search after finding nothing more intriguing than a few waterlogged tree branches, old tires and some fishing gear.

At least one important element of the mystery surrounding Heather's whereabouts seemed to have been solved. She was believed to be with the Kentucky teenagers. And the runaway teens were thought to be in Richard Wendorf's missing Ford Explorer. Investigators suspected they were on their way to Kentucky or Louisiana and alerted law enforcement authorities in both states to be on the lookout.

Early Wednesday, two days after the murders and the day before Thanksgiving, Lake County authorities issued first-degree murder warrants for four of the runaway teenagers. A warrant was also issued for the arrest of fifteen-year-old Sarah ''Shea'' Remington, aka Charity Lynn Keesee, on charges of being an accessory to murder after the fact. The murder warrants, signed by Lake County Circuit Court Judge Mark Hill, authorized the arrest of Rod, Scott, Dana—and Heather—as suspects in the murders of James and Naoma Wendorf. Roderick, Dana and Sarah (Charity) were identified as being from Murray, and Howard (Scott) was from Mayfield, a small town in adjoining Graves County.

Lake County Sheriff's Department spokesmen, who only

a day earlier had stated that the teenagers were merely wanted for questioning, confirmed to the press that they were suspects in the murder. "The evidence in the case reached the level of probable cause," said Captain Chris Daniels.

The police spokesman also responded to the stories and rumors that were swirling around the murder investigation linking the grisly crime to vampirism or other blood cult activities. "We haven't found any evidence of that in this case," Daniels told reporters. If the law enforcement officer hoped that speculation about an ominous occult link to the slayings was laid to rest with his remarks, he was in for a big disappointment.

The unsettling possibility that a blood-crazed vampire cult had gained a toehold among teenagers in the rural central Florida community and in western Kentucky captured the public imagination, and events were progressing too rapidly to ignore the tie-in. It was too frightening, repulsive—and fascinating—a prospect to be glossed over. In Eustis, Mount Dora, Tavares, Murray and Mayfield parents were increasingly calling their teenagers aside for serious father–son and mother–daughter talks.

While homicide detectives from the sheriff's department were preparing for an overnight dash to Kentucky to confer Tuesday morning with local police about the case, the first signs of jurisdictional friction began to appear. A story in the *Paducah Sun* quoted an unnamed police department detective in Murray as saying that the Wendorfs had been bludgeoned to death with wooden clubs. Daniels groused that "police up there" were apparently releasing information that investigators in Florida didn't have. The autopsies pointed to "blunt trauma to the head," he said, but did not pinpoint the murder weapons used in the killings. Kentucky police were also complaining about not getting enough information from authorities in Florida, but Daniels said that data produced as the investigation progressed was being shared on a need-to-know basis. "There's a lot of stuff I don't even know."

Another unspeakable question that none of the law enforcement officers yet had an answer for had been whispered and talked about by classmates of the sisters and friends of the Wendorfs since shortly after the double murder was discovered, and still persistently hovered over the investigation: Did the rebellious fifteen-year-old daughter of the Wendorfs play a personal role in the brutal murder of her parents? At the moment, Heather was an enigma, a contrasting puzzle to solve: child of darkness or victim of plundered innocence?

While local and national media converged on central Florida and western Kentucky, a reporter for the *Orlando Sentinel* wheedled an exclusive interview with Ferrell's mother in Murray. Sondra Gibson had something shocking to say about the missing Florida girl who called herself "Zoe" and paraded around with a dismembered doll dangling from her backpack. The woman confided that Heather had told Rod she wanted her parents dead, and the prospect of their deaths was a frequent topic during the phone calls between her son and the girl. Sondra confided that Heather "was saying she was going to kill her parents for a long time."

3. VASSAGO

Roderick Justin Ferrell was a sad misfit whose home in Murray, Kentucky, was about as different as it could be from the comfortable, loving nest that Richard and Naoma Wendorf strove so hard to create in Florida for their daughters.

He was born in Murray on Friday, March 28, 1980, when the dark hollows and sunsplashed mountain ridges, and the flatlands and gently sloping hills of the western part of the state were just beginning to burst with bright pools of yellow and purple from the freshly budding beds of goldenrod, wild violets and bluebells. His sign in the zodiac was the ram, his planet was Mars and his element was fire. To people who take stock in such things, his birth sign meant he would grow up to be impulsive, bold, confident and independent. But somehow he seemed to have been born under an unlucky star, and the glitches in his life began showing up early in his life. Even his first name was misspelled on his birth certificate as ''Roderrick'' with three ''r's'' instead of two.

The lusty, squalling infant entered the world the same year *Playboy* magazine centerfold Dorothy Stratten was murdered by her husband, a former Vancouver pimp who then committed suicide, because she was planning to marry movie director Peter Bogdanovich. Before the year was out an even more electrifying murder shocked Beatle fans around the world when Mark David Chapman assassinated John Lennon outside the Dakota apartments in Manhattan.

It wasn't long after the tiny newcomer was carried home from the hospital in his mother's arms, that his life began sliding inexorably downhill. Both his parents, Sondra Joann Gibson and Rick Allan Ferrell, were seventeen when their son was born. The young parents only lived together about thirty days before splitting up. In the mid-1990s, when Rod's name began making headlines across the country, his father hadn't seen him for years, and was not taking an active role in the boy's upbringing.

Rod's mother had legal custody, and her parents lived in Murray. Harrell and Rosetta Gibson were loving and attentive grandparents who helped their youngest daughter raise the little boy who had intruded into their lives. The elder Gibsons were hard-working Christians who considered Jesus Christ to be an important part of their lives, and attended a Pentecostal church in Murray twice a week, on Sundays and Wednesday nights. Their grandson often went to church with them when he was a little boy. Long before he and his mother moved back to Murray from Florida, however, his interests had changed and he stopped attending services.

One time after Rod was old enough to appreciate the experience, his grandparents packed up the boy and his mother and set off on a trip to New Orleans, Louisiana, and Texarkana, Texas. The family holiday was the thrill of the boy's young life. Wandering among the moist sights and sounds of "the Queen City of the South," peering at the wrought-iron courtyard gates and iron-lace balconies of the French Quarter, smelling the magnolias and the fresh, sweet olives, and drinking in the town's unique history and personality was an unforgettable experience.

The exotic Mississippi River city that grew up on swampland amid the bayous and canals of southern Louisiana between Lake Pontchartrain and the Gulf of Mexico also has a darker side to its history. The city is steeped in the eerie incantations of Voodoo, an exotic blend of West African

animism and shamanism with Roman Catholicism that has
never lost its darkling reputation for spine-chilling midnight
rituals, hungans and mambos, loas and black magic that is
such an indelible part of the New Orleans mystique. The
stories of shuffling zombies with vacant minds and eyes as
sallow and lifeless as pus would eventually be replaced in
the boy's psyche by another kind of monster with a sinister
immortality that would become part of the city's more modern legend. But that was for later.

The New Orleans that Rod experienced with his mother
and grandparents accounted for a pleasant interlude in his
life, but it didn't last. By the time Rod was in his early teens
he was already doing pretty much whatever he pleased,
whenever he wished. As a sixteen-year-old he was every bit
as stubbornly willful as his friend Heather. Rod became the
type of child studied and fretted over by sociologists, crim-
inologists, mental health professionals and experts in other
methodologies in their efforts to understand causes of the
rising tide of teenage violence and other juvenile crime. Before he was out of his teens he was destined to come to the
attention of professionals representing all those vocations.
He experienced more than his fair share of the kind of en-
vironmental trauma and emotional deprivation that experts
tend to factor in as causes of serious juvenile misbehavior.

In Eustis he had serious trouble at school, performing far
below his potential. After returning to Kentucky, some of
his former friends in Murray noticed that he seemed more
self-confident than he had been when they knew him earlier.
Before he moved to Florida with his mother, he had complained of feeling like "a big geek," one of his chums later
recalled. After he returned, there was no evidence of the old
self-doubts, and he behaved as if he was desperate to be
noticed. He boasted of having been trained in the martial
arts and was an ominous, if slightly ridiculous, figure who
dressed totally in black.

Like "Little Orphan Annie," he seemed to have only one
outfit to his name. The long, straight, naturally brown hair
that fell to the middle of his back was dyed black and

combed to one side across his face. Even his fingernails were painted black. At times Rod experimented with a goatee, but it was a losing effort for the adolescent, and the sparse, scraggly crop of facial hair was only a sometime thing. It made him look like he had a dirty face, and after trying to cultivate it for a few days, he would tire of the effort and shave it off.

Except for his thin, pale, pimply teenage face, Rod Ferrell looked as black as a crow. The ebony fashion was apparently carefully chosen to project an image of implied threat. Black absorbs and obliterates other colors, and symbolizes menacing power and mystery. It is surrounded by an aura of evil. Hitler's dreaded Waffen SS wore black uniforms. Far earlier, Russia's frightful first czar, Ivan the Terrible, who has been compared by some historians with Transylvania's dread Vlad Tepes, son of Vlad Dracul and the inspiration for Bram Stoker's classic *Dracula*, was protected by a palace guard called the *Oprinikn*. The *Oprinikn* dressed totally in black and rode black horses. More recently, the predominant color favored by outlaw biker gangs, punk rockers and the S&M crowd is black. In the Western world it is also the color of mourning and of the grave. Bela Lugosi, Christopher Lee and other actors famous for playing the prince of vampires always dressed in black.

Back home in Kentucky, while Rod slid deeper into his "Vassago" persona, drifting through the streets of Murray looking as insubstantial as a moonbeam, his problems in the community and in his home rapidly multiplied and he was soon brought to the attention of local welfare and social services agencies. Sondra Gibson was a single mother subsisting on welfare. After she and her son moved back to Murray they shared their Broad Street apartment in a housing complex known as South Side Manor, near the southern outskirts of town, with her boyfriend, Kyle Newman. Newman was a tattoo artist and the South Side Manor maintenance man. Most people who knew him well called him by his nickname, "Smoke."

Rental for the apartments is based on income, and occupants who can't even raise the full amount of the moderate fees are assisted with government subsidies. Many of the residents are people like Sondra Gibson and her son, single mothers with children, and others who have especially low incomes. The complex is composed of a half-dozen brown, two-story buildings. Each of the buildings has eight apartments. Public areas inside the buildings, and the grounds outside, are generally neat and tidy. Among the most distinguishing features of South Side Manor are the old rattletrap cars that are almost always parked outside. The living arrangements of Sondra and her boyfriend were apparently accepted with easy tolerance by most of her close neighbors in the apartments, but there were others in the larger community, who attended church on Sundays and Bible study or prayer meetings during the week, who whispered and clucked their tongues.

Murray is smalltown insular and a majority of its 15,000 residents, roughly half of Calloway County's total population, are firmly wedded to fundamentalist Christian beliefs and lifestyle. Kentucky is a local option commonwealth, meaning that citizens of individual cities and counties can choose to be "wet" or "dry." In communities that choose to be "wet," residents and visitors can legally buy beer or harder booze at package stores, or buy and drink alcoholic beverages in properly licensed taprooms or restaurants. Murray is "dry," and residents, visitors, or local college students attending Murray State University who have a yen for a six-pack or a taste of something stronger can make a fifteen-minute drive due south through the hamlets of Tobacco and Hazel, then cross the Tennessee state line to the lickspittle town of Puryear. Or they can make a forty-five-minute trek in the opposite direction to Paducah. There is one other option. They can look up a local moonshiner and buy a quart jar of "white lightnin'," a fundamental element of Kentucky mountain legend, as transparent as fresh spring water and as powerful as a mule's kick.

Although a strong sense of spirituality and religious fidelity runs through Calloway County, there is, like any other community in the United States, a rowdier element that drinks, gambles and fornicates. Much of the county's 384 square miles of land is heavily wooded, or planted in burley and dark-fired tobacco, corn, soybeans and wheat. Tobacco is the leading legal cash crop, although the same climate and other weather conditions that produce the sturdy waist-high burley are said to work similar wonders for more clandestine plantings of marijuana sown in some of the more isolated areas of the county.

Murray is only eight miles north of the Tennessee state line, and some of the backroads stretch for miles without passing a city, a house or any sign of human activity. Local rowdies with a yen for gambling a part of the paychecks earned in the tobacco fields, in the cabs of longhaul trucks or in the manufacturing plants that are a staple of the economy in Murray and Calloway County know where to look among the backroads for a rousing cockfight between savage little roosters outfitted with razor-sharp metal spurs that slash and gouge, or a blood-and-guts battle-to-the-death dogfight between scarred pitbulls and powerful Labrador–German Shepherd mixes specially bred and trained for ferocity.

Ever since Colonel Richard Callaway moved into Kentucky with Daniel and Squire Boone, then helped found Boonesboro in the late eighteenth century, there has been an element of rugged individualism in Calloway County. The frontiersman and Calloway County namesake, who was appointed colonel of the militia and justice of the peace, and elected as a representative from the frontier area of Kentucky in Virginia's General Assembly all in the same year—1777—was killed by Indians a few years later at Boonesboro. But he left his name behind him, in slightly altered fashion, when Calloway County was formed from part of Hickman County in 1780. During those frontier days, proper spelling occupied a far lower priority than survival.

The streak of rebelliousness that still runs through the area today was reflected by the attitude of most of the local residents when they sided with the Confederacy during the Civil War. Kentucky was a border state, and local Johnny

Rebs and Confederate sympathizers in Calloway County joined with troops from other Southern states during clashes with Union forces in several small encounters.

The nocturnal carousing of more modern local individualists aren't the kind of activities and local color promoted by the Murray–Calloway County Chamber of Commerce. Local movers and shakers prefer to stress the attractions of a strong economy and brisk job market, along with the recreation and educational opportunities, the profusion of churches, and Murray's national recognition as a highly rated retirement community.

Murray is the local center of industry and offers jobs in plants manufacturing everything from toys, college books, scoreboards and clocks to small engines, electric motors and concrete products. Mattel Toys, the makers of Barbie dolls, is the area's largest industrial employer, with a local workforce of about 1,500 people. A deep feeling of religion and spirituality has always exerted a powerful influence in Murray, and a century-and-a-half after the town was incorporated in 1844, the community was supporting 111 churches. One of the churches is Roman Catholic, and the rest are Protestant, predominantly Baptist, along with a strong cross-section of other fundamentalist, evangelical and Pentecostal Christian denominations. Among the church-goers, a certain element believed that if someone didn't participate in the rich religious life of the community and receive the baptism of the Holy Spirit, they were outsiders. Teenagers were urged to attend church and Sunday school, Bible study, youth groups and other evening and weekend activities. Rod marched to a different drummer.

Murray State University, a liberal arts school with an enrollment of almost 9,000 students and a national reputation for outstanding basketball teams, occupies choice acreage at the north central edge of the downtown business and government area. Another well-known feature at MSU is the Boy Scouts of America's National Scouting Museum, which is constructed on campus, and is a vivid testament to the atmosphere of Middle-American wholesomeness that pervades the school and the small town. There is an air of *American Graffiti* about Murray which, although it is gradually disappearing, might remind a visitor of the quieter and safer times of the 1950s.

Like most small towns in the South and much of the rest of the country, teenage boys and girls cruise the downtown area on weekend nights during the school year, and almost every night during the summer. In Murray, Court Square is in the center of the downtown business district, and girdles the Calloway County Courthouse. The old nineteenth-century courthouse on Main Street houses the Calloway County Sheriff's Department, but court activities are held in a more modern building known as the Robert O. Miller Courthouse Annex. The annex is on Maple Street, just behind the courthouse. The Murray city hall, fire station and other city and county departments are all located either on the square or within a one-block walk. The square is the center of local government and business, and for Murray teenagers it is the center of the dry town's limited nightlife.

On weekends, Main Street becomes a bewildering cacophony of ear-splitting blasts from car stereos, roaring beefed-up engines and boisterous teenagers loudly honking horns and yelling at friends. The drivers make the circuit of the square, then roar west along Main Street to the Hungry Bear restaurant. They either make the turnaround there and head back to the square, or park and crowd inside to order Cokes and hamburgers or merely hang out. The Hungry Bear is just across Main Street from the Dairy Queen and Corvette Lanes, the town's only bowling alley, where some of the kids stop to play video games. A clutter of restaurants and fast-food outlets ranging from McDonald's and Hardee's to Taco Bell are within a fast five-minute drive from just about any location in the town. Several of the fast-food outlets are clustered along Twelfth Street (U.S. 641), which is the main north–south route through town. Many of the younger teens hang out at the Circus Skate, north of town, which was known locally for years as the biggest roller rink in the United States.

Rod didn't have a car or a driver's license, and the brooding, skinny youth with the long, greasy black hair and sallow, pimply face wasn't part of the younger crowd that hung around the Circus Skate. He missed his friends in central Florida, and a few weeks after his mother moved back to Murray with him he ran away and returned to Lake County. After he was returned home, he ran away a second time. One time he was tracked down in Leesburg, one of the scattering of smalltown Lake County communities within a few miles of Eustis. After Rod was returned to Kentucky, Heather wrote to her friend Damion about her despondency over Rod's failure to help her escape from "hell." The teenagers hadn't forgotten the psychic and emotional bond they had formed in Eustis and built on after Rod trekked north to follow his mother. Rod told friends in Murray that he planned to lead his comrades from Kentucky to Florida and take control of the vampire culture there.

Rod designated Heather and Damion as a couple, according to the scenario pieced together by investigators who examined some of the letters that had passed back and forth between Eustis and Murray, and talked to teenage friends or acquaintances of the youths. She was to be his "queen" and he was to be her "sire."

Rod spent so much time on the phone talking to Heather that his mother couldn't keep up with the bills, and the telephone company disconnected service at the apartment. Then, after Heather's father put his foot down on the collect calls, he turned to the post office to keep up his friendships in Eustis. Rod wrote to Heather, and he also used the mails to continue a relationship with his former girlfriend, Jeanine. The girl's mother, Suzanne LeClaire, considered the first letter she found to be a "sweet puppy love kind of thing." As the correspondence continued, however, the letters grew more devilishly ominous. In one of them, Rod talked about wanting his mother to "cross over." That was terminology he and some of his gradually widening group of friends in Murray used for drinking blood in order to become a vampire.

Finally, Mrs. LeClaire read a letter written to the fifteen-year-old schoolgirl that was more alarming than any that she had seen previously. "It sounded like violence and blood and murder," she later told a reporter for the *Lake Sentinel*. Jeanine's parents ordered her to get rid of some novels with vampire themes which she had borrowed, and clashed with her over her increasingly disturbing friendship with Rod and her interest in the world of the occult. Suzanne LeClaire eventually became so distraught that she warned Heather's mother about the ominous direction the relationships between Rod and their daughters was taking.

While Rod was becoming one of the major sources of family dissension in the homes of two teenagers in Lake County, he was also stirring up trouble as a tenth-grade student at Calloway County High School. He was apparently capable of doing passable work, but he was an undisciplined student who rebelled at authority and refused to cooperate with his teachers. Playing at being a vampire had more appeal than boring classes in ancient history or such mind-boggling mysteries and esoteric puzzles as algebra. He skipped school whenever he felt like it. Even on the days he attended class, instead of bearing down and paying attention, he refused to do his assignments and played what he later described as "mind games" with his teachers. Much of the time he idled away his time doodling, creating the same kind of morbidly sinister pictures he'd sketched when he was a student at Eustis High School.

One frustrated teacher at CCHS wrote in a report about the troublesome student: "He has not caused any discipline problems because he puts his head down. I have not been able to get him to do anything. . . . His attitude was, 'So what?' "

An assistant principal added in another note that Rod's mother had said her son was threatened by someone or by some gang he hung around with and was told they would kill him if he didn't do what they said. About a week after returning to Murray from Eustis, he told his grandmother that he was afraid to ride the school bus. So Rosetta Gibson drove him to school.

The concerned adults who were responsible for his education found him difficult to communicate with. The surly teenager was openly defiant and had a reputation for being disrespectful to teachers and tardy for classes, and for smoking. Between January and May 1996, twenty-two separate infractions of school regulations were recorded on his student record.

Frustrated authorities at last expelled him from school and banned him from the campus after he cursed one of the teachers. The uncooperative, rebellious youth was instructed not to return to classes until the spring semester the following year. The official reasons for his expulsion were listed on his records as "willful disobedience, defiance of school authority and incorrigible bad conduct." During his brief, chaotic experience as a student at Calloway County High he earned "F's" in every class that he was signed up for. A few months after he was kicked out of school, Rod remarked that he could neither read nor write. But like most of his teachers, he knew he was capable of learning and claimed that when he worked at his studies he received "A's" and "B's." Most of the time he stopped working—or never started.

His expulsion didn't seem to bother him, although he got into trouble for continuing to hang around the school. Principal Jerry Ainley warned him a couple of times to stay away from the campus after he was observed hanging around. Near the end of October, Ainley learned that the boy was seen in the rear parking lot, then inside the main CCHS building. Ainley escorted Rod off campus, then filed a formal complaint with juvenile court authorities charging him with criminal trespass. Rod's troubles were rapidly piling up.

He believed he was treated as an outcast by other students and his teachers, and he may have been right about that. He was a weird kid with a long, thin nose and long hair who wandered listlessly along the edges of local teenage society, looking as gaunt and wasted as a model in a Calvin Klein ad. He talked increasingly about vampires and blood and was known to slash his own skinny arms with a razor or a knife. Along with the scars, he sported a couple of tattoos, including a handsome, professionally rendered sketch of a colorful dragon, and an ankh—the ancient Egyptian symbol of reincarnation.

His mother's boyfriend believed the teenager was getting a bad rap, and wrote off Rod's infatuation with vampires as nothing more serious than youthful curiosity or exploration. He indicated that other more discreet people who were into the vampire scene weren't hassled if they pursued their interests in private and dressed more conventionally than Rod did. Some people thought the boy was a freak, Kyle Newman later told a newspaper reporter, because he was an individualist who didn't go along with the local Bible-thumping. But every kid wanted to be seen as different, he said, and Rod had "a good heart."

Although Rod wasn't a part of the in-crowd who hung around with the high school jocks and cheerleaders, and didn't make the scene at the courthouse square tooling up and down Main Street in souped-up junkers, his anti-social behavior, outrageous costumes and teenage rebelliousness appealed to certain girls. For a while after registering at CCHS, he dated an older student named April Doeden. He was romantic in his own unique way, and told the eighteen-year-old girl that he believed they were soulmates and would live forever.

Soulmates or not, after April left Murray to live with her mother, Rod began dating a high school freshman named Charity Lynn Keesee. The hazel-eyed girl was fifteen years old and lived with her father, David Keesee, on Rainbow Lane in Murray. After April returned to Murray with an infant son named Robert, she continued her friendship with the strange boy who dressed in black, was obsessed with vampires and liked to hide in people's houses, then jump out and scare them when they got home.

Although Charity had taken over April's place as his

steady girl, Rod and the older teenager still hung around with many of the same people. After awhile, a rumor began floating around that Rod wanted to use April's little boy as a human sacrifice in some dark ritual. April was eventually quoted in a weekly magazine story as confirming that the rumors had a basis in fact. " 'He sees Bobby as being like the child-of-light type of deal.' . . . 'So basically, to give his father [Satan] a gift,' he would give 'the ultimate gift—sacrificing her baby.' "*

As part of a statewide workfare program for welfare recipients, Rod's mother, Sondra, held a part-time clerical position in the Murray–Calloway County office of the state's Department of Social Services, and she talked to Edna Cothran, who was a family service worker there, about some of her problems with Rod. Even though Sondra was personally interested in so-called New Age mysticism, she was worried about her son's preoccupation with a darker side of the occult.

Sondra said that Rod was involved with a big cult in Florida, and engaged in self-mutilation and other frightening activities. She told the social worker about her frightening experience on Memorial Day before leaving Florida, when she discovered Rod and the girl sharing blood. Rod had also carved an inverted cross into his skinny chest with a razor blade and his wrists were scarred with slash marks.

If the disgusting stories told by Rod's mother were true, it seemed obvious that he was a severely disturbed teenager—but it was also apparent that he wasn't the only person living in the upstairs apartment at the South Side Manor who might benefit from the intervention of outside counselors and agencies. Sondra told the social worker that she was afraid her boy would kill himself if outsiders attempted to intervene in their tangled family affairs, and she cautioned that meddling with Rod might even put both women in danger. Rod told her that she knew too much, Sondra said. Then she

*Who Weekly, December 16, 1996.

added the ominous warning: "... and they will kill me and you if you tell anyone."

Drugs were part of the noxious mixture of diabolism and juvenile delinquency that Rod was involved in, according to her story. She said he used "cat," an especially potent designer drug that is undergoing a frightening spurt in popularity among young people across the country. "Cat" is the street name for methcathinone, a chunky, dirty white powder that can be snorted, smoked or mixed with water and injected. It is a powerful amphetamine similar to crack cocaine in appearance and potency, and it is cheap and easy to manufacture. Ephedrine, a chemical that can be derived from certain over-the-counter energizer pills and diet suppressants, is a key component. Other ingredients may include lye, paint thinner, battery acid and drain cleaner.

Manufacturers often set up makeshift laboratories in the woods or mountains, just like Kentucky moonshiners have done for centuries while brewing white lightning. Cat is fiercely addictive and can lead to uncontrollable shaking, depression, paranoia, and hallucinations.

His mother also hinted at another distasteful family secret. Rod had threatened to tell authorities that she had had sex with one of his teenage friends, and have her sent to prison, she said. When the family services worker pressed for more information about the threat, the troubled woman told a strange story about a night when two of Rod's buddies stayed over at the apartment. One of the boys brought a bottle containing a purple-colored liquid, and when he screwed off the lid, smoke and a strange odor wafted through the room. Sondra went to her room, closed the door and fell asleep. Sometime later, she became aware of the weight of a body on her. Then she fell back into a heavy sleep and didn't awaken again until morning. She told the social worker that although she had previously believed the experience was merely a dream, she had become certain that someone had had sex with her that night. She said she thought she had been drugged.

Rod's obsession with the darker mysteries seemed also to

have spilled over and gotten caught up in his mother's imagination in other ways, leading to her active involvement. She talked about occult symbols, which she said included the image of a wizard with a star. Occultists recognize the five-pointed star as a pentagram, or pentacle, one of the most powerful of all magical symbols for protecting oneself from evil spirits or controlling and bending them to one's will. A star with one point projecting upwards so that it resembles a human body with arms and legs outstretched, symbolizes the dominance of the divine spirit. When the odd-tip is pointed down with two points projecting upward like the horns of a devil, the pentagram becomes a symbol of black magic and evil. Pentagrams have been used by black magicians and sorcerers along with other paraphernalia, rituals and incantations in efforts to call up powerful demons like Asmodeus, Beelzebub, Belial or Leviathan.

Sondra sometimes called herself "Star," and used the symbol as part of her signature—drawn with one point protectively projecting upwards. Some nights she heard sounds that she believed were caused by demons tapping on the windows of her apartment, the woman said. One night something in a gray robe swooped through her room.

Sondra said her son talked of having no soul, and of being convinced that he was possessed. He burned candles in the apartment, and filled a bowl with chunks and pieces of something she described as looking "like slop." Black curtains were hung over the windows of his room. At times he led other members of his cult on nocturnal trips to a black tombstone at the Murray Cemetery, next to the Murray–Calloway County Park on the north side of town, where they performed obscene blood rituals and left objects on the grave. At other times the would-be vampires trekked to a more ancient burial ground, the Old Salem Cemetery just outside the southern outskirts of the city.

The petite, brown-eyed, brown-haired woman told the social worker that Rod was sometimes physically abusive toward her. She said that she took him to her parents for help but they didn't take his behavior seriously, and covered up for him. Her mother passed off the boy's weird actions as merely "a teenage thing," she said. Ms. Cothran advised Sondra to go to the local spouse-abuse shelter if she was afraid her son would injure her.

The conversation was exceedingly troubling and seemed to indicate that conditions in the household were on the verge of spinning out of control, threatening to expand into a maelstrom of destruction that could reach out and harm members of the family, and possibly other people as well. Ms. Cothran passed the information and her concerns up the line of the social services agency. She telephoned Lana Lewis, a protective services specialist, and recounted the conversations with Sondra in detail. Ms. Lewis kicked the knotty problem up another level to the DSS's main office in the state's capital city at Frankfort and asked superiors if the DSS should intervene in the relationship between the mother and son. She explained that Sondra volunteered the information to the family service worker and did not desire intervention. After they talked the matter over, Ms. Lewis was advised not to take a report, but to document everything and to tell Ms. Cothran to do the same while assuring Sondra that she was available to discuss options with her.

Ms. Cothran and a colleague, meanwhile, drove by the Murray Cemetery on their lunch hour and found the tombstone Sondra had described. The woman said a psychedelic mushroom with a sunset in the background was inscribed on the headstone, and a guitar pick was lying by the grave. The image of a wingless angel was engraved near the top. The grave belonged to Eric Allan Moore, a Calloway County High School student who was seventeen when he died in a car crash on April 14, 1995, while he was driving to Tennessee to be with a friend who had been shot.

The DSS wasn't the only local government agency to become concerned with Rod's strangely threatening behavior. Sondra and her son had barely settled in after returning to Murray before she referred him to mental health authorities, but he kept only a couple of appointments with counselors. In July 1996 Sondra filed documents with juvenile court authorities complaining that he was "beyond parental control." In the official complaint she claimed that he was involved with a Satanic cult, smoked marijuana, and had several times threatened her life. The distressed parent complained that when she grounded her son, he ignored her. He slept during the day and stayed out at night, refusing to recognize any curfews. Sondra said she was afraid that if he continued his pattern of behavior he would harm her or her father.

About the time he was expelled from school, Rod appeared with his mother before Judge Leslie Furches in the Juvenile Session of the District Court. During the proceeding in the Miller Annex, he admitted to the charge of being "beyond parental control," and promised to give up his rebellious ways. In a pre-trial interview with a family service worker he had already admitted using marijuana, LSD and "herbal things" during the summer months. In a "Predisposition Investigation Report" prepared for the court by social worker Phil Kilby, he added cocaine to the list of drugs the boy may have abused. Kilby also noted that Rod was involved with the occult during that period.

Kilby observed in his report that family strengths included the professed willingness of Rod and his mother to accept outside help and intervention in their family problems. The social worker added that it was reported to him that Sondra's boyfriend, whom he described by the slightly archaic term, "paramour," was a positive influence on Rod, and that they shared some activities. He quoted Sondra as saying that Newman attended AA meetings and had "reformed his life since he was in the 'pen.' "

Other potentially favorable factors cited in the report were Rod's desire to be free of court restrictions and to see his girlfriend. Kilby said that Rod accepted the responsibility for his behavior and considered it to be in the past. "It appears to this worker that while Ms. Gibson and Mr. Farrell [sic] may be resolved to change their family functioning, it is unreasonable to expect a complete about-face so quickly," Kilby wrote. However, "There are discipline issues which seem to be incompletely addressed. While it is commendable that Mr. Farrell can rely upon his girlfriend, it would be better to establish more skill in self control.'' Rod's last name was alternately misspelled and correctly spelled in the report.

More importantly, the social workers seemed to realize that the youth's professed desire to change his ways needed to be taken with a grain of salt. Kilby had undoubtedly been down that road before with other clients, and his doubts showed a rare insight. He recommended that the court suspend any time to be served by Rod, with the stipulation that the troubled juvenile and his mother comply with certain conditions. They included requirements that both mother and son enroll in a program called Life Education to Empower People (LEEP), which utilized group therapy and weekly lessons for troubled children and their parents. The non-profit program began in Paducah and later extended into Murray, and adults and children attended separate sessions.

The court complied with the social worker's recommendation, and tacked on some additional tough rules for Rod to live by. He was ordered to remain in counseling with Murray mental health authorities; submit to random screening by the agency for substance abuse; re-enroll in school for the next semester, and remain in school until he graduated or turned eighteen; abide by a curfew of 10 p.m. weekdays and 11 p.m. on weekends; obtain his mother's permission to go out, and abide by her rules about when he was to return home and who he was allowed to be with; make no more threats against her; avoid associating with anyone involved with drugs or the occult; and create and submit to the court a two-page single-spaced typed essay ''chronicling the detrimental effects drugs, the occult and defiant behavior has had in his life.'' That sounded good, but it was like telling the sun to rise in the west.

Rod avoided juvenile detention and walked out of the courtroom in the Miller Annex side-by-side with his mother, but if he was truly contrite about his misbehavior it was a fleeting emotion. The recommendations might have turned his life around if he had made a serious effort to comply with them, but he had barely left the shadow of the annex before he went straight back to his old ways. He continued to sleep most of the day and then venture out at night to see his girlfriend, Charity, hang around with his other friends and haunt the dark shadows of cemeteries.

The rebellious youth didn't keep any of the promises, including writing the essay. Frustrated court officials ordered him to return to the court on November 25 and explain to the judge why the paper was never written. Rod wasn't even in Kentucky that day. The unruly teenager from the Bluegrass State was in Florida. It was the day Naoma and Richard Wendorf died.

As the last days of summer played out in western Kentucky, local farmers began harvesting their rich fields of tobacco. The thin-leafed, bright-colored burley was cut and brought in from the fields, then stacked on frames inside tobacco barns for drying. Waist-high rows of rougher, dark-fired tobacco were also harvested and transported to the barns, where it was loaded on racks four feet off the floor. Then hickory logs and limbs, or other carefully selected aromatic woods, were spread over a thick blanket of sawdust on the floor and ignited. It was the beginning of a long process that hadn't changed in Calloway and the surrounding tobacco counties for more than a century. The sawdust smoldered for weeks, while the rich aromas and flavors of the scented wood worked their way into the leaves that would eventually be turned into snuff and other smokeless tobacco.

In the city of Murray, while leaves on the poplars, oaks and maples turned into brilliant splashes of red, orange and yellow, students were unloading luggage from car trunks, pinning posters to apartment walls, checking into dormitories and generally settling into the routine of the new school year at Murray State College. But Rod and his adopted vampire kindred were largely oblivious to the rich, pulsing life of the larger community around them. He and his friends were moving increasingly deeper into a bleak and miserable fantasy world of black magic and depravity.

One night he was hanging out with a nineteen-year-old crony when he picked up a stray kitten by the hind legs, then swung it around and smashed it against a tree.

It was possible to absorb the energy and hunting intelligence of animals by killing them, he believed.

4. VAMPS

"I played it with him. It's hard enough to find something you can do with your kids today, and the game was fun."
— Sondra Gibson, Reuters interview

The time would come when jittery residents of Calloway County talked in hushed tones about a mysterious stranger from New Orleans who showed up one day and introduced many of their most impressionable young people to a fantasy role-playing game constructed around a mythical society of vampires. Then, his job completed, he faded back into the mists.

Based on the work of investigators who later probed the genesis of the game's local popularity, it seems there was no Pied Piper–like character in Murray at all. There was no need for one. Young people all over the country had discovered "Vampire: The Masquerade" and other role-playing games featuring gothic and mystic characters ranging from the undead and werewolves to fire-breathing dragons and dashing heroes.

Two decades earlier, in 1974, another widely popular role-playing game called "Dungeons & Dragons" exploded onto the American scene, attracting thousands of gamesters who spent periods ranging from a few hours to weeks at a time creating the rich characters and complicated plots and subplots. Other role-playing games were developed by TSR, Inc., the creators of D & D, and new competitors quickly sprang up.

In an age when many of their contemporaries had their noses stuck to computer screens, dealing with modems, CD-ROMs and brilliant graphics, the role-playing games provided participants an opportunity to bond and interact with other human beings while losing themselves for a few hours or a few days in safe fantasy worlds. Role-playing games sell by the millions.

The most successful of the newcomers was White Wolf, based originally in Stone Mountain, Georgia, and later in nearby Clarkston, a DeKalb County suburb of Atlanta. In 1991, White Wolf introduced its most successful game, "Vampire: The Masquerade." By 1996, more than half a million copies of "Vampire" had been sold, another game, "Werewolf: The Apocalypse," was marking up huge sales and White Wolf was recognized as the forty-fifth fastest-growing company in the United States. "Vampire" even had its own home page on the Internet. One sample home page message lured prospective players with the leading question: "What is a claim of age for ones who are immortal? What is a claim of power for ones who defy death? . . . We shall see whom I drag screaming to hell with me."

"Vampire" was the first of the popular games that allowed players to move away from boards, card tables and dice, and assume roles by dressing the part, speaking in dialogue believed to fit the characters and time and acting out the scenarios. Players can still square off over a card table form of the game if they prefer that to live action, however. And if they prefer, they can play either version of the game casually dressed in bluejeans, sweats, or T-shirts and skirts. It is not unusual for gamesters, especially when squaring off in the live action version of "Vampire" to take a year or more to complete a game. White Wolf's fictional vampires belong to a series of clans, who are often warring members of a larger vampire society known as the Camarilla. Following a terrible inquisition that wiped out almost all the world's vampires, the Camarilla was formed as an underground government in order to avoid total annihilation of the race, according to the game's creators. While warring

among themselves, however, the vampires cooperate in
"The Masquerade," an effort designed to prevent humanity
from learning of their existence.

Players are guided by a handbook outlining a loose set of
rules, and individual sourcebooks called "Clanbooks," that
define the characteristics of individual clans, such as the
powerful and business-oriented "Ventrue," the artsy "Toreadors," crazed "Malkavians" and grotesque "Nosferatu,"
to create their own characters according to their personal
tastes or whims. A gamemaster, or storyteller, presides over
sessions of the game, sometimes hiding riddles or clues
while vampires work to solve individual problems. Specially
manufactured dice, some with ten sides and some with the
more traditional six, are also components of the games and
play a part in maintaining the challenge and unpredictability
of the adventures. Consequently, the narrative direction of
the game is partly up to the players, partly based on the roll
of the dice, and partly controlled by the rules created by the
manufacturer.

Although all vampires are "kindred" to each other, they
don't always get along, and nasty schisms occur within and
between individual clans, leading to struggles for dominance. Players, who choose vampire names, personalities
and characteristics such as strength, perception and dexterity,
are expected to resolve the conflicts. Vampires have ghouls
as slaves to do their bidding and may also run into troubles
with Lupines—werewolves—or other dread and mysterious
creatures that inhabit the more darkly gothic role-playing
games.

The Georgia-based company maintains the enthusiasm of
players by continuously publishing new volumes, scenarios
and versions of their games. One popular followup on
"Vampire: The Masquerade" is titled "Vampire: The Dark
Ages," and set in Medieval Europe. White Wolf even pub-
lishes its own "World of Darkness" series of novels tied to
the characters and clans in their game worlds.

Significantly, perhaps, one of the more ominous male
characters among "Vampire: The Masquerade's" "Torea-

dor" clan is known as "The Outcast." He is a sullen, renegade tattoo artist who refuses to take orders or follow the rules—and his most glaringly traitorous acts lead to the destruction of his closest companions.

Rod became deeply involved in "Vampire: The Masquerade." He and his longtime friend, Damion, had participated in role-playing games since they first became chums in elementary school. But after his return to Murray from Florida, Rod was either unable or unwilling to separate the fantasy of the elaborate role-playing game from the grim realities of his everyday life, even though an excellent example of how the game could be given the positive, innocently entertaining spin it was designed for was available practically on his doorstep. Rod attended a few sessions of VAMPS, but never became seriously involved with the role-playing group.

VAMPS was an acronym for the Victorian Age Masquerade Performance Society, organized by James Yohe. Yohe was a twenty-five-year-old married student at Murray State carrying a major in theater and minors in business and graphic arts who was a fan of role-playing games. Yohe settled on the game as a handy gimmick to attract people to participate in skits and other performances produced to raise money for charity. The organizer contacted local humane societies and charities benefitting children and offered to help raise money with VAMPS activities. Members of VAMPS and their supporters used the live-action gothic fantasy game as an improvisational tool, writing loose story lines, then permitting the players to fill in the blanks by developing the characters and working through whatever problems they were faced with. Rules taken from White Wolf gamebooks were used as the guidelines.

It appeared to Yohe that the timing for launching VAMPS was good, because interest in vampire books and movies was at a peak. Author Anne Rice's best-selling novel *Interview With the Vampire* had been turned into a blockbuster movie starring teenage heartthrobs Brad Pitt and Tom Cruise, other books with similar themes were practically leaping off the shelves, and additional vampire-related films were in the works in Hollywood.

Recent television series also featured the undead, including a Fox Entertainment Network show based on "Vampire: The Masquerade" called *Kindred: The Embraced. Kindred* aired for only eight segments during the 1995–96 season, but that was long enough to create a hard core of fans who continued to debate the characterizations and plots on the Internet. Television vampires sometimes even appear as the good guys. *Forever Knight*, appropriately aired in a late-night timeslot during the 1992–93 television season, attracted its own fan club for the series, and a couple of others formed around the star, Geraint Wyn-Davies, and actor Nigel Bennett, who played a character named "LaCroix."

With any kind of good luck at all, it seemed to Yohe that VAMPS could successfully ride the crest of the dark wave of vampire mania that was sweeping the country, especially among young people. VAMPS was based on a theatrical premise, so players dressed for their vampiric roles. Some of them wore white face paint or emphasized their mouths with thick slashes of scarlet lipstick. Some also spoke in what they believed was gothic or other dialect that they considered to be appropriate to the times and to their characters.

Since it was a masquerade, many of the players also adopted aliases to fit in with the personalities or characters. Yohe used the name "Giles." Rod apparently never used the name Vassago while participating in VAMPS activities, though he used the name at other times, in other situations, just as his longtime friend John Goodman used "Damion," and another close friend, Steven Murphy, called himself "Jeremy S. Fulcher" and other times, "Jaden."

The VAMPS players utilized the Murray State campus, the Murray–Calloway County Park which bordered the school to the west, and sometimes met at Yohe's home. VAMPS enforced strict rules against anyone bringing drugs or alcohol to the performances. At its peak, the society had about twenty-five people who regularly participated in the activities, and a few others who attended performances or held lesser roles. Some players drove to Murray from as far away as Nashville, a two-and-a-half-hour journey, in order to participate in the nocturnal games that were scheduled about every two weeks.

Rod hung out with some of the people involved with VAMPS but never became a member. Most of the more active players were a few years older, and Rod and most of his closest teenage cronies were unable or unwilling to pony up the $25 initiation fee. He attended two or three of the game sessions or performances, and Yohe was introduced to him by other teenagers. Looking back later on his first meeting with Rod, Yohe speculated that he was probably introduced to the youngster by either April Doeden or Steven Murphy.

Steven was approximately three years older than Rod and was an especially close friend of his at that time. They first met while attending Calloway County High School, where Steven believed he had been stereotyped as a Satanist. Other students tried to set up a fight between the peculiar boys with the oddball interests, but Steven figured that he and Rod were too much alike to allow that to happen. He crossed up the troublemakers and introduced himself to the younger boy.

The two high school mavericks quickly became close companions and confidants, sharing their cryptic interests in vampires and other aspects of the dark side. It was Steven who watched Rod kill the cat. The boys shared long, serious talks about death and killing. Steven later recalled that the discussions were always about fantasy, never reality. But one of the most serious subjects of discussion focused on exactly what they would do to avenge the death of someone they loved. Sometimes their morose discussions of revenge occurred at the Old Salem Cemetery. It was one of their favorite places to while away the night hours, strolling among the silent dead and through the eerie shadows of the tombs, stone slabs, granite angels and spires. According to Murphy, the boys decided they would get their revenge by beating their unfortunate enemy "to shit or slice them up, 'cause shooting them would be too easy.''*

The boys didn't discuss such things at the VAMPS meetings. It wouldn't have been allowed, and they wouldn't have been welcome to continue hanging around with the serious players. Rod treated the meetings and other VAMPS activities primarily as social gatherings, and the few times he participated, his character never really helped resolve the conflicts posed by the story lines. His friends were there, so Rod tagged along, but he treated the situation merely as an opportunity to hang out instead of becoming very actively involved. He spent most of his time quietly observing the activity of others, and didn't do much talking. "He was just very laid back and relaxed," Yohe later recalled.

Another of Rod's friends, Howard Scott Anderson, also showed up at VAMPS events a couple of times. The boys had been friends since they were in the first grade together, and Scott was even more quiet and laid back than Rod. He sat around watching and listening to others who participated more actively in the games. Scott and Steven once teamed up with Rod to pose for a local comic book artist who photographed the boys in the Old Salem Cemetery. Rod was shown jumping on a grave in one picture, and another depicted Steven stretched out face-up on a gravestone, Rod beside him holding a long-bladed knife above his head with both hands, as if he were about to plunge it into the older boy's chest. Another of the photographs captured a bare-chested Rod hanging upside-down by his legs, bat-like, with his arms crossed over his bony chest. Role-playing vampires supposedly become invisible when they cross their arms over their chests. The artist planned to use the pictures as models for drawings she was creating. The comic book had a dismal, vampiric tone that was very much in the style of VAMPS, and the boys were excellent models.

Eventually, Rod and some of his closest pseudo-vampire kindred quit showing up at the VAMPS activities. VAMPS

*Who Weekly, December 16, 1996.

may have been too tame for his tastes, but whatever the reason, he began veering off in another more ominous direction, leading his own games that were expanded to include mock killings. While other Calloway County High School kids were cruising around Court Square, harmlessly yelling at each other and flirting, Rod and his brothers and sisters of the fang were prowling through the shadowy alleys and backroads playing diabolic blood games.

Steven later recalled that the all-night exercises were "a major adrenaline rush," and the youths usually wound up the games by gathering at a twenty-four-hour Hardee's restaurant to relive the adventures and boast of their prowess as imaginary killers. Rod was always hyper after the games and Steven thought he talked and behaved as if he were wired on speed. It took him a while to come down.

After a while, Rod and some of his small band of companions began to talk about the imaginary vampire subculture as if it really existed; as if there really were Nosferatu, Toreadors and Malkavians. The strange, brooding boy acted as if he believed it was indeed possible to cross over and become one of the mystical immortals. The small group of renegade gamesters were crossing the line, and were becoming a cult.

An especially macabre element of participation in the clan was an act they called "embracement," the mutual sharing and sucking of blood. Embracement was also the most important element of "crossing over," the ritualistic first-time sharing of blood that served as the initiation for a new vampire. According to Steven, Rod and his comrades believed that it was necessary that the "crossing over" occur on consecrated ground such as a cemetery. Rod loved the feeling of power and control that the ritual gave him.

Rod was rapidly slipping deeper into a nightmare netherworld filled with gruesome images of blood, murder and sheer horror, and the menacing new direction in which he was leading his most devoted followers cost him some of his closest friends. Damion was designated as the clan's second-in-command, but he dropped out of the circle after

Rod accused him of plotting a coup attempt. As the boy later recounted the incident to homicide investigators, the old friends got into a fight after Rod learned that Heather wanted Damion to take over the vampire clan. Rod wound up kicking out some of Damion's teeth. Then he began looking around for a new second-in-command, and for a new "sire" for the fifteen-year-old would-be vampire queen waiting in Eustis.

In one of Heather's letters, she wrote about the nasty split between Rod and Damion that put her in the middle of a ferocious tug-of-war and reputedly led to the two boys plotting each other's murder. Was the letter nothing more than the darkly romantic fantasizing of a bored teenager with an overactive imagination? Or did it provide the first ominous hint of the bloody detour the vampire obsession was about to take from harmless fun to deadly reality?

The fledgling Vampire Clan was becoming too weird, too frightening, and the teens were behaving as if they were no longer playing a game. Rod also clearly realized there was room for only one leader, and his disagreements with other males capable of launching threats to the throne were uniformly violent.

For awhile Vassago and Jaden were as close as Damon and Pythias. After whiling away the night playing at being vampires, listening to records or watching vampire movies on a VCR, Rod often slept over at his chum's house just off Kentucky State Road 94, which becomes Main Street when it cuts through the center of Murray. Like Rod, Steven favored black clothes, but he had his own special touch. The older boy liked heavy metal bands, and he usually wore black T-shirts with the image and name of one group or another on the front. Rod also liked rockers; most of his peers did, even the kids who faithfully attended church. The church-goers were likely to listen to Christian-oriented musicians such as Amy Grant, Steven Curtis Chapman, Kirk Franklin or the Washington-based group, "D. C. Talk." Their costumes and lyrics were more acceptable.

Rod and most of his close friends preferred listening to

groups and performers like "AC/DC," Ozzy Osbourne and Marilyn Manson that were generally off-limits to their more conventionally religious neighbors. The costumes and lyrics of the bands Rod was drawn to tended to be as darkly threatening to his Bible-thumping neighbors as a swarm of thirsty vampire bats.

There is also a strong middleground between Christian musicians and Marilyn Manson or "AC/DC," and Rod and his friends were perfectly willing to take advantage of the opportunities for a little harmless fun whenever a local group appeared at a concert on the Murray State campus. A couple of times Rod attended outdoor shows by a locally-based five-member band called "Trippin' Lizard." The lead singer was a tall, slender dude named Jim Mahanes, who wore his long, blonde hair pulled back into a ponytail when he wasn't performing at concerts for the MSU Student Government Association. "Trippin' Lizard" steered away from Marilyn Manson material, and specialized in "grunge rock," like the music of "Pearl Jam" and "Alice in Chains."

For a while the close friendship between Rod and Steve included frequently sharing the telephone during lengthy collect calls to Heather. They talked for hours, chatting about "Vampire: The Masquerade," joking with Heather—and sometimes extending the talks to include Jennifer. Steve later recalled talking with Heather's older sister more than once. Eventually, however, the boys had a falling-out over what Rod depicted as a struggle for supremacy.

The friendship ended abruptly at about midnight, Wednesday, August 28, 1996, when Rod and Steven clashed in a brief fracas next to a stairwell downstairs from the Gibson apartment. Steven was six feet tall and a solid, muscular 192 pounds, and the younger boy lost the uneven contest. Rod was scrappy and quick to resort to violence to settle a disagreement, but he was as thin and lean as a strip of Bob Evans bacon, and he was no match for the bigger boy.

Steven was already becoming increasingly disenchanted with the behavior of Rod and some of his other friends, and his girlfriend didn't want him hanging around with the younger kids. They behaved like a bunch of weirdos. Steven was in a bad mood and his temper was as prickly as a porcupine when he showed up at Rod's apartment. His nasty humor intensified when he realized that Rod was quarreling with his mother again. Recalling the incident later, Steven said that when Rod began mouthing off, he grabbed the younger boy by the throat, slammed him against a wall and choked him until he started turning blue.

As soon as Steven released his hold, Rod lurched upstairs to his room. Steven began to feel bad about roughing up his friend and went upstairs to apologize. He was standing outside Rod's room when the blade of a knife was suddenly jammed through the wooden door, he said. When he peered inside the room, Rod was pacing back and forth carrying a baseball bat.

According to Rod's account, disclosed in an affidavit he filed in Calloway County District Court as part of a fourth-degree assault charge against the older youth, Steven choked him and threw him against a wall. Rod said that he was at home with his mother when Steven and another youth stopped by to visit a few minutes before midnight. After awhile Rod and the other boy went downstairs to smoke, and about the time he finished his cigarette, Steven joined them.

Continuing with the statement, Rod said that after a few minutes of talk, Steven demanded to know what he had to do with another youth "messing" with his girlfriend. Rod protested that he didn't have anything to do with the situation, and Steven accused him of lying. At that point, Steven grabbed him by the throat and slammed his head against the brick wall. Steven snarled, "Don't fuck with me," while choking him. The younger boy said he thought he was going to pass out while Steven continued cussing and choking him, before he was finally released. As Rod began shakily climbing the stairs to his apartment, Steven shouted a harsh parting shot at him: "Now you know I'm superior and you're under me."

Rod's mother provided a slightly different version of the

confrontation. She said the older boy pushed her son and told him, "Now you know who's the Prince of the City." That was an apparent reference to one of the more powerful characters in "Vampire," and both boys had played the role at different times while they were gaming.

Steven saw Rod the day after the encounter and apologized, but it was too late. A few minutes before noon on Tuesday, September 3, six days after the brawl between the two longtime chums, Murray Police Department officers arrested Steven on a warrant for fourth-degree assault. He was freed on $500 cash bail, with instructions that he have no contact with the complaining witness. Rod stated in the affidavit that he believed Murphy would try to hurt him if he had a chance. Almost a month later, on September 30, Steven appeared in the district court at the Miller Annex and pleaded guilty to the charge. He eventually spent seven days across the street in the Calloway County Jail, the remainder of a six-month sentence was suspended, he paid a fine and costs totalling $82.50 and was ordered to stay at least one hundred feet away from Rod.

The former close kinship between the two teenagers was permanently shattered, and each of the boys assembled his own circle of friends. According to Steven, soon after the fracas at the South Side Manor apartments, he and his most loyal friends became the targets of threats from his former chum. He heard that Vassago had formed a vampire clan and was going to take control of the city from him. His former vampire kinsman wanted his power, Steven believed.

Rod's abrasive, trouble-making ways didn't change after he was roughed up by Steven, even though his efforts to enlist new blood from among the youths he hung around with in Calloway County were modest. Most older teenagers, and some of the younger ones, thought that the carefully crafted air of ebony malignancy he surrounded himself with was more ludicrous than intimidating. But trouble clung to him and followed him wherever he went.

One of the people Rod tried his vampire spiel on was nineteen-year-old Jason Scott Jones, who lived across the hall from him at the South Side Manor Apartments with a wife and a year-old baby. One day Jason saw Rod putting together firebombs, and didn't even ask what the boy planned to do with them. Some things it's better not to know. Another time Rod casually mentioned that he was going to kill some people and move to Florida. The young family man apparently didn't take the statement seriously. Rod was always popping off with far-out remarks. That was the way he was: a skinny, pimply-faced blowhard who was full of cock-and-bull stories.

Jason had a job with a construction company and wasn't as footloose as younger boys, who stayed out half the night roaming through Murray and rural Calloway County with his strange neighbor, but they did some buddying around—and it led to trouble. That was becoming routine for people who became too friendly with Rod.

At about 10 or 10:30 on the night of November 5, Jason drove Rod and another juvenile named Michael to April Doeden's home at Grogan's Trailer Park in Murray. April had a house full of friends, including Steven Murphy, who was sitting on the front porch with a teenage girl. Michael got out of the car and asked Steven to tell another boy named Joey who was inside the house to come out. But Steven was worried about getting in trouble because of the court order prohibiting him from having any contact with Rod. So he went inside the trailer and telephoned the sheriff's department to tell them Rod had just shown up. April joined the girl who was still outside on the porch.

Rod got out of the car and told April that he'd heard she and Joey were looking for him, but she said that wasn't true. Then Rod began ranting about being a nine-foot demon, and said he wanted Joey to kill him in order to free him of his worldly existence and make him more powerful.

It was classic Rod Ferrell, but dying violently in order to be reincarnated as a powerful supernatural entity such as a demon or vampire wasn't a unique idea. It is a common element of some diabolist beliefs. In rural southern New Jersey, near the city of Vineland, several years before Rod was born, a teenager who believed that his violent death would lead to his reincarnation as a mighty demon who would command forty of Satan's legions convinced a couple of his high school chums to tie him up and throw him into a lake, where he drowned. Rod had claimed to be a nine-foot demon before. April wasn't impressed, and she ordered him to leave.

Her friends began drifting back into the trailer, and Rod climbed back into the car with his pals. He was in the front passenger seat, Michael was in the back seat by himself, and Jason was driving. As the driver began slowly pulling out of the trailer park, April stepped up behind the vehicle to write down the license plate number. That was when she heard someone, who sounded to her like Rod, yell, "Back up," she later related. According to her account, Jason suddenly slammed the car in reverse and it lurched backward. April leaped out of the way, but the right rear tire of the car ran over her right foot.

The young mother was treated at the local hospital emergency room, where X-rays failed to show any broken bones. She also told her story to Murray police, and said she believed Jason knew she was behind the car and deliberately tried to run her over. The lanky, six-foot-two-inch driver was arrested at his apartment at the South Side Manor on charges of reckless endangerment in the first degree. The charge is a felony, and Jason was in serious trouble. He was freed on $2,500 bail, and ordered to have no contact with April, the complaining witness.

Rod was getting into one mess after another, and was developing a reputation for dragging just about anyone who hung around with him into his troubles. Most of the young people who knew him gave him a wide berth. By the time the friendship between Rod and Steven dissolved in the fracas outside the Ferrell apartment and in the courtroom, VAMPS and Jim Yohe were folding their tent. Interest in the club was flagging, the effort to attract new dues-paying members was dead in the water, and Rod and a few other hangers-on were veering off into a frightening new direction.

For a sixteen-year-old, Rod inhabited a wildly chaotic and dangerous world. Trouble seemed to surround him on every side.

His relationship with his mother was especially curious and contradictory; at one time it might appear strained almost to the breaking point, and the next day or the next week the mother and son were sharing activities, including the boy's morbid fascination with vampires. Sondra sometimes joined in the role-playing game with Rod and his friends, and later indicated to a reporter that it seemed harmless. "I played it with him," she said. "It's hard enough to find something you can do with your kids today, and the game was fun. It was something, anyway."

Sometimes she was so determined to exert parental discipline that she virtually dragged him to the mental health clinic or to court. At other times, however, she behaved as if she had surrendered to his will. And if his accusations and those of the angry mother of one of his pals were based on solid evidence, Sondra crafted her own vampire game, giving it a personal predatory sexual twist that plunged her into deep trouble with the courts.

The troubled five-foot-one-inch, 105-pound woman was served a criminal summons accusing her of two misdemeanors for allegedly trying to seduce Steven Murphy's fourteen-year-old brother by telling him that sexual relations with her were part of a vampire initiation ritual. (The boy's last name is different from that of his mother and older brother.) Police caught up with Sondra at her job at the DSS, and served the arrest warrant. Sondra later contended that she understood the boy to be over 18 and in college, yet in one letter to him she ungrammatically noted, "If you was 18 . . .". She was later permanently removed from the position, and an agency spokesman blamed the dismissal on her work performance as well as the criminal charges.

She was charged with criminal solicitation to commit rape in the third degree, and criminal solicitation to commit sodomy in the third degree, after Penny Murphy swore out an affidavit complaining about Sondra's behavior. The outraged mother said her younger son was also a friend of Rod's and was frequently at Sondra's home. She claimed that Sondra once kissed the boy against his will, the statement continued, and after he was sent to live with his father in Gallatin, Tennessee, she wrote letters to him describing sexual fantasies of the two of them together. The woman added that Sondra sent the boy a key to her apartment, and in her letters made Satanic references and talked about "becoming a vampire and being his bride."

The scandal began to break into the open on September 16, when Penny Murphy marched into the DSS office carrying a handful of letters Sondra had written to the boy. The family services office supervisor referred Mrs. Murphy to Calloway County Attorney David Harrington. While the angry parent was huddling with Harrington about the embarrassing development, local bureaucrats at the DSS were immersed in a flurry of telephone calls, memos and note-writing aimed at tracing the agency's dealings with Sondra in her dual roles as client and employee. The communiques passed from family service workers, to protective services specialists, to supervisors and directors. They were peering under every rock and into every dark corner, seeking to determine if the agency could or should have made greater efforts to help or intervene in the problems of the dysfunctional family.

The inquiry was all very private and conducted as an internal probe. In Murray, the DSS and allied arms of the local social service apparatus are reluctant to share sensitive information with the public about matters like the mortifying scrape their client and former part-time worker had gotten herself into. The social workers can be as jealous of the secrecy and inner workings of the public agencies as any fund-raising political hack or highly paid White House legal advisor.

Authorities eventually released a sexually explicit letter Sondra wrote to the boy on June 23, five days after her thirty-fourth birthday, after he was sent to Tennessee. Two other notes she wrote to the boy in May, including a three-page letter fantasizing about sex with him, were later disclosed in court documents.

In the four-page June love letter, which was marked with occasional misspellings, she talked about her anguish after learning that he had returned to Tennessee, and said a neighbor drove her around town, then to his mother's to look for him. But it was too late. He was already gone. She wrote that she dreamed of his return, embrace, and "Yes [boy's name], to become a vampire, a part of the family, imortal [sic] and truely [sic] yours forever." She talked of her hopes that he would return to Murray and "cross me over and I will be your bride for Eternity and you my Sire," she said.

Sondra wrote that she had heard rumors that he was afraid of her "because of sex," and agreed she knew a lot about the subject because of her age and experience. She assured him she would never do anything to make him uncomfortable, and said she figured "Steven and them" had told him she was "wild and a slut." The truth was that she had only been with two men since moving to Murray, and it had been months since she had had sex. She recalled times when she had wished that he would stay at the apartment and spend the night with her.

The woman also wrote about her desire to put on her blue denim sundress and perform oral sex on him before moving on to regular sexual intercourse—which she described in some detail. "I've dreamed of you crossing me over while your [sic] getting off," she wrote. She noted that he had his own key to her apartment and suggested that he could probably talk his father into letting him move in. His brother was welcome to visit as well, she said. The steamy letter was signed "Forever your Star." A five-pointed star trailing a pair of interjoined wavy lines forming a huge heart was drawn under the signature.

In one of the earlier letters, written May 17, she fretted about her boredom and talked of moving to a new job in a few days as a receptionist at the Social Security Administration offices. She was proud that she would have her own computer at work. Turning to news of her son, she told the boy that Rod and "Shei [sic] are still together," although he was still talking to other girls in Kentucky and Florida. Sondra said she was looking forward to a trip to Florida on June 13, and planned to stay a week so she could continue a custom of always spending her birthdays on the beach. She suggested they exchange pictures and said she planned to go to the mall that weekend and buy him a necklace she had seen and wanted him to have. "So you can wear it & know that your [sic] thought about & missed a lot!" The dot on the end of the exclamation point was formed into a heart.

Sondra told the absent teenager how sexy she thought he was, and said if he were eighteen she would find a way for him to return to Murray so he could move into her apartment "and we could have some wild sex every night." She wrote that the first time they met she thought he was a college student, and she loved the way he was "so mysterious." The letter was signed: "Love your friend eternally Sondra." A large heart dripping what appeared to be two drops of blood from the tip was drawn at the edge of the page. She included several pictures of herself wearing a swimsuit in one of the letters, and one of the poses was especially sexy.

The entire incident was a terrible mistake, Sondra later claimed. The correspondence was all part of the fantasy vampire game. In other remarks to reporters she blamed the legal ruckus on Penny Murphy, whom she said was looking for revenge because of the charges filed against Steven after he beat up on Rod. There would never have been any trouble over her interest in the younger boy if Steven hadn't been arrested. Steven's mother didn't complain about the matter until less than one month after he was arrested for roughing up Rod, Sondra added. She was nevertheless ordered to appear in the Calloway County District Court on October 14 for a hearing on the charges. When she failed to appear, the hearing was postponed for several weeks. Ultimately, Sondra pled guilty to trying to entice the 14-year-old boy to have sex.

Rod was unfazed by the menacing storm clouds and the

chaos and turmoil that blew up and flashed around him, his mother and just about everyone else he was closely associated with. His life was becoming like one of the fierce thunderstorms that formed and burst over the mountains east of Murray with such regularity during the rainy season, drenching the peaks and roaring through the hollows and gulleys.

The gloomy youth who floated through the shadows of the night with such a gathering sense of foreboding was behaving as if the intellectually challenging fantasy game was totally merged and confused with his real life. Instead of playing the roles and harmlessly flirting with the darkly romantic fictional universe, he had become a permanent denizen of a real vampire world. Steven and other gamesters who had previously joined him and his dwindling band of close friends in long, challenging adventures, avoided him as though he were an accident waiting to happen.

5. THE VAMPIRE HOTEL

"I feel this case will end in a tragedy, due to escalating behaviors. I feel it won't be long."
          —*Social worker Edna Cothran*

Despite the loss of Steven Murphy's friendship and his ostracism from other gamesters who were alarmed at his behavior, Vassago had assembled the core of a vampire family in Kentucky, and was almost ready for a third and final return trip to Florida to pick up Zoe and any other Eustis teenagers they were able to recruit. He adopted a personal "V"-shaped mystical sign with dots added to each side signifying the number of members in his vampire clan, he told friends.

The vampire kindred whom the developing cult leader gathered around him in Kentucky were the misguided and non-conformists: gullible teenagers ready to follow him for love or a sense of belonging.

For Rod, the fantasy vampire universe he had entered was more appealing than the dreary realities of his life in the rent-subsidized apartment he occupied with his mother and her boyfriend. And he was pulling his friends along with him inside a labyrinthian nightmare world of sinister shadows and monstrous acts that was about to fill with blood, cruelty, pain and savage violence.

Howard Scott Anderson was also the product of a severely dysfunctional home that was even more filled with depri-

vation and neglect than Rod's. He was the oldest son of four
boys in a family whose struggles with alcohol, violence and
crushing poverty had been the subject of intervention by
local social service agencies since 1993. His father, Howard
B. Anderson, had a nasty drinking problem that turned him
as mean as a coal field bully, ravaging his family and frightening neighbors and social workers.

During the early 1990s the Andersons lived in Hazel, a
rustic hamlet about a ten-minute drive south from Murray
along U.S. Highway 641 that is best known for its antique
mall and flea market. The town is within easy hollering distance of the Tennessee state line. The peak-roofed, two-
story, wood-frame house the Andersons lived in was a
disaster, and had been allowed to deteriorate horribly. A
wooden porch running across the front and along one side
was falling down, and the yard was littered with beer cans,
bottles, broken pieces of lumber, old tires and other debris.
Inside the rickety structure, gaping holes loomed from the
floor and walls, and even during the worst of the Kentucky
winter most of the windows were broken or left open. Doors
hung at odd angles from broken hinges, or were leaned hap-
hazardly against walls. The rooms were cluttered with cardboard boxes, ragged splintered boards, beer bottles and other
trash.

Two television sets and a window fan squatted among the
litter in one room, and a dilapidated bunk bed was in another. Much of the time there was no electricity in the house
because bills hadn't been paid, and at least once a long ex-
tension cord was strung through one of the windows, snaked
across the lawn and plugged into a hookup at a neighbor's
house so the Andersons could watch TV.

Social workers were frightened of Howard, and he told
them that alcohol didn't account for his only substance abuse
problem. He claimed he also had a long history of using
cocaine, LSD and marijuana. One time when a social worker
noticed a couple of clubs in a corner of a room, Anderson
boasted that he had made them and could use them to kill
someone if he wished. He assured the woman she didn't

have to worry, however, because he wouldn't hurt her.

In January 1994, Howard was charged with felony assault in the Calloway County Circuit Court after allegedly hitting his wife on the head with a bottle. She refused to testify, so the charge was lowered to a misdemeanor count of wanton endangerment. Circuit Judge David Buckingham ordered Howard to spend thirty days at an alcohol treatment center, and to leave the house and live away from the family pending a psychiatric evaluation. According to the court order, the husband and wife were permitted to see each other only in public places. Howard moved into a mobile home, and about the time he changed his address to Grogan's Trailer Court, Martha was admitted to the psychiatric unit at the Murray–Calloway County Hospital. She had been pestered by thoughts of suicide.

While all that was going on, social workers from the Calloway County office of the DSS, in concert with local court and medical authorities, applied themselves to the task of trying to repair the damaged family and protect the children. One of the easier jobs was taken on by Family Preservation workers, who saw to it that the broken windows were replaced, other repairs were made to the house, the yard was spruced up and the beer cans and other trash were carted away.

Successful intervention aimed at making the family more functional was a more difficult task. Martha wasn't out of the hospital very long before a family service worker was writing more troubling reports about neglect of the boys and difficulties with both parents. Edna Cothran, the same social worker who later shared disturbing conversations with Sondra Gibson, wrote a memo to her supervisor urging fast action in dealing with the family's problems. Mrs. Anderson spent most of her time with her husband, leaving the children without food or electricity, the concerned social worker said. Ms. Cothran added that Hazel municipal authorities believed the house should be condemned, and she agreed.

Early in June, Hazel's town constable, Max Parrish, notified a social worker that the Anderson children had been left alone for three days. As a town constable, Parrish also functioned as one of six Calloway County constables, and juggled an additional job as the Calloway County animal control officer. It was Parrish who later rounded up some of the dogs that escaped from the shelter in Murray. Shortly after 9 p.m., five-year-old Nicholas "Nicky" Anderson was found huddled on the steps at the front of the house, crying because he was locked out and didn't have anything to eat. He told Parrish that his mother had gone to Grogan's Trailer Court and was never coming back. Parrish contacted social workers and was advised to round up the other boys, who were believed to be hanging around Hazel, and bring all the Anderson children to the Murray Police Department. The day before Nicky was rescued from the front steps, his mother had angrily advised social workers that the state was welcome to take the children. "I'm going to be with Howard," she said.

Parrish was a busy man, but he located the other boys. Before he could transport them to Murray, however, Howard and Martha Anderson showed up and began quarreling with him and a neighbor who had become involved in the family troubles. Ruth Daughaday, a social worker with the DSS who was on call that night for emergencies, also parked her car at the house at almost exactly the same time that Howard and Martha drove up with milk and other groceries. Mrs. Anderson claimed they were going to take the boys to her mother's house in Marshall County, which was Calloway County's next-door neighbor to the north. But the older woman told DSS authorities that she was old and sick and couldn't take care of the boys. Deputy Sheriff Joe Lawrence was finally dispatched to the house, where he collected the boys and drove them to the police department. The parents followed him to headquarters in their car, but at the request of the social worker they were advised to leave.

Various neighbors had temporarily sheltered one or more of the boys, but they turned down requests by DSS workers to take them in that night because they were scared of the father. They said they were afraid because of threats he had made. Eventually a member of a local church gathered up an armload of blankets, pillows and some food and sat up with the boys for the remainder of the night in the Hazel city hall. The DSS provided sleeping bags for the impromptu camp-out. The boys spent the next day at a local shelter, and the day after that a judge signed a custody order and they were placed in foster homes. One family took Scott and thirteen-year-old Robert, and another family took Nicholas and twelve-year-old Sam. A couple of days later Howard Anderson was reported to authorities to be outside of his mobile home at Grogan's Trailer Court beating on the sides of his car and screaming, "God damn Ruth Daughaday."

Ms. Cothran concluded her two-page memo to the supervisor by pleading for assistance and pointing out that there was "a high potential for violence. I feel this case will end in a tragedy, due to escalating behaviors," she wrote. "I feel it won't be long."

After Howard and Martha moved to Mayfield, the DSS set up a program of supervised visits for the family at the Graves County Family Services Office there. The early visits were marked by anger and disappointment. Howard staked out of the first meeting without speaking to any of his boys. Martha tangled with one of the foster parents when he walked in and began reading her the riot act for neglecting her children and failing to contact them at his home on birthdays. He complained she didn't even bother to telephone the boys to say hello.

Three weeks after Ms. Cothran first warned of the high potential for violence, the worried social worker forwarded another one-page memo to her supervisor, asking for advice about handling supervised visits at the DSS office by Howard Anderson with his children. He had come to her office and screamed at her in what she described as "a threatening manner." And when he "becomes violent Mrs. Anderson's behavior escalates," Ms. Cothran wrote. Supervising a visit at DSS put the social worker, staff and other people in the building at risk, she warned.

Ms. Cothran included copies of psychological and psychiatric evaluations showing that, according to the diagnosis of Howard's mental state, he suffered from major depression—"irritability"—and anti-social personality disorder. She warned that he was reportedly seen with a pistol by children at the trailer court, and during a court appearance a sheriff's deputy suspected that a bulge in Howard's pocket was made by a handgun.

Scott and Robert spent two years in foster care in the little north Calloway County community of Dexter living in the home of a Church of Christ deacon. They attended church regularly. The two younger boys spent a year at their first foster home, then were moved in with another family in Graves County. Robert graduated from the eighth grade at the Calloway County Middle School, and Scott was attending Calloway County High School when he met up with Rod, his longtime friend from the first grade. The boys began hanging around with each other. Scott was a much better student and generally much better behaved than his strange new sidekick. While he was at CCHS he maintained a "B" average in his courses, attended church two or three times a week, and took classes in Tae Kwon Do. He loved the Korean martial art, and seemed to understand the underlying philosophy of discipline and self-control. People who knew him then recalled that he did not normally behave violently, and rarely showed any displays of temper. Adults considered him to be "a nice boy."

In February 1996, after the senior Anderson got his drinking problem under control, and Martha had worked for a local hotel, then moved to a job as a cook in a cafe, the boys were reunited with their parents. Social workers believed the couple were making significant progress in putting their lives back together, and were ready to take on the responsibility of providing a better home with fit living conditions for their boys.

The boys moved back under their parents' roof—such as it was. After the boys were taken away and the house in Hazel was condemned, Howard and Martha Anderson eventually moved to another home in the nearby town of Mayfield. The two-story house wasn't a palace, but it was an improvement over the family's former home. The parents had undergone counseling, Howard consented to outpatient treatment at a substance abuse agency and they cleaned up their home, tossing out old clothes and trash, storing things in boxes and making improvements to the interior walls. Howard had been sober for months, but his health was broken and he was permanently disabled. He had survived three heart attacks and a couple of strokes, so the family hadn't broken the ugly grip of poverty. The Andersons still needed, and received, financial and other help from social agencies.

Scott preferred using his middle name, and it was easier for his family because it eliminated the confusion of sharing his father's first name. But like so many of the youngsters he hung out with, Scott also used other names. His parents usually called him by the affectionate, if unimaginative, nickname "Scotty." But the boy often referred to himself by a favorite nickname, "Nash." Regardless of his apparent efforts to alter the perception other people might develop about him by playing the name game, Scott didn't look all that different from many other teenage boys in western Kentucky. He was an unimposing, slender youth who wore glasses and parted his wavy shoulder-length brown hair in the middle—like his friend Rod. Most of the time he wore a scraggly pencil-thin mustache that peaked just under the tip of his nose.

Even though Howard B. Anderson was facing down the devil in the bottle, he was still unable to hold down a job and the family lived in grinding poverty in a wood-frame house. At times they had no heat or running water. During the coldest weather, blankets were stretched along the walls to capture and preserve heat. The Andersons sometimes borrowed money from a neighbor when they didn't have food in the house.

Incongruously, considering his miserable surroundings, or perhaps as merely one more testament to the electronic age, Scott had a computer which he kept turned on for hours while roaming through mythical electronic worlds of hunters and the hunted. Sometimes he was predator; sometimes prey. Often when Scott wasn't busy playing his computer games after school, he was romping with his mongrel pup, Tippy. Sometimes when it was impossible for him to shut out the misery of his surroundings, he exploded into anger and punched one of his bony fists through a wall. Those times were unusual. Unlike his friend Rod, who constantly sought to be the center of attention, Scott was quiet for the most part, and satisfied to stay out of the limelight, preferring to be part of the background. He was easily led, according to his father.

Scott had figured a way out of the quagmire of poverty and near hopelessness he found himself mired in, although he was dead-set on completing his final two years of high school before he would be prepared to put his plan into action. The flatland Kentucky boy who had never seen an ocean was planning to join the Navy and save up his money so he could eventually attend college. In the Navy he would no longer be the poor kid whose family lived like Erskine Caldwell's unforgettable character, Jeeter Lester, and his tribe of backwoods ne'er-do-wells in *Tobacco Road*. He would merely be one more faceless sailor with a roof over his head, three good solid meals a day, decent clothes to wear, a regular paycheck and an opportunity to learn a trade or profession he could use in civilian life. Importantly, he would belong, if not to a strong family unit, then to the next best thing. He would be part of a tradition-honored fraternity of seagoing swab-jockeys who sailed the world and were called on to help fight their country's wars.

It was true that the boy's parents were unable to provide him with many of the material advantages of other children his age, but they loved and were proud of him. Scott obtained a part-time after-school job as a fry cook at a McDonald's in Mayfield, opened his own checking account in a local bank and obtained a driver's license. When Howard Anderson swapped a rattletrap 1982 Chevy truck straight up for a red 1987 Buick Skylark, the father and son also cut a deal. Howard made some repairs to the turbocharged Skylark so it could be used as the family car, but he and his wife told Scott that if he kept up the insurance payments it would be his to drive to and from work and to tool around in nights whenever his parents weren't using it. The car was considered to be Scott's present for his sixteenth birthday on December 18, 1995.

At times Scott clearly did a good job of handling his responsibilities as the oldest son in the family. He behaved himself and attended to his studies at Mayfield High School, where he got along with other students and impressed teachers with his upbeat, can-do attitude. In a media class he attended, Scott was known as a willing volunteer for various projects.

He was also an attentive big brother to Nicky, and showed the younger boy how to play with his Lego blocks. At other times, he played Nintendo on his computer, rode three-wheelers around the neighborhood, or worked on bikes, motorcycles and cars. He was developing into a pretty good mechanic.

By the time the summer of 1996 was winding down, however, he was spending more and more of his free time with Rod and their small circle of intimates. He confided to his younger brother Sam that he was a vampire, and one night took the boy along with him and some of his friends on an eerie journey to an old cemetery south of Murray. Sam later told a newspaper reporter that the teenagers talked about making human sacrifices. Rod used a razor to slash three cuts on his own arm, the boy added, then a girl named Cindy sucked up the blood. When Sam's companions tried to talk him into cutting his arm, he refused. "Uh-uh, that's stupid," he said.

On another night, Rod showed up at the Anderson house and he and Scott played a board game called "Dungeons & Masters" until dawn. They were totally absorbed in the game, and the intricate challenges they were faced with as players. It required concentration, imagination and a sharp mind. When the boys had at last had enough of the game for a while, they stuffed the board and other components under Scott's bed. They never played the game again.

Martha Anderson picked up bad vibes from her son's visitor that night. She thought Rod was a "weird" kid, and didn't like the idea of Scott continuing to hang around with him. After that night, Rod became a sensitive subject around the Anderson household. The strangely morbid boy who dressed all in black and floated in and out of her home like some malignant revenant from an old Bela Lugosi movie was her son's closest friend. But wherever Rod went, trouble seemed to stalk him—and his companions.

The Andersons could tell when their boy had been hanging around with Rod. He dyed his hair jet black, like his friend's. Sometimes he would react defiantly, and ignore the rules they attempted to lay down. There were also times, according to Scott's father, when the boy behaved like a zombie. Eventually he would snap out of the funk, and then he behaved like any normal teenager.

One morning Martha Anderson went to her eldest son's room and found him lying in bed, shaking uncontrollably. He had been beat up, hit in the head and suffered a concussion during a parking lot fight after mixing it up with some other boys he found with the bicycle of one of his brothers. Despite his choice of Rod for best friend, occasional evening-to-dawn game-playing and other all-night activities, Scott was an attentive student at school who cooperated with his teachers and had never been considered a serious discipline problem. Martha Anderson was so concerned about his condition, however, that she didn't send him to class that day. The next morning he was sitting on the edge of his bed, still shaking, when she walked into his room. The distraught boy grabbed her by the arms and said: "Mama, I'm losing my cookies."

"Are you losing it cookie-by-cookie, or crumb-by-crumb?" she asked.

"Cookie-by-cookie," he replied.

It was a frightening statement, and Mrs. Anderson took her son to a mental health counselor. The counselor talked to the boy, gave him some medication, told him to go back to school, get his job back and stay out of Calloway County, Scott's parents later recalled.

By November 11, Scott was feeling better—good enough to run away with his troublesome best friend. Mrs. Anderson figured the boys were together and she and her forty-two-year-old husband drove to the apartment on Broad Street to look for him. The boys weren't there, and Rod's mother said she had ordered them out of the apartment, along with another juvenile, because they had a gallon of gasoline and were making Molotov cocktails. Sondra later told authorities that a couple of hours after she kicked her son and his chums out of the apartment he returned to pick up some baseball bats, then left again and she didn't hear from him for a while.

Scott was still missing when an in-home family therapist dropped in to see how the family was doing. There were signs of deterioration in the household, and Howard Anderson was resting on a mattress lying on the floor when the caseworker visited. The last time he had stopped by, Howard was sitting on the mattress, and clothes littered the floor, chairs and couch of the living room. Martha said she needed to do some tidying up.

Howard told the therapist about Scott running away and said he had already filed a missing persons report with the police. In reply to questions, Martha said the children hadn't visited therapists at the mental health agency for a while, and the social worker told her he would arrange some appointments. He made one for the parents in December, and began working to set up another visit for the entire family in January 1997.

Scott remained out of touch with the family for several days before he simply walked in the door one night in the middle of November. His mother took him to the mental health clinic in Murray, which recommended counseling. Rod's mother also traipsed back to juvenile court authorities and filed a petition accusing her son of being an habitual runaway. She added that she was planning to move to Paducah before the end of November, and would notify the court of her new address.

Although the suspicions weren't immediately confirmed, it was generally believed that the boys moved in with Dana Lynn Cooper during their disturbing hiatus from home. Dana was older and maintained her own home in an apartment in the same complex where Rod and his mother lived. She supported herself with earnings from a job as a cashier at the Murray Wal-Mart and was free to choose her friends without parental interference. But as an independent nineteen-year-old, she didn't have many close friends and was a lonely young woman before Rod sidled into her life.

Dana was born in the southern Chicago suburb of Oak Lawn on April 8, 1977, but spent most of her childhood in Kentucky and graduated from CCHS while Rod was a freshman at Eustis High. The brown-haired, blue-eyed teenager was neither cheerleader pretty, nor homecoming-queen popular. She was quiet, even more subdued and unobtrusive than Scott, preferring to find a corner of a room somewhere where she could fade into the surroundings while watching and listening to her companions.

Dana had a placidly pleasant oval face, a silky smooth complexion, and dark, curly hair, but she was huge. When she was in school she towered over many of her male classmates, and weighed more than most of them. By the time she began hanging around with Rod Ferrell and his friends her awkward pear-shaped body tipped the scales at slightly more than two hundred pounds. Rod and other members of the loose-knit group that people eventually began referring to as the Vampire Clan accepted her as one of their own. Suddenly she had friends: other teenagers who came to her apartment, telephoned her or showed up with a car to pick her up and go for a ride somewhere. They shared confidences—and feedings.

Dana was accepted into the group because she agreed to "cross over," and participated in a ritual that Rod said must be carried out in order to transform a mortal into a vampire. According to her explanation, each person present at the ceremony, including the new initiate, slit three incisions into either arm and allowed blood from the cuts to drain into a cup. A small amount of water was added—then she drank the entire scarlet concoction. Rod, Scott and eventually Heather all crossed over, according to Dana. She said she thought Charity probably crossed over, as well, but she wasn't sure.

Modern society produces large numbers of people who feel left out, and consider themselves to be sad rejects while contemporaries who are no more deserving, or no more anxious for companionship, are handily accepted by their peers. It didn't matter to Rod and his band that Dana was big, or that she was three or four years older than her companions. She immediately became part of the group. Her apartment also served as a handy refuge for her younger friends when they wanted to get away from parental pressures for a while.

Charity Lynn Keesee was a slender five-foot-three-inch-tall girl with the supple young body of a high school cheerleader and a heart-shaped, pixie face, who weighed eighty-three pounds—considerably less than half as much as Dana. When Rod returned to Murray and registered for classes at Calloway County High he carried a certain mystique with him and an attraction for fellow students such as Charity. He was the new kid in school. The distinctive appeal of newcomers is a small school phenomenon, and is especially noticeable in rural communities like Calloway County, where many teenagers get their most vivid impressions of the outside world from MTV. Rod's strange maverick behavior and spiel about vampires and immortality added to the air of mystery for some of the fifteen- and sixteen-year-olds like Charity, both before and after he was kicked out of school. He was a rebel who bucked authority, and that is a surefire attraction for many teenagers.

Charity was born on September 12, 1980, in Montana. She had loving, attentive parents, but was a child of a broken home. By the time she met Rod, she was living with her father a few miles outside Murray. Her mother, Jodi Remington, lived hundreds of miles away in Piedmont, South Dakota, where she worked for the local county sheriff's department. Relatives in Montana and Wyoming later described Charity as brilliant but emotionally immature. The impressionable schoolgirl was a fine student, but she was entranced by Rod's darkly glamourous vampire fantasies and stronger personality.

Like some of her closest chums, the teenager with the long brown hair that she dyed black, like Rod's, sometimes used different names. Rod and other close friends usually referred to her as "Shea," but she was also known at times as Sarah Remington. After a boy a few months younger than Charity quit hanging around with Rod and his pals, she also became the baby of the fledgling Vampire Clan.

The boy didn't volunteer to abandon his pseudo-vampire friends. His mother shared some of the same doubts about her son and the company he was keeping that troubled Scott's parents. He was obsessed with the occult. Her concern deepened after the boy dyed his hair and painted his nails black, and she noticed cuts on his arms and found vampire novels in his room. The mother confronted Rod and told him to stay away from her son, but her warning fell on deaf ears.

The willful fourteen-year-old ran away and spent a week with Rod and Scott while they were AWOL from their own homes, before he was tracked down by police and returned to his mother. She arranged to have him treated as an in-patient at a local mental health agency. Discussing her younger brother later with a reporter, the boy's seventeen-year-old sister described Rod as "very manipulative." He made the other youngsters who hung around with him feel important. "I knew he'd gone off the deep end," she said of her brother.

Months later, the people of Calloway and Lake Counties would find themselves trying to figure out how a skinny misfit like Rod could attract any kind of following with such an obviously shallow act. He didn't have the good looks or the photographic memory and encyclopedic knowledge of a David Koresh, the cult leader who took more than eighty of his Branch Davidian followers with him to their deaths in a bloody shootout and fire at Waco, Texas; the religious charisma and political know-how of a Jim Jones, who led hundreds of his People's Temple followers to death through suicide and murder in Guyana; or even the crazed New Age spirituality and pseudo-scientific huckster spiel of a Marshall Applewhite, who led his zombie-like acolytes in self-mutilation and mass suicide so they could ride to glory on a spaceship they were convinced was trailing the Hale–Bopp Comet.

Rod had something else. He had vampires, with their message of power, of surrender and of the siren promise of immortality. The immortality of the undead was not the same as the immortality offered by his fundamentalist Christian neighbors in the numerous churches that the Calloway County faithful attended. The everlasting life promised from the pulpits was more difficult to obtain, an elusive reward for goodness in this life that would be realized only after the Apocalypse, when the souls of the chosen would be summoned to rise up and take their places beside the golden throne.

Vampire immortality was not some hazy concept of heavenly reward that was offered at some time in the distant future. The immortality that the kindred hoped to achieve was seductive and sexy, apparent and immediate.

Various forces were at work in the community and across the country that may have helped Rod maintain his friends' fascination with vampires, and their readiness to believe his pronouncements about such weighty matters as crossing over, or embracement and immortality. For a while, until he became too much of a maverick for the group, VAMPS helped keep their interest high. But he was also captivated by *Kindred: The Embraced*. The TV series was about a family of vampires who lived secretly among mortals—much like his own emerging Vampire Clan.

Vampires have another important attraction for certain teenagers who are pestered by feelings of insecurity, self-doubt and alienation. The undead, if they existed in reality as they do in popular fiction, would be society's ultimate outcasts. Many teenagers can relate to that. Rod had another advantage going for him as well. He somehow developed an eerie talent for exploiting the weaknesses and cravings of his fellow adolescents for a non-parental authority figure who shared and understood their insecurities. He trolled the schools and local teenage hangouts for the most vulnerable recruits he could find. He was a scavenger who fed from the wounded, the naive and the unwary.

Rod and his friends began traipsing up to the ruins of an old hotel overlooking Kentucky Lake in adjacent Marshall County. The ruins are known locally as "the Vampire Hotel." It is a spooky place, which, if one believes in such things, looks like it could indeed be a vampire aerie. It's especially scary at night when a pale moon casts just enough light over the ruins to make the broken stone and charred wooden timbers stand out in ominous silhouettes that can be easily shaped by the imagination into lurking vampires, werewolves or other monsters. Long before Vassago put together the nucleus of his Clan, local legend had it that real vampires had their graves there and lurked in the ruins of the old resort hotel.

The Vampire Hotel is hidden deep within an area of woods, thick, prickly underbrush and steeply sloping hills overlooking an even more rugged spread of forest land known as the Land Between the Lakes. The LBL, as it's known locally, is a slender, ragged finger of land between Kentucky Lake on the west and on the east, Lake Barkley—named for one of the state's most illustrious sons, former Vice President Alben W. Barkley. It was created by the Tennessee Valley Authority in the 1930s out of parts of Lyon and Trigg Counties in Kentucky, and Stewart County in Tennessee when the Kentucky and Barkley Dams were constructed. Campers, hikers and fishermen haunt the LBL, and most of the heavily wooded acreage is set aside as national parkland. It is home to wild turkey, rabbits, squirrels, raccoons, deer, an occasional bobcat and other wildlife.

The approach to the ruins is steep and rugged enough to challenge a mountain man of the likes of a Grizzly Adams— or a healthy teenager. At the top of the rise, the Vampire

Hotel looks out over the wilderness, and after the sun goes down the mournful hoot of owls and the eerie call of loons and other nightbirds drift up to the lookout from the dark surface of the land and the man-made lakes below. The scattered remains of the concrete walls, walkways and columns of the old hotel are surrounded and littered by empty liquor bottles, beer cans, decaying condoms, burned matches and small glassine envelopes and other drug paraphernalia. When Rod and his friends trekked to the ruins, trees and the crumbling wood and concrete were covered with ugly graffiti that included some especially morbid phrases and symbols. "PLEASE DEPOSIT DEAD BODIES HEER," one misspelled message instructed. "NO LOVE, ONLY DEATH," "ME KILLA," and "FOLLOW ME TO DEATH," others advised. Swastikas, the number "666" of the Beast of Revelations, and the peace sign—which some people are convinced is a devilish symbol—were also spray-painted among the ruins, along with common graffiti obscenities.

A refreshing smattering of scribbles reflecting more innocent times were also scrawled on the ruins, such as telephone numbers and girlish names. "KEN LOVES VIVIAN," was sprayed on a crumbling wall, amid all the obscenities, dark warnings and black magic symbols, by one young romantic. The Vampire Hotel was a choice destination for teenagers like Rod and his Clan, a private redoubt where they could be alone to play at being vampires and lay their dark plans. It was one of their favorite hangouts.

Some strange doings were known to be going on under cover of darkness in Calloway County and neighboring communities, and very little of the funny business was occurring at the Vampire Hotel. At least one crank laboratory was set up inside the town of Murray and operated for a while before it was shut down by city police, sheriff's officers and Kentucky State Police. But local law enforcement officers were also seriously concerned with an outbreak of hellraising running through a certain segment of the teenage population that was darker and more arcane. The troubling shenanigans were evidenced by cemetery vandalism, late-night seances, and reputed blood rituals.

And although authorities weren't immediately aware of it, Rod and his Vampire Clan were a big part of the problem. Their misbehavior was becoming far more serious than mere "kid stuff." Kid stuff didn't extend to mutilating and killing small animals, or performing weird rituals that led them to slash their own arms with knives and razors, then drink each others' blood. The Calloway County Vampire Clan was involved in deadly serious sociopathic behavior that was inexorably escalating.

Some imaginative predators have lured naive children into vampire cults so they can sexually molest them. Early in 1996, a few months after Rod moved back to Murray with his mother, police in Virginia Beach arrested a furnace and air-conditioning repairman who claimed to be a vampire, on charges of rape and carnal knowledge for sexual assaults on teenage girls. Jon Christopher Bush wore a cape and plastic snap-on fangs, and strolled around local malls with his arms crossed over his chest, while recruiting more than thirty thirteen to sixteen-year-olds into his depraved cult. During the mall crawls, members of Bush's clan painted their faces white and their lips and the fingernails of their left hands black.

According to police investigators, the bespectacled imitation vampire with the shock of dark brown hair, thin black mustache and goatee, outlandish costume and twistedly vivid imagination accepted about a half-dozen boys into the cult. They were used as enforcers and recruiters to help him lure some of the prettiest girls from junior high and high schools in Virginia Beach and nearby Chesapeake. Girls who underwent the initiation rite were expected to submit to oral sex with the leader, have sexual intercourse with him or permit him to bite them under their breasts. Boys were initiated into the clan with a tiny nip on their shoulders that was barely hard enough to leave a bite mark or bruise.

Bush used another version of the role-playing game, "Vampire: The Eternal Struggle," to help lure the underage boys and girls into the cult, and charmed his followers with fanciful stories about a vampire universe, a fourteen-level vampire hierarchy and his role as a powerful elder of the vampire family. Following a two-day bench trial without a jury in the Virginia Beach Circuit Court, Bush was convicted of twenty-two felonies and eight misdemeanors, including carnal knowledge, crimes against nature and contributing to the delinquency of a minor. Early in January 1997 he was sentenced to twenty-six years in prison.

Law enforcement authorities in the Atlantic Ocean resort city were especially sensitive to the dangers of misdirection or the negative exploitation of role-playing games, because of a notorious double murder of two elementary school boys by a teenager who was an avid player of "Dungeons & Dragons." Seventeen-year-old Shawn Novak slit the throats of the younger boys in the spring of 1991, and defense lawyers at his murder trial argued that he was so caught up in the fantasy game that he believed the victims were inhuman creatures whom he had a right to kill. Novak was convicted of two counts of capital murder and sentenced to life in prison.

In mid-October, Murray residents were shocked by the atrocity at the animal shelter, and their outrage extended far beyond the borders of Calloway County. The local chapter of Crimestoppers established a reward fund and more than $1,000 was raised for information leading to the arrest of the vandals. Ken Alsobrook, who operated American Justice Security, a business in nearby Paducah, donated his time and expertise to install a laser-activated alarm system at the shelter after watching a newscast about the atrocity on a local television station. Alsobrook also donated the wiring, and community contributions paid for the remainder of the equipment, which the business provided at cost. Murray's six-day-a-week newspaper, The *Ledger & Times*, and the *Paducah Sun*, along with area radio and television stations, helped keep the story alive and in the public mind.

Sheriff Scott and his investigators had a rough idea of what had occurred, but hadn't yet filled in all the spaces. It seemed from the outset of the investigation that some kind of black magic or Satanic cult was involved. And the sheriff had a pretty good idea that the cultists were teenagers. One of the teenagers whom investigators talked with was Rod Ferrell. The deputies approached the boy after receiving a tip developed through the local Crimestoppers program.

Sheriff Scott, who has a passing resemblance to a younger version of the Southern sheriff played by Carroll O'Connor in the television series *In the Heat of the Night*, was rapidly closing in on the suspects. The sheriff announced to the press that he was almost ready to file formal charges in the case. Although only two suspects were expected to be immediately charged, he said the investigation was continuing and the incident was believed to be tied to cult activity. As many as ten juveniles might be involved with the group, he added.

On Wednesday evening, October 30, the night before Halloween, Rod's friend April Doeden visited him at his South Side Manor apartment and he confided a chilling secret as they were talking about the outrageous act committed at the shelter. "Remember what I did to the cat?" April later quoted him as asking. "I did a lot more out there." Soon after the conversation, Deputy Sheriff Dennis McDaniel took a formal statement from April about her talk with Rod.

On Halloween night and early the next morning, deputies picked up Rod Ferrell and another sixteen-year-old Calloway County High School student. When Rod walked into the sheriff's headquarters, he had a surprise for the chief law enforcement officer. The boy was wearing white makeup on his face and his lips were rouged. Scott had seen many strange things during his years on the force, but the black-clad juvenile's get-up was a new one for him. The boys were charged in juvenile court with second-degree cruelty to animals, criminal attempt to commit third-degree burglary and third-degree criminal trespass. Rod arrogantly advised the sheriff that it didn't matter what authorities tried to do to him. He couldn't be harmed because he was immortal.

Even though Rod had never previously been in serious

trouble with the law, he had already developed a pretty good idea about how to manipulate the system. His cavalier attitude may also have been helped along by his youth, and knowledge of the great care and leniency authorities in Kentucky tend to take in the handling of most juveniles who get into trouble with the law.

In keeping with Kentucky law designed to shield most juvenile offenders from publicity, the names of the boys weren't publicly disclosed when they were charged in the attack at the animal shelter. The commonwealth has some of the strictest shield laws in the country protecting the confidentiality of juveniles involved in court proceedings. Victims aren't even allowed to attend juvenile court proceedings, and are not advised of the disposition of most criminal cases involving adolescents.

Sondra Gibson later told a reporter that her son couldn't have been involved in the grisly mutilation of the puppies because he was at home asleep in their apartment the night of the crime. She expanded on the story during a later interview with a reporter, claiming that her boy was home in bed after getting drunk and passing out. Rod thought Charity was cheating on him, so he went out with one of his buddies from school and got roaring drunk, Sondra said. When the boys showed up at the apartment that afternoon at the tail-end of the drinking spree they were in such horrible shape that it frightened her. Rod passed out on the bathroom floor, and was ice cold and limp as a dish rag. Sondra said her boyfriend, Smoke, picked him up and put him to bed. Rod later learned that he was wrong about Charity; she hadn't been running around on him at all.

Despite the high-minded intentions of the framers of Kentucky's statutes dealing with juvenile crime, the boys' shaky anonymity wasn't preserved very long. And the alibi provided by Rod's mother was destined to be submitted to a long, hard look by skeptics in two states.

The break-in and mindless atrocity committed at the animal shelter was especially troubling to Sheriff Scott, not only because of the cruelty of it, but because of the signal the savage act appeared to send. Exhibiting the percipience that good cops seem to have been born with, or tend to develop after a while on the job, the sheriff was concerned that the senselessly barbaric act at the animal shelter might be only the tip of the iceberg and a precursor of even more shocking outrages. Rod might not be satisfied with the carnage at the shelter, and might be about ready to give the ratchet another turn to crank up the horror.

Sheriff Scott wasn't the only person who was worried about the ominous direction the vampire obsession was taking. Harrell Gibson had a heart-to-heart talk with his quirky grandson. He told the boy he believed it was time to get out of the vampire cult. "They won't let me," Rod replied. "They'll kill me."

Calloway County law enforcement authorities had had a bellyful of the kooky shenanigans and were determined to put a stop to the foolishness. The young vandals were becoming dangerous. Rod and his following of bogus vampires had been whittled down to four hard-core members—the two boys, Dana and Charity. The pressures on the teenagers, especially Rod and Scott, were mounting, and talk among the quartet increasingly focused on Florida, New Orleans and other possible destinations in Louisiana. Rod had never forgotten his childhood visit to the mysterious, moist city along the Mississippi, and the lure of the Pelican State was further enhanced for the fledgling vampires by its prominence as a locale for the blockbuster novels of preternatural evil by author Anne Rice.

About the middle of November, Scott startled his parents with a surprising question. "How would you feel if I came back from Florida with a wife and baby?" he asked. The query sounded to the Andersons like typical teenage blather; nothing really to get in a dither over. If their eldest son continued to behave in character, the next time they had a serious talk he would have a totally different eye-popper to spring on them. But Scott was almost ready to journey south and meet the "queen" who was once promised to "Damion."

The plans of Rod and his acolytes to run away weren't a very closely held secret, except from their parents. On Friday night, November 22, Steven Murphy saw "Vassago," "Nash," "Shea" and Dana at the Hardee's talking about their plans to clear out of Murray and head south.

The next day Dana Cooper abruptly quit her job at the Wal-Mart.

Rod Ferrell said goodbye to his grandparents, Harrell and Rosetta Gibson.

Charity Keesee slipped into a clean pair of jeans and a blouse and left her house to spend Saturday night with her friends. She never returned to her home.

Scott Anderson told his parents he was going to Murray to see a movie, then drove away with his brother, Robert, in the old Buick. When they got to Murray, Scott dropped Robert off in front of the Circus Skate at U.S. 641 and Utterback Road, and told him he would pick him up at closing time. Scott never showed up. Instead, Dana and Charity walked to the roller rink and told Robert his brother had been beaten up and left somewhere. Then the girls walked away into the night.

The sand was rapidly filling up the bottom of the hourglass.

6. THE MANHUNT

"There was a little girl, who had a little curl,
right in the middle of her forehead.
When she was good, she was very, very good.
When she was bad, she was horrid."
                                        —children's ditty

The chill slid and curled through Eustis and north-eastern Lake County like one of the early winter freezes that periodically slips down from the north to glaze citrus crops with ice and shrivel the fruit. The news that spread through the city, and especially the high school campus, about the horror inflicted on the Wendorf family produced a chill as devastating as the crop-killing cold, but in a far different way.

The runaways were still low on cash and food, and during their drive west, they stopped overnight in remote locations along the highway in order to save money and avoid attracting the attention of police. They fed on snack cakes, bread, soda pop—and blood. Dana was their willing larder. By serving as a quiescent vessel to provide perceived sustenance for her friends, she not only belonged, but with her blood coating their stomachs she was a part of them. And they were part of her.

After everyone had transferred into the sports utility vehicle in Sanford, the teenagers steered the Ford onto I-95 and drove north to Jacksonville and I-10. Then they followed the interstate highway west across the Panhandle, through Alabama and Mississippi all the way to New Or-

leans. They spent the first night in Tallahassee, Florida's
capital city, and charged a purchase to Richard Wendorf's
credit card before continuing their dash to New Orleans.

When Rod and his entourage drove over the long cement-
and-steel causeway spanning the eastern edge of Lake Pontchartrain into the clinging moisture and lurking menace of
the Big Easy, there was no Mardi Gras with street parades,
masked balls and twenty-four-hour carousing underway.
And there was no one waiting to welcome a ragged band of
adolescents from rural Florida and Kentucky into local vampire society. New Orleans is a big, sprawling, rugged city
of a half-million people with a malignant underbelly infested
with ruthless gang-bangers, crackheads, pimps, hookers and
other assorted low-lifes. The real-life dangers must have
been mind-boggling and terrifying to immature children with
no friends there, no pocket money and no idea of how they
expected to survive.

New Orleans is one of the most dangerous cities in the
United States, with one of the highest rates of violent crime.
In 1993, only three years before the young adventurers drove
over the causeway, New Orleans earned the unenviable reputation as the murder capital of the country. FBI statistics
show that 389 homicides—76.6 slayings per 100,000 people—were recorded that year, giving New Orleans the highest murder rate of any American city with a population of
250,000 or more. The dismal picture hadn't changed much
in the interim.

Tourists wandering among "the cities of the dead," New
Orleans' exotic above-ground cemeteries, are robbed and
gang-raped by thugs from nearby housing projects, and others are mugged in the French Quarter. The police department
has been rocked by one scandal after another. The Big Easy
was still what it has always been: a rowdy, ribald, Mississippi River town. Danger lurks around every corner, and any
mortal—or vampire—who carelessly ventures into the
streets after dark is taking a chance of getting mugged, or
worse.

The New Orleans that civic boosters focus on, with its

storied jazz impresarios, boozy tours of the historic seventy-block French Quarter, the Superdome and fine Cajun cooking, was off-limits or beyond the financial reach of the vampire-obsessed teens because they were too young and too broke. The runaways spent only one night in the Big Easy, and they barely had enough money left for a tank of gas when they piled into the powder-blue Ford Explorer and drove it back onto I–10. They headed northwest across St. John the Baptist and Ascension Parishes into the heart of the plantation country. Skirting the edge of the bayous, they drove past old restored antebellum mansions, built for wealthy planters more than a century earlier, that sat far back on broad lawns dotted with stately, moss-shrouded tulip and live oak trees. Any one of the mansions might have served as a perfect backdrop for a Hollywood vampire movie.

While Rod and his followers were exploring Louisiana, the possibility that members of a suspected killer vampire cult might still be hanging around Lake County had several senior officers and detectives with the sheriff's department working through their Thanksgiving holiday, and many civilians feeling the effects of seriously jangled nerves. About mid-afternoon on Thanksgiving Day, police checked out a report that Richard Wendorf's Ford Explorer was seen at a convenience store in Mount Dora. It wasn't the same vehicle. Reports were also broadcast by an area radio station that some of the fugitive teens had telephoned friends in Eustis, but the stories were based on faulty information. For many residents of Eustis, Mount Dora and other nearby communities, Thursday wasn't a typical Thanksgiving Day. The turkey and ham on dining room tables were served along with a big helping of apprehension and fear.

Nerves were even more frazzled in Murray. Widespread fear that the runaway teenagers were headed back to their home turf set off a wave of concern and false sightings. Calloway County residents worried that, like the vampires of East European legend, the homegrown revenants might be returning to their roots to rest and regather their strength

The Vampire Hotel, the abandoned ruins of an old resort near Murray, Kentucky, overlooking a rugged area known as the Land Between The Lakes. The isolated ruins were popular with Murray's would-be vampires, and other teenagers who climbed the bramble-covered hills to drink, do drugs, or make out. *(Jim Mahanes)*

Court Square in downtown Murray, Kentucky, where local teenagers cruised at night. *(Jim Mahanes)*

Dana Cooper, the first of the reputed Vampire Clan to be returned to Florida from Louisiana, is escorted by a sheriff's officer from the sally port into the booking area of the Lake County Detention Center. *(Marsha Hunt/Daily Commercial/Sygma)*

Charity Lynn Keesee, also known as Sarah Remington, is surrounded by female guards and officers with the Lake County Sheriff's Department as she arrives at the detention center in Tavares, Florida, following the long journey from Baton Rouge.
(Marsha Hunt/Daily Commercial/Sygma)

Howard Scott Anderson begins the booking process after he and his companions return to Florida to face charges in the grisly double murder of Richard and Naoma Wendorf.

(Marsha Hunt/Daily Commercial/Sygma)

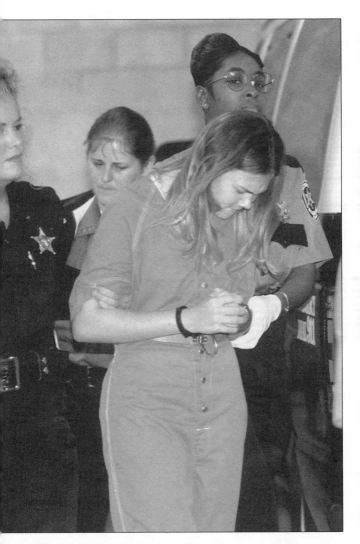

Heather Ann Wendorf, younger daughter of the slain couple, is led into the booking area of the Lake County Detention Center with her hands cuffed in front of her. *(Marsha Hunt/Daily Commercial/Sygma)*

Rod Ferrell, sixteen-year-old leader of the bloodthirsty clan of would-be vampires, clowns around and sticks his tongue out at photographers as he is led into the jail in Tavares.

(Marsha Hunt/Daily Commercial/Sygma)

Jennifer Lynn Wendorf, the vivacious Eustis High School senior and cheerleader who returned home and found her parents murdered and her younger sister missing.
(Chris Livingston/Daily Commercial/Sygma)

Officers with the Lake County Sheriff's Department use evidence tags to mark the location of a pair of high-top shoes found on the lawn, while colleagues continue to inspect the inside of the three-bedroom Wendorf home for clues to the brutal double slaying.
(Chris Livingston/Daily Commercial/Sygma)

in the rich, dark soil of their forebears. Rod's former neighbors were seriously spooked.

For a few days, the Murray Police Department and Calloway County Sheriff's Department were bombarded with nervous reports from citizens about phantom sightings of Rod or threats from him and his friends. About a dozen reports were telephoned to the sheriff or the Murray Police Department by people claiming to have seen one or more of the fugitives in the area. All kinds of wild stories were making the rounds. The fears were especially prevalent among people who had feuded with Rod, or otherwise crossed his path during the would-be vampire's violence- and trouble-plagued sojourn in western Kentucky. Steven Murphy left town and went to Tennessee for a while to live with relatives of a friend.

At about 6:30 p.m. Tuesday, the night after the murders, a tipster had telephoned the sheriff's department and reported that Rod was seen inside the Wal-Mart. It was the same store where Dana had worked before suddenly quitting her job and leaving town with her friends. Sheriff Scott alerted the Murray Police Department, and sent officers to the store to supplement the smalltown law enforcement agency. Store employees were notified about the reputed sighting, and armed lawmen surrounded the building until the report was checked out and determined to be false.

Later the same evening, the Murray Police Department logged a call from Harrell Gibson reporting that his grandson had telephoned him at his home in the Fox Meadows apartments. "Grandpa, it's me," Rod nervously announced. He talked only a few minutes, and at first claimed that he wasn't sure where he was, but said he had been in a traffic accident. Gibson, whose first name was mistakenly transcribed by police as "Harold," said that he believed Rod told him that he was by himself in Sedalia. Sedalia was uncomfortably close to home. It is a little crossroads town of about 300 people, approximately twenty miles west of Murray in Graves County. Sedalia is even closer to Mayfield, which is only seven miles north, straight up State Road 97.

After talking a few moments, the shaken sixty-seven-year-old grandparent asked, ''Rod, would you do me a favor? Would you turn yourself in to police?'' An approximate twenty-second silence followed, then the boy hung up.

If Rod was back in the area, with or without his fellow runaways, local law enforcement in western Kentucky had a serious problem on their hands. Duty officers at the police station notified Detective Mike Jump and Kentucky State Police about the report. Then, while other officers were logging in a report from an angry resident on South 14th Street who said that his dog had been barking and a grumpy neighbor threw a garbage can at it, an extra patrol was ordered for the 500 block of Poplar Street. One of the residents there had previously reported being threatened by the Clan leader. Rod had a nasty reputation for throwing temper tantrums, for wild emotional blow-ups and savage violence that erupted in the blink of an eye. Without warning, some of his closest friends had suddenly been redefined as blood enemies by the volatile youth and almost everyone who had had previous contact with him was edgy. It was no time to take chances.

Late Wednesday, the evening before Thanksgiving, a couple of Calloway County sheriff's deputies were dispatched to the home of a sixteen-year-old boy who had returned from school and told family members that he was confronted by one of the fugitives at CCHS, and his life was threatened. He said the incident occurred in the parking lot after classes were dismissed, and the cultists were driving a white Bronco.

The boy's relatives were already badly shaken by the story, but while the lawmen were taking the statement, the fear skyrocketed when the lights suddenly blinked off and the house was plunged into total darkness. Worried that the blood cultists might be moving in to carry out their grisly work, the alarmed deputies quickly radioed the information to their headquarters. Almost every available unit, vehicles and patrolling deputies, were dispatched to the house on the double. Some of the police cruisers were still on their way to the scene when the jittery officers learned that a car had slammed into a utility pole, causing the blackout several miles away at the boy's house.

The frightening blackout was no more than a bizarre fluke, but Sheriff Scott had to take the boy's report seriously. He ordered a surveillance team to position themselves outside the house, and notified the Kentucky State Police and other area law enforcement agencies that members of the reputed Vampire Clan were reportedly seen in the area. A short time later a KSP highway patrol car became involved in a high-speed chase after spotting a white Bronco in Graves County and taking off in pursuit. When the vehicle was pulled over, the KSP officer quickly determined that the driver had nothing to do with the fugitives. He was on parole, had had a few drinks and didn't want to be stopped.

After repeatedly asking the high school boy if he was telling the truth about the confrontation at CCHS, Sheriff Scott learned that the story was just a bunch of Kentucky flapdoodle. Although the teenager initially insisted that the confrontation had really occurred, he eventually broke down and admitted he had been lying. He didn't see Rod, Scott or any of their perceived companions at the school or anywhere else on Tuesday. The sheriff, along with other local law enforcement agencies, had invested considerable effort, including time, manpower and equipment into protecting the boy and his family and putting out an area dragnet that was all for nothing. Scott talked with the county prosecutor, and the boy was charged with a class D felony offense of hindering prosecution and apprehension by giving false information to law enforcement. An extra charge of possession of prescription drugs not in the proper container was added to the offenses.

In accordance with the commonwealth's practice of protecting juvenile offenders, the boy's name and the disposition of the case were not publicly disclosed. But the blabbermouthed youth wouldn't be the only teenager to get in trouble because of an apparent misguided desire to become part of the story that was swirling around the two semi-rural communities. Florida authorities would eventually have their own tall-tale-teller to deal with.

While the teenagers were on the run, Murray police disclosed that Rod was wanted for questioning in the armed robbery of the local Days Inn motel on the Saturday before the murders. The bandit had stepped out of a car carrying several other passengers, stalked into the hotel and stuck up the clerk, and police figured Rod might have pulled off the job before leaving for Florida. He was quickly cleared of any involvement in the case after an older man was arrested and charged with the crime. According to police, the gunman's companions in the car didn't even know he was robbing the motel.

Rod wasn't a stickup man, but he had a reputation for subterfuge, cunning, deceit, treachery, lies, violence, and doing the unexpected. He was unpredictable and clearly dangerous, so police charged with responsibility for patrolling and protecting the people who lived on his home turf couldn't afford to take anything for granted. He could be a thousand miles away, or lurking somewhere in the shadows of Murray, Mayfield or rural Calloway or Graves Counties. He didn't have to jump out from behind a corner, like April and other former familiars had seen him do so many times, just for the fun of scaring someone. People were already scared.

Jim Yohe heard some frightening new stories about the dangers to anyone foolish enough to trek up the hillside and through the brambles to the Vampire Hotel. The most frightening rumor, however, was a story that Rod had a little notebook or memo pad that he used to record the names of people he planned to eradicate. The Murray State College graduate student was pretty sure his name was on the list, and spent the twenty-four hours immediately after hearing about the list watching doors, peering cautiously out of windows and looking for anything suspicious and unusual that might indicate he was being stalked.

Yohe wasn't the only person who was looking over his shoulder, nervously anticipating a glimpse of the angular, black-garbed, Ichabod Crane–like frame of the self-appointed vampire lord drifting down the road clutching his trademark long stick wrapped in black electrical tape. Since the story had broken across the country, a lot of people were keeping an eye peeled for the young fugitives.

Dana's father knew that members of a savage blood cult might be slinking around murdering parents, and he was ready for them if they came for him. When a carload of teenagers pulled into the driveway next to his modest house off a two-lane highway about three miles west of Murray, Otha D. Cooper's reaction provided a sobering demonstration of how extensively the pall of fear cast by the Vampire Clan had cloaked the community. Andrew D. Hannigan, his sister, Crystal, and two other boys stopped a few minutes after 9 o'clock Thanksgiving night to pick up a girl from Arkansas who was staying at the trailer home of friends when the sixty-two-year-old man stormed down the front steps of his house. Cooper was armed with a .357 Magnum and he ran across the yard toward the car.

Kaylee Smith, who was waiting outside for her friends a few yards east of the Assembly of God Church, had just climbed into the eight-year-old white Ford Taurus when Cooper loomed in front of the driver's side window and pointed the powerful weapon at Hannigan's head. "Please don't, sir," the startled youth pleaded with the lanky, gray-haired man with the blazing blue eyes and a pistol that looked as big as a cannon. When Cooper ordered Hannigan out of the car, the youth slammed it into reverse and backed out onto Road 94. Cooper began blazing away with the pistol and emptied all six shots. One slug slammed into the hubcap of the left rear wheel, and another went through the left front tire.

While his terrified passengers screamed for him to keep going, the driver steered the crippled Ford down the highway, ignoring the flat tire and the bumpy ride, until he reached a convenience store where the teenagers piled out

and telephoned the Calloway County Sheriff's Department.
A sheriff's deputy arrested Cooper at his home, took away
the pistol and collected six empty shell casings from the yard
and driveway. Cooper was put in the back seat of a patrol
car and driven to the Calloway County Jail, where he told
Sheriff Scott that he had seen Rod Ferrell and Dana in the
white Taurus. The jittery parent was charged with first-
degree wanton endangerment. Cooper was bailed out of the
jail by Friday morning, and charges were amended to five
misdemeanor counts of second-degree wanton endangerment. There was one charge to represent each of the teenagers in the car.

Cooper's wild exhibition of gunplay and the high-speed
car chase in Graves County were the most seriously dangerous incidents tied to the wave of fear spread by the cultists, but it seemed that just about everyone in Murray was
preoccupied with the story. Teenagers and adults at the Hungry Bear, at Hardee's and at Rudy's Restaurant on Court
Square were confiding that they had heard Rod had contacted his mother, his grandfather, or some friend from a
secret location in Calloway County, or from Florida. Before
Steven Murphy left town he claimed to have heard from a
dependable source that Charity had phoned someone in Murray and said she was frightened and sorry she ever ran away
with Rod and the others.

That may or may not have been a fact, but it was certainly
true that the grand adventure, if that's what it was, was already beginning to lose some of its luster for the runaway
fifteen-year-old. There was some talk among the fugitives
about trying to get to Spokane, Washington, where Charity
had grandparents. But she also had relatives in other states
whom the cash-strapped and increasingly desperate teenagers figured might be approached for an emergency hand-
out.

Sheriff Scott was busy in Murray contacting the parents
of the Kentucky fugitives. His contacts included Charity's
father, in Murray, and her mother, Mrs. Jodi Remington, in
Piedmont, South Dakota. The lawman asked all the relatives

he talked with to notify him of any calls they received from the teenagers. He figured they were short of money, and one of the first places they were likely to turn to for help would be their parents. That would be especially true of the younger members of the group, Scott believed. He was right on target.

On Tuesday night, Rod telephoned his grandfather. On Wednesday, Charity placed a collect call to her grandmother in Wyoming, and said she would telephone her mother on Thursday. She kept her word and called Mrs. Remington several times from pay phones. The Remington home in Piedmont, a tiny settlement of about 300 people, is about an hour-long drive east of the Wyoming state line near Ellsworth Air Force Base and Rapid City. It's at the east edge of the Black Hills National Forest, and is surrounded by other small towns with names like Deadwood, Silver City, Black Hawk, Nemo and Tilford. Farming is the principal source of income for most of the residents of the area, but mining for gold, silver and other ores also provides jobs for the local population. Compared to Piedmont, the town of Murray where Charity lived in Kentucky is a major metropolis.

Mrs. Remington worked for the local sheriff's department and was using a telephone with a caller ID box. Each time Charity called, her mother telephoned Sheriff Scott in Murray and shared the information she had gathered, including the pay phone numbers. She hated the idea of turning her own daughter in to police because she was worried Charity would hate her for it. But she was worried about her daughter's safety, and she wanted Charity and her friends off the street and away from Rod so they would be safe. Turning the runaways in was an act of love and something she felt in her heart she had to do.

After one call, Mrs. Remington told the Kentucky sheriff that she had heard a tugboat in the background and her daughter had said they were near a Howard Johnson's motel. Charity was frightened and sorry she had joined in the ill-fated adventure. She told her mother that she and her com-

panions were somewhere in Louisiana and needed money.
She also mentioned seeing a big battleship that was moored
on a river. The ship was actually a destroyer from the World
War II and Korean War era, the USS Kidd DD-661, which
was moored on the Mississippi River along South River
Road in Baton Rouge. The runaways had driven seventy-
five miles across the floodways and bayous into the Pelican
State's capital city. They were only a few blocks from the
historic white Gothic revival–style capitol building.

After learning the runaways were near the hotel, Sheriff
Scott told Mrs. Remington to instruct her daughter to go
there with her friends and have the desk clerk telephone her.
He suggested she tell the clerk she would pay the hotel bill
for the teenagers and promise to drive to Louisiana to pick
them up, and she agreed. In the meantime the Kentucky
sheriff passed the number of the pay phone Charity had used
on to Baton Rouge police. They traced it to a pay box near
the Centroplex, and radioed patrol officers to be on the lookout for the powder-blue Explorer and a gang of teenagers.

As soon as Scott learned they were at the hotel, he called
Baton Rouge again and relayed the information to his police
contacts there. The sheriff telephoned Baton Rouge several
times that night, and while he was talking to his colleagues
in Louisiana during one of the calls, deputies a few feet from
his desk were logging in the report about the shooting next
door to Otha Cooper's house. When Scott phoned in the
information that the fugitives were at the hotel, the Louisiana
lawmen were already closing in.

At about 9 p.m., Officers William Clarida and Jimmy
Wellborn spotted the dusty sports utility vehicle pulling into
the parking lot at the Howard Johnson Plaza–Suite Hotel on
North Third Street. Clarida and Wellborn radioed police
headquarters for backup, then watched as two girls climbed
out of the Explorer and walked into the lobby. Moments
later the backup officers arrived, and Charity and her companion were taken into custody in the lobby on the fugitive
warrants from Florida. Outside, another team of officers, accompanied by a couple of police dogs, converged on the

remaining teenagers in the parking lot and placed them under arrest.

Within fifteen minutes from the time Sheriff Scott alerted his colleagues in Louisiana to their location, the teenagers were handcuffed and loaded into cage-cars. They were tired, frightened and hungry and submitted to arrest without any show of defiance. They spent the remainder of Thanksgiving night in custody. It was the first of many nights they would spend in juvenile detention centers or jails in two states.

The vampire brood had been on the run and the subject of a rapidly burgeoning manhunt for only three days, three nights and part of a fourth. Until Charity began making the calls to her mother and grandmother, much of the attention of law enforcement agencies involved in the search was focused on the home area of the Calloway County youths and the states they would likely pass through on their way from Florida to Kentucky.

Parents and other close relatives of the runaway Kentucky teenagers, and members of Heather's family, greeted the news that they were safely in custody with relief. In Murray, Charity's father said that "basically" his daughter had run away from home, and he believed she didn't realize the trouble she was getting into. He told reporters he was relieved that she was safe. Charity had never been in trouble before, Keesee added.

Howard Anderson said he was glad police didn't have to "gun down" the teenagers.

Harrell Gibson voiced similar sentiments to a reporter for the *Tri-County Sun* in Lady Lake, Florida. He said he was thrilled because hope had been restored. "We know they won't be out killing anybody else." Harrell conceded that some prison time was obviously in the future for the suspected killers, but said he was hopeful there would be no death sentences. He also said that he believed the murders were tied to drug abuse that had messed up their minds.

Then the heartbroken retiree added an observation that few people following his grandson's recent exploits would have been likely to agree with. "You hate [to] see good children wasted, but Rod is really a good little boy.''

Rod's mother suggested that he may have merely had the bad luck to show up at the Wendorf home after the couple was murdered by someone else. "If I can see him and look straight in his eyes, I'll know what happened," she told a reporter with the *Orlando Sentinel*. She also denied that her son was the darkling lord of a vampire cult, and said that she believed the runaways were all in it together. Sondra conceded that she had dabbled in vampirism, but said she had gotten out of it after becoming frightened.

She didn't bother reporting Rod as missing when he vanished from Murray because Charity was two months pregnant with his baby and she and her boyfriend figured the young lovers had eloped, she said. Scott's parents reported him missing as soon as they realized he was gone with the family car, and they searched his room in an effort to figure out what he had been up to and where he might have gone. The only unusual item the search turned up was a single pornographic magazine.

In Umatilla, James Wendorf told reporters that his granddaughter was in good health.

Sheriff Scott was also pleased with how easily the Vampire Clan was rounded up, and said he was amazed they were gullible enough to walk into the trap at the hotel.

After Heather and the Kentucky teens were taken to the Baton Rouge Police Department homicide headquarters for questioning, the Ford Explorer was transported to a police auto pound, sealed and held for Florida authorities. Lake County Sheriff's Sergeant Wayne Longo and Detective Alvey Gussler were already on their way to Kentucky to look for the fugitives when they were notified of the arrests in Baton Rouge. The LCSD detectives made a quick change in their travel plans, and drove across the Florida Panhandle, then through Alabama and Mississippi to Louisiana's second-largest city. Longo and Gussler traveled in the cab of a flatbed truck that was piggybacking one of the LCSD's crime scene processing vans.

Shortly after arriving in Louisiana, the Florida detectives

conducted a meticulous inspection of the sports utility vehicle and an inventory of its contents. Detective Ben Odom of the Baton Rouge Police Department obtained a search warrant after filing an affidavit in the local courts that listed weapons among the items being sought, including a "heavy-blade, chopping-type tool or kitchen utensil," and a hunting knife. A string of pearls missing from the Wendorf home, papers or diaries, and lug-sole boots and tennis shoes, along with several other items, were also listed on the affidavit. The footwear was sought in order to make comparisons with prints left at the murder scene.

Pictures were taken of the outside of the Explorer before the search began, and additional photos were snapped during every step of the process. The detectives and evidence technicians worked systematically, carefully examining the outside of the Explorer, checking tires and the undercarriage for unusual particles of dirt, mud or other debris. Inside the vehicle, they inspected the surfaces, the floors, between and underneath the seats and the upholstery on the sides. They emptied the glove compartment, meticulously packaging and sealing everything they found in evidence bags or vials. Tags were attached to each of the containers, and marked with the exact location, time and date the material was collected.

The team of law officers collected road maps, numerous cigarettes and butts, two pocket knives, a hunting knife with a black handle, a razor blade, a two-and-a-half-foot-long stick wrapped in black electrical tape, a mesh backpack with a dismembered Barbie doll attached to it books including Anne Rice's 1988 horror novel, *Queen of the Damned*, *The Ultimate Dracula* and *The Necronomicon*, several videotapes of children's movies, including *The Lion King* and *Aladdin*, and two teddy bears. The pearls were draped over the neck of one of the stuffed animals.

The bears and the animated Disney films were an incongruous discovery that evoked a distressing image of babies playing at being monsters. The titles and subjects of the books were darker, seemingly more fitting for fugitives suspected of involvement in such a ghastly crime as the Wendorf murders. The title *Necronomicon* was coined by horror and science fiction writer H.P. Lovecraft in one of his stories as the title of a fictional book of black magic spells that involved gross rituals utilizing dead human bodies or body parts. Since that time the fictional black magic tome has become a staple of occult novels, and the paperback found in the car carried Lovecraft's fictional title along with reputed spells for calling up demons.

Swabs of six small stains that resembled blood were also collected from the interior of the truck and stored in special containers for later analysis by serologists and other forensics experts in police laboratories. If the stains were confirmed through laboratory analysis to be blood, and were matched to other samples collected from the Wendorf house, they could possibly provide an important link between the runaway teenagers and the murder victims. Finally the interior of the dusty Explorer was vacuumed, and the bag was preserved to be emptied later and examined for hairs, fibers and other trace evidence.

The search of the vehicle continued for thirteen hours, but it was a necessarily slow procedure that was vital to establishing and maintaining the integrity of the process and avoiding possible legal repercussions down the line when prosecutors and defense attorneys squared off from each other during a trial—or trials. Even the smallest omission or variance from established procedure could conceivably lead to key evidence being ruled inadmissible by the courts because it was contaminated or improperly collected and stored. The Explorer was carefully gone over again after it was driven onto the flatbed and hauled back to the sheriff's department in Tavares.

A similar meticulous search had already been conducted on the Andersons' Skylark and its contents after it was transported to the LCSD in Tavares. Homicide detectives and technicians eventually collected nearly four hundred separate items of possible evidence, including samples of blood stains and smears, from the house and the two vehicles.

Four of the five teens were under eighteen years old, so

information released to the public immediately after their apprehension was sketchy because of laws protecting juvenile offenders. But police disclosed that they were questioned and had cooperated to a certain degree. For the time being, while hearings were being scheduled in juvenile and adult courts of East Baton Rouge Parish, former neighbors of the runaways in Florida and Kentucky were kept in the dark about most of the details surrounding the statements to homicide investigators.

Photographers and reporters were waiting early Friday evening, however, when the suspects were led out of the police headquarters after a night of questioning and formal booking as fugitives from justice. They were handcuffed with their hands behind their backs. The two younger girls looked frightened, confused and miserable. Heather, her hair parted in the middle and pulled back into a single, long pigtail, held her head down. Despite the cuffs and the awkward position of their arms, the two girls held hands while passing through the press gauntlet.

When reporters shouted a question at Rod asking if he had anything to say, he replied: "God bless America." Scott kept his mouth shut but exchanged a smirk with the Clan leader. After Charity was helped into a police car, she leaned her head wearily against the back seat and closed her eyes. Dana looked steadily down toward the sidewalk as she was led through the phalanx of reporters, and kept her head down after she was seated inside one of the police cruisers. Except for the single outburst from Rod, the prisoners ignored the flurry of shouted questions from the gang of reporters and photographers.

It had been a long, exhausting night and day, and the stress and lack of rest was showing. The teenagers looked bedraggled and washed out. Dana was driven to the parish prison and locked up. Her former companions were taken to the juvenile detention center to spend the rest of the night.

When Scott was led to the waiting police cars for the ride to the detention center, it marked his second trip outside the police headquarters building since his arrest. At about 5:30

p.m., Ben Odom, Baton Rouge Detective Dennis Moran and
the Florida detectives escorted him to the Mississippi River
levee a few hundred yards from the bridge over I–10, where
they briefly searched the banks and the water for the murder
weapon. It was rotten timing to be looking for anything. The
late autumn weather was rainy, cold and miserable and the
surface of the river was choppy and as gloomy and dark as
a vampire's heart. It was difficult to see anything, and the
search was quickly postponed.

Baton Rouge police and their Florida colleagues resumed
the search early Saturday morning under a rusted-out dock
near a graffiti-speckled pipeline. The location is a popular
hangout for local teenagers who use the area for beer-
drinking parties and as a lovers' lane. After a few minutes'
search, police divers recovered a loaded double-barreled
shotgun in about fifteen feet of water. The Wendorfs weren't
shot, and the short-barreled shotgun wasn't the murder
weapon. Investigators concluded that the shotgun had been
stolen in a house burglary, and speculated the fugitives may
have planned to sell it so they could buy food.

Later in the afternoon, divers moved to a new location
between the bridge and the Belle of Baton Rouge, a river-
boat that was outfitted as a casino and moored on the river.
During the sweep of the river bottom, the mud and weather
made it impossible to see, and the divers had to feel with
their hands. The farther into the river they moved, the more
risky the operation became, and senior officials at the scene
finally called the divers in after they had extended the search
about sixty feet from shore. No crowbars, tire tools or anything else resembling the weapon used to fatally bludgeon
the Wendorfs were found.

While divers cruised along the muddy river bottom, officers working along the levee cut a two-foot section out of
a large tree with a chainsaw and loaded it into a crime scene
van that was parked nearby. In response to questions from
reporters, detectives said that the teenagers had carved something into the bark. They refused to identify the words or
symbols, but said there was nothing about the carvings to

indicate Satanic or other occult behavior. Later, however, reports surfaced that the carving was indeed some manner of vampire-related symbol. Identification papers belonging to one of the youths were also found near the tree.

Some authorities in Louisiana and Florida tried their best to downplay the occult angle in the case, and LCSD spokesmen said there wasn't any evidence of vampire rituals connected with the twin murders. But there were simply too many slashed arms, stories of ritualistic blood-drinking, graveyard ceremonies and histories of wearing outlandish black clothing for the element of vampirism to be ignored. A flood of information was developed by law enforcement officers and other agencies linking the runaways to an obsession with blood and a fantasy world of the undead.

In Baton Rouge, Police Corporal Don Kelly reported that the arms of all five of the teenagers showed evidence of what appeared to be self-inflicted cuts. Except for that, they didn't show any behavior that was vampire-like, although some of them were dressed in black, he said. But there were no fangs or black capes. "They just look like screwed-up kids," he told the *Orlando Sentinel*. "There's no shortage of those."

In Kentucky, Mike Jump told reporters that the reputed cultists were blood-suckers. "They cut each other's arms and suck the blood. They cut up small animals and suck the blood," the MPD detective said. "They honestly believe they're vampires."

The murders of the Wendorfs and apprehension of their youngest daughter with the runaways dominated the news in Lake County and Murray. On November 30, the *Daily Commercial*, which is based in Leesburg and competes for subscribers with the *Orlando Sentinel*'s local edition, the *Lake Sentinel*, ran a front-page story headlined, "POLICE INTERVIEW SLAYING SUSPECTS . . . VAMPIRE CULTISTS STILL JAILED IN BATON ROUGE." The story was illustrated with a headshot of a wholesome-appearing young girl with long hair. The caption under the photo identified her as "H. Wendorf."

Inside the paper, the banner headline on the sports page

advised, "Eustis Girls Advance to Tipoff Final." The accompanying story traced the hoop team's come-from-behind 46–44 win over Cocoa Beach, and noted that "Eustis survived a scare . . ."

The day after Thanksgiving, the Panthers boys' football team was trailing host Crystal River in a game that could drop them out of the 4-A playoffs, but that only deepened the gloom that many of the students already felt. One of their most vocal cheerleaders, Jeni Wendorf, wasn't at her usual post leading cheers from the sidelines. Her fellow yell leaders were uncharacteristically subdued.

Tom Graham, the Eustis High student who wore the mascot Panther suit at the games, showed up for the contest with two black armbands pulled snugly over the sleeves of his jersey. The black bands represented the parents of his schoolmates, Jennifer and Heather. Beth Ann Crow told a reporter that the cheerleaders were feeling the shock, and described Jeni, her fellow co-captain on the yell squad, as "the loud one." Leslie Watson, another cheerleader, hadn't even thought about the game for a week, and said that the girls were praying for their friend.

The contrast between the world of high school thrills, basketball games, cheerleading and puppy love that Heather had just left behind, and the dreadful reality of the brutal murder of her parents and her legal predicament was dismally apparent. While Jennifer was grieving for her parents and Heather was seven hundred miles from home, held in a juvenile detention center on a first-degree murder warrant, former schoolmates of the sisters were continuing on with their lives.

As the only member of the Vampire Clan considered to be legally an adult, Dana was handled differently from her companions. While the younger runaways were lodged in the juvenile detention center, Dana was issued a loose-fitting orange top and a pair of yellow pants, and locked up with other adults in the parish prison. She was held without bail.

On the Monday morning following the arrests, she appeared in Baton Rouge District Court where Florida authorities presented Judge Jewel "Duke" Welch with waiver of extradition documents and an affidavit of probable cause for the young Kentucky woman's arrest. Dana missed the hilarity shortly before her arrival in the courtroom when an assistant district attorney placed a black coffee cup on the judge's empty desk. A little red stuffed pig with black horns and a red pitchfork was propped up inside the cup. An inscription on the toy read: "You little devil." The prank was good for a few chuckles, but the ADA whisked the infernal imp away from the desk before the judge walked into the courtroom.

The indelicate attempt at black humor was indicative of the attitude of a growing number of people who were intrigued by the story of a bizarre band of blood-sucking wannabe vampires who mutilated animals and murdered humans. The reality of lives lost and other lives squandered by teenage foolishness that got out of hand was too grim to focus on. So they treated the murders and the flight of the runaways as black comedy. The teens were the subject of jokes on talk radio shows, and idle conversations in barrooms, beauty shops, offices and factories in three states.

The mess Dana found herself in was no joke to her. The nineteen-year-old woman looked drained and empty of emotion as she stood before Judge Welch with her wrists cuffed in front of her and chains on her ankles. She spoke in a strong, confident voice, however, when she said she understood her Constitutional rights and agreed to return to Florida voluntarily. Public Defender Bert Garraway, who was assigned to represent her in the proceedings, advised her not to fight extradition by insisting on a hearing because it would simply delay the inevitable.

The proceeding was sterile and swiftly efficient, and ten minutes after it began Dana was led awkwardly back to her cell. In the courtroom, Garraway stood at his client's side, but there wasn't much he could say that would be helpful to her either at the hearing or later. He gave her the best advice he could. He told her to keep her mouth shut when she was around the Florida officers. Anything she said to them, even the most casual remark, could be used against her.

After the hearing, Judge Welch added his own spooky touch to the tableau when he was asked about the eerie aspects of the case. "We don't get many vampires around here," he said. "They're usually all down in New Orleans."

According to the waiver signed by the judge and by Dana, law enforcement authorities had thirty days to take custody and transport her to Florida. But police and prosecutors in the Lake County–seat town of Tavares weren't in a mood to waste time. Early Tuesday morning, Dana was awakened at the parish prison, fed a light breakfast, and at almost exactly 9 a.m., with her hands and feet securely fastened in manacles, she was helped into the back of a Lake County Sheriff's Department cruiser. Moments later the prisoner and her escorting officers began the seven-hundred-mile trip back to central Florida. The chunky, heavy-hipped girl, who had become used to being perceived as merely part of the background most of her life, was suddenly the center of attention and when she left Baton Rouge she rode in the middle of a three-car caravan.

Late Tuesday evening, December 3, the green-and-white cruiser she was riding in pulled up to the east end of the three-story box-shaped Lake County Detention Center in Tavares. A large overhead door was automatically slid open from inside, the cruiser carrying Dana and her armed escort moved into the sally port and the door slid shut behind them. After checking to make sure the door was closed, the officers got out and put their sidearms in lockers and turned the keys. Then they helped the shackled woman out of the car and led her a few feet away to the prisoner intake area.

Dana was already wearing a pair of wrinkled jailhouse trousers and a loose-fitting shirt, and she had been thoroughly searched before leaving Baton Rouge, but in accordance with regulations she was ordered to spread-eagle and was patted down. If she had been a newly arrested prisoner still in civilian clothes, she would have been ordered to empty her pockets and remove jewelry such as earrings, bracelets and rings.

In a jail, or "detention center" as most of them are called in these days of political correctness and concern for prisoner sensibilities, jewelry is valuable contraband that can be traded among inmates or stolen. Rings, watches, necklaces and similar baubles can provide an excuse for violence and other trouble in any jail, and the only jewelry that corrections officers in charge of the Lake County facility permit inmates to keep are plain gold wedding bands. If a piece of prohibited jewelry can't be removed because it's too tight or is permanently welded on, a corrections officer cuts it off.

Dana wasn't wearing any jewelry, and she was led from intake into the booking area, then placed in a holding cell to await her turn for further processing. At the detention center every newcomer awaits his or her turn, regardless of the seriousness of the crime he or she is charged with. Rambunctious drunks, shoplifters and wife-beaters are given the same treatment during the booking process as people like Dana, who are facing murder charges. The wait can be five or six hours if a busload of prisoners happens to come into the jail just ahead of another newcomer. That happens sometimes. There is constant traffic between inmates moving in and out of the jail, including prisoners who are housed for the federal government on a per diem basis.

Several holding cells are located in the booking area, enough to separate troublemakers from each other and to segregate men from women. Dana was placed in a cell of her own until the paperwork that arrived with her had been checked, and it was her turn. Then she was moved to the booking desk and seated in front of a thick sheet of shatterproof glass. Booking officers were seated on the other side of the glass, each one in front of a computer. Once she was seated, Dana was assigned an inmate number and began answering questions, including her address, first, last and middle names, date of birth, hair color, eye color, occupation, next of kin, the name of her attorney, phone numbers, location and description of scars, blemishes, tattoos and medical history.

Answers to the questions were carefully checked by the booking officer against the paperwork brought with her when she was transferred to Lake County from Baton Rouge. Dana's arms were scarred with thread-like lines from old wounds inflicted with razors or other sharp instruments during blood-sharing rituals. The information about the scars was duly noted and typed into the computer.

Fingerprinting was the next step in the process. Dana was printed in Baton Rouge, but the process was repeated in Tavares. Although the jail was first put into use in June 1992, and was an example of a modern structure built with an eye toward taking advantage of technological and other recent advances in corrections, one of the few areas it was still lagging behind in was fingerprinting. Jailers in Tavares didn't yet have a computerized fingerprinting system which works by photographing the hand to capture the distinct patterns. Instead, they used the old-fashioned method. Dana's fingers and thumbs were inked, then one at a time an ID officer pressed and rolled them onto a thin sheet of white cardboard.

After the new inmate was fingerprinted, her picture was taken. The photographer used a video camera to take a still shot of Dana looking straight into the lens. There were no profile shots, but the single picture was automatically fed into a computer that contained all the other information collected about the new inmate since she began the booking process. The information in the computer, including the picture and the fingerprints, are available to officers throughout the facility. Senior officers at the jail expect that sometime a few months or a few years down the road, booking information will be shared with other law enforcement authorities.

When the booking officer was finished with the new inmate, Dana turned in the clothing she brought with her. Clothing from outside the jail, along with other personal items such as jewelry, are placed in a bag and stored until the inmate's transfer or release. Any money brought into the jail by new inmates is placed into a commissary account. Regardless of whether they have one thousand dollars or one dollar, it goes into the account. Inmates are issued a document similar to a credit card, which they use to make purchases.

The next step for Dana was delousing and showering. She was sprayed with a chemical agent for lice and any similar parasites she may have carried into the jail with her, either on her body or in her clothes. Then she was allowed to shower. The delousing and showering process is humiliating and dehumanizing, but there are no exceptions to the rule. A single inmate carrying head lice, body lice or crab lice could spread the parasites to every other prisoner and corrections officer around her and cause the quarantine of an entire cellblock.

At last the young woman was issued a two-piece orange uniform that included a pair of pants and a shirt. Males and females wear the same style of loose-fitting uniform, and the only differences between the clothing of some inmates is the color. According to the color code, orange is worn by pretrial inmates. Inmates whose cases have already been settled and are serving short sentences at the detention center for misdemeanors wear blue. Kitchen workers, who are all selected from among sentenced inmates, dress in white. Occasionally an inmate will be held on two custody levels, serving a misdemeanor sentence while awaiting trial on a more serious felony charge. In that case he or she is considered to be an escape risk and is issued an orange uniform. Like Dana, about ninety percent of the roughly six hundred men and women at the detention center were pre-trial inmates and were issued orange uniforms.

Underwear and socks aren't issued along with the jail uniforms and, like other inmates, Dana was permitted to keep her own. The jail has two washdays per week, and inmates who want additional underclothes or socks are permitted to buy them through the commissary. Dana also kept the softsoled sandals she wore on her trip from Louisiana. If she hadn't worn the sandals, she would have been issued a pair of rubber flip-flops. No inmates are permitted to wear hard-soled shoes, because they may be used as weapons. Even inmates who wear sneakers have the shoelaces confiscated in order to minimize the risk of suicide. After they have been evaluated and are released from the classification pod to general population, inmates are allowed to write formal requests for return of the shoelaces.

Along with the uniform, Dana was also issued two clean sheets, a couple of pillowcases, a light blanket and a six-inch-deep plastic bucket about fifteen inches around at the top. The bucket was for personal items such as writing paper, pens, photographs, letters and any legal papers she might collect during her stay. The buckets are stored under the bottom bunks of cells, and anything that is too big or too voluminous to fit inside is banned.

Dressed in the rumpled orange uniform, and carrying her bucket and the bundle of bedding, Dana was at last led along the concrete-and-steel corridors of the jail to her cell. Throughout the ordeal, Dana was quiet and unemotional, and moved as automatically as a zombie. When she was told to look straight ahead for the camera, she looked straight ahead, unblinking. When she was told to stretch out her fingers for printing, she stretched out her fingers. When she was told to lift her arms for the spray from the delousing chemical, she obediently lifted her arms.

Moving through the booking process and making the silent trek to her temporary home in the starkly secure structure was an ignominious, sobering experience that stripped away humanity and individuality. The detention center is no place for someone with claustrophobia, or for someone who is used to the personal freedom and open spaces of rural western Kentucky. In Tavares, Dana was surrounded by the ugly confining reality of thick walls that were constructed of solid concrete block, and reinforced vertically and horizontally with steel bars.

The young woman who had shared blood while indulging in dark role-playing fantasies of vampires was being buried alive in a grim stone-and-steel tomb with hundreds of other people. For an unknown number of days, she would spend most of every day locked inside a two- or four-woman cell with a small common area, or dayroom, just outside. The cells are outfitted with double bunks, a stainless-steel lidless toilet and built-in sink at the top. Mirrors made of stainless steel instead of glass, which could be broken and used by an inmate as a weapon against herself or someone else, are located directly above the combination toilets and sinks. The new prisoner was able to control the flushing mechanism of the toilet herself, a function that isn't left up to inmates in every jail or prison. The sink also had a built-in fountain, and Dana could take a drink of water any time she wished, merely by pressing a button. There weren't many other choices left to her control. Confinement, boredom and regimentation were all in her immediate future.

Except for pre-trial hearings and the trial itself, when she would be secured in chains and manacles, then escorted through an enclosed overhead walkway across West Main Street leading from the jail to the Lake County Judicial Center, the only times Dana would be allowed out of her "pod" (cellblock) would be to talk with attorneys, for occasional visits with friends or family, for showers and for brief exercise periods. Contact with other inmates and corrections officers was kept to a minimum, even during meals. The rest of the time she would be confined to her cell from lockdown at 11 o'clock at night to 6:30 in the morning, and to the dayroom throughout the day and early evening, along with approximately seventy other women in her pod.

Inmate trusties accompanied by guards deliver meals, slipping the trays of food through horizontal slots in the cell doors that prisoners and staff alike refer to as "bean holes." Although most jail inmates are allowed into the dayrooms inside their own particular pods during the day, at mealtime they are always locked up in their cells until the food is delivered. When the detention center was first opened, meals were served at the tables in the common area. But some inmates either stole meals from fellow prisoners or bullied them into turning over choice treats like cake, fruit, meat or beverages. So jailers reverted to a system designed to ensure that each inmate receives his or her meal. It is only after the trays have been slid through the bean holes to all the inmates within a cellblock that the cells are unlocked and the meals are permitted to be carried into the dayrooms. From that point on it is up to the individual inmate to defend his or her food from hungry predators.

Breakfasts are slipped through the cell door slots at about 6:30 to 6:45 a.m., and typically consist of cold cereal, fruit and bread. Milk is provided for the cereal, and juice is frequently served as the beverage. Orange juice is a staple. Trusties begin delivering lunch at about 10:45 a.m. and a typical meal consists of a cold sandwich, a piece of fruit and a chunk of cake. Milk, Kool Aid, some other soft drink or fruit juice are alternated as beverages. Hot food is usually provided for the evening meal, and a sample menu could include a hamburger, veal, meatloaf or chicken, a vegetable and a beverage.

Every inmate, unless he or she is on a special diet approved by a physician, is served the same food and the same amount. Jailers feed everyone the same, regardless of whether the inmate weighs ninety pounds or three hundred pounds. There are no seconds, no refills on beverages, and no inmates are served coffee. Jailers eliminated coffee from the inmate menu a couple of years before Dana checked in. It was too expensive, and an unnecessary luxury. Corrections authorities also figured that inmates didn't need any kind of stimulants, including caffeine, that might fire them up and make them more unruly.

Dana's new world was dismally bleak and compressed; filled with the screams, moans and sobbing of other inmates, the clanging of solid metal cell doors sliding open or shut and the regular heavy footsteps of crisply uniformed guards echoing along the floors of the corridors. Dana had already known a degree of loneliness in her life, but it was nothing like what she would experience in jail. She was one of the youngest women in an all-female cellblock designed to accommodate 128 inmates, and the charges against her were among the most serious faced by any of them.

The cellblocks range from the smallest, which have a capacity of thirty-two inmates, to others with more than one hundred beds. The center was constructed with priority given to security and the safety of staff and inmates. It was a huge improvement over the former jail, just behind the old courthouse a couple of blocks down West Main Street. The former jail was renovated and turned into the Lake County Sheriff's Department headquarters. Sheriff Knupp has his offices there, and the civil, criminal investigations and road patrol divisions are also headquartered in the former jail.

Outside the jail, Dana's arrival back in Lake County was big news, and reporters from newspapers and television stations flocked to Tavares to obtain photos of her and interviews with police and prosecutors. When she was led through the crush of photographers and reporters in Louisiana, and later in Florida, her behavior was the same. She looked straight ahead, and kept her face as stiffly expressionless as a corpse while shuffling awkwardly in the leg chains.

She didn't look the way most people expected a vampire to look. In most vampire movies, the females of the species are almost uniformly sensuous with slender bodies, shapely breasts, long legs and long hair. Dana looked huge and disappointingly lumpy in the first newspaper photos taken of her after her arrest. Even her hairstyle belied the general Hollywood image of female vampires. Instead of cascading over her shoulders in a lustrous fall, the most distinctive thing about Dana's naturally dark, naturally curly hair was the ringlet that draped in a lazy loop over the center of her forehead.

On December 4, Dana made her first court appearance in Florida, but she didn't even leave the jail. Dana was showing the effects of the physical and emotional strain of the last few days, as she and four other women were led past a group of reporters and photographers at the jail into a holding cell. The other women were dressed like she was, in bright orange jail uniforms, but they were accused of far less serious local crimes that had nothing to do with the sensational Vampire Clan murders. One of the women covered her face with her hands when she saw the assembled reporters.

Dana didn't even look at the journalists, and when it was her turn she was led into a small courtroom where she stood stolidly and without any noticeable emotion, in front of a small video-phone. Then, while a female guard stood at her side, and with her wrists securely cuffed, she awkwardly raised her right hand to be sworn in. On the other end of the hook-up, in a courtroom directly across West Main Street from the jail, Lake County Judge Donna Miller denied bail. The judge observed that Dana had no ties to the local community, and there was a risk of flight.

Miller assigned the Public Defender's Office to the young woman's case after Dana said she didn't have money to pay a lawyer, or a car she could sell to raise cash. The no-fuss, no-muss proceeding was over in a few minutes and Dana was led back to her cell. A local criminal defense attorney, Mary Ann Plecas, was later named by the court to replace the public defender, at taxpayers' expense, as the young woman's lawyer in the local proceedings.

The downstairs courtroom with the video-phone and closed-circuit TV to permit video conferences with judges across the street is a good security feature and an excellent example of the up-to-date technology that is typical of the new jail. Judges can go to the jail to conduct business if they wish. Except for videotaped bond hearings, however, the courtroom isn't used much. Most of the local judges prefer conducting court business in their own chambers and court-rooms across the street.

In Baton Rouge, where juvenile court proceedings were closed to the public and only the barest details were released to the press, the Florida police officers ran into a temporary roadblock in the person of Judge Pamela Taylor Johnson when they appeared in her court seeking to extradite Dana's companions. Instead of smoothly moving forward in the same manner as Dana's hearing, the proceeding before the juvenile court judge immediately bogged down in a spider-web of legal technicalities and curiously incongruous events and statements.

When Dana left, her companions hadn't yet had their detention hearing, a requirement of Louisiana law to determine if Baton Rouge police had sufficient reason to hold the runaways as fugitives from justice. The judge dealing with the juveniles was required by state law to give their parents an opportunity to be present during the hearing. Charity and Scott indicated that they wanted their parents to attend the proceedings, and authorities began arranging for the trips to Louisiana. Judge Johnson gave them forty-eight hours to get to Baton Rouge and scheduled the detention hearing for the quartet of adolescents for the following Wednesday. "They're children," she said. "The law allows them to have their parents present."

Rod didn't ask to have his mother attend the hearing, but at his request he was provided with a personal counselor. Assistant Public Defender Steven A. Dixon was also named to represent him in the criminal matters, and lawyers were appointed for Scott and Charity. Heather's parents were dead, so the judge appointed a temporary guardian to protect those of her interests that were not specifically tied to the criminal accusations and extradition proceedings. A Baton Rouge lawyer was appointed to represent her on the criminal and extradition matters. All the teens waived their right to demand a hearing on the fugitive charges within seventy-two hours.

Judge Johnson withheld making a decision on the extradition status of the youths until after the detention hearing, and she had an opportunity to take a closer look at the paperwork and other elements of the process. The judge confirmed that she also planned to look into details surrounding the police interrogation of one of the juveniles. She didn't disclose which of the teens she was referring to.

Although the goings-on in juvenile court are normally closely guarded, some latitude is provided to judges, and Johnson called a brief news conference to help clear the air about her involvement and responsibilities in the notorious case. She told reporters that Florida hadn't filed an official extradition request for the two boys and two girls. While the judge was making that statement, a copy of the Florida affidavit of probable cause for extradition was lying on a table a few feet away. Judge Johnson nevertheless stated: "I have not seen any probable cause affidavit. There is no paperwork at all."

The trickle of information and apparent contradictions merely added to the public confusion. The judge's statements were in direct contradiction to earlier remarks by LCSD deputies, who told reporters that they had filed the necessary paper work. It also conflicted with the presence of the affidavit on the desk in her courtroom. It was the same affidavit that Judge Welch had accepted as satisfactory earlier in the day when he issued his ruling allowing Dana to waive extradition and return to Florida. Apparently, the Florida affidavit had not been officially entered into evidence in the juveniles' case. Also, the judge wanted to hear from the juveniles' parents before extraditing them. Thus, the four companions Dana left behind were ordered to remain in the juvenile detention center, while the judge met with them and their attorneys, and with police. The meetings, conferences and hearings eventually extended over three days.

The judge's objections caught Florida authorities by surprise, and while the teenagers remained in Baton Rouge, Lake County prosecutors began scrambling to comply with her mandate. Prosecutors preparing the paperwork in Tavares were breaking new ground, because Florida and Louisiana statutes governing extradition and transportation of juveniles were rarely used. There were no easy-to-fill-out forms, and they wrote out the requests from scratch, then Federal Expressed them to Baton Rouge. Additional material was faxed to the judge.

Lake County police and prosecutors had a final ace-in-the-hole available in case everything else failed and their efforts to return home with the teenagers continued to be frustrated by legal technicalities. They had obtained a war-

rant from Florida Governor Lawton Chiles requesting release of the criminal suspects to the Lake County officers.
The governor's warrant wasn't expected to be used unless
it came down to a worst-case scenario, and Lake County
authorities were forced to ask the state of Louisiana to return
the fugitives. That would mean more frustrating delays,
which they hoped to avoid by satisfying the demands of the
judge in Baton Rouge.

The Lake County contingent was facing an inescapable
fact: It was Judge Johnson's court, and they had to play by
her rules if they wanted to expeditiously extradite the juveniles. The out-of-state lawmen also learned that they were
mired in the middle of the first waiver hearings involving
juveniles held in Louisiana in ten years. The confounding
tangle was further complicated by the fact that Louisiana
law is based on the Napoleonic Code, while conduct of the
courts in every other state is based on English Common
Law.

Lake County sheriff's deputies and the runaways were
still waiting for authorities to sort through the complex bu-
reaucracy of the courts in two states, when Charity's father
and Scott's mother arrived in Baton Rouge to be with their
children and attend the detention hearing. David Keesee, a
slender man with a neatly trimmed beard and mustache, traveled from his home just outside Murray, and Martha Anderson made the long trip from Mayfield. She and her sister,
Esther McMahon, scraped up the gas money for the trip and
drove all night. They arrived in Baton Rouge at 5 o'clock
in the morning. Mrs. Anderson told reporters that Scott
seemed to be under Rod's influence. "He seems to be able
to hypnotize people," she said of Rod. "He's scary."

Howard Anderson remained at home in Mayfield to take
care of the younger boys, and to deal with the flood of news
reporters who found their way to the shabby wood-frame
house from as far away as Louisville. There was no electricity in the Anderson home when the reporters began
showing up, but the lights had been turned back on by the
time a family service worker from the DSS visited the next

day. When Anderson first saw the social worker he worried that the DSS agent was there to take the rest of the boys away, but was quickly reassured that no such thing was in the works. The social worker asked if the family needed grocery money, help paying for gasoline for the trip to Louisiana, or any other assistance. The distraught father assured him that he and the boys were getting by. The house was cleaned up, but cardboard was still propped against some of the broken windows to keep the cold out. The social worker arranged to get some medicine for Anderson, and after learning from Nick that the family had no Christmas tree, he arranged to have one delivered to the house.

Rod's talk at the detention hearing about not needing his mother appeared to be more teenage bluster than a true indication of his feelings. As soon as he had an opportunity, he placed telephone calls to his mother and grandparents in Murray. His grandparents assured him that they still loved him and were standing by him. Sondra later told reporters that when she talked with her son, he sounded and behaved like a frightened child. He told her he didn't know what was going on, and that he was going to be in court. She also disclosed that she was planning to go to Florida, and didn't know until an *Orlando Sentinel* reporter told her that parents would be allowed to address the judge in Baton Rouge. "No one has told us anything," she said. "No one has called us about anything at all."

While the runaways were waiting in Baton Rouge for the fuss over their extradition to be sorted out, the autopsies on the bodies of Richard and Naoma Wendorf were completed. The heads of both husband and wife were smashed like eggshells, with horrendous blows from the murder weapon—which police finally identified as a crowbar. Richard Wendorf was struck twenty-two times in the face, on top of his head and on the chest. A half-inch slash was also cut into his left thumb. Naoma Wendorf was clubbed once in the face, and twenty times on the top and back of her head. The blows were delivered with such ferocity that her brainstem was severed.

Curious burn patterns were found on both bodies. Nine oval-shaped burns were scorched into Richard Wendorf's upper right chest and they were so deep they penetrated his muscle tissue. Five of the burns were connected to form a rough "V" shape and the other four were outside—two dots on one side and two on the other. Naoma Wendorf's upper right abdomen and both her arms were scarred by a curious series of burns.

After the bodies of the murder victims were at last released to the family, mourners said their final goodbyes during services at the Baldwin–Fairchild Funeral Home chapel in Goldenrod–Winter Park. More than two hundred men, women and children gathered at the chapel for the 1 p.m. closed-casket ceremony. So many people turned out for the service that latecomers stood in the foyer or against the walls in the back, while Pastor Peter D. Nordstrom gently led them through the emotional ordeal. When referring to the deceased, he called them by the names most of their friends and family members used—"Ruth" and "Rick."

It was a time when families needed to come together, to stick together and to pray together. That may have been made more difficult by the absence of one of the family's youngest members. Outside the funeral home, terrible things were being said about Heather in the press and within the larger community. Mourners at the funeral couldn't pray with Rick and Ruth's youngest daughter because she was locked up in a juvenile detention center hundreds of miles from Winter Park. So they prayed for her.

The pastor urged the the somber assemblage to share their love with the missing girl. "Although there are all sorts of speculations at this point regarding Heather, one thing is sure: God loves Heather," the clergyman declared. "And nothing is ever going to change that." The mourners also loved Jennifer and, although she was being comforted and cared for by loving relatives, they showed their concern for her before and after the service with hugs, kisses and sympathetic words.

Richard and Naoma's older daughter was seated with relatives in the front row of the chapel. During the eulogy Stoothoff sat beside the girl, who occasionally broke into sobs. The final, mournful farewell to her parents was being carried out exactly one week after she returned to her home from work and found them dead. On the final morning of her parents' lives, Jennifer was one of the most popular girls at school and was looking forward to beginning her college career in a few months. She had a handsome, affectionate, steady boyfriend, classmates who looked up to her, teachers who respected her and two loving parents and a little sister to share confidences and family activities with.

Then she walked in on the murder scene and her life turned into a cheap slasher film. It was like the earth had collapsed under her and she was plunged screaming into a black pit. She was abruptly orphaned; her sister was missing, then sought as a suspect in the murders of their parents; and the ghastly mutilation of her parents was indelibly imprinted in her psyche and in her mind. Through no fault of her own, her innocence had been stolen and forever despoiled.

"They understood that life isn't seeking to get, that the part of life that enriches us is also in the giving," the pastor of the Rolling Hills Church in Zellwood told the assembly about Rick and Ruth Wendorf. The Reverend Nordstrom also talked about how the Wendorfs had worked and saved their money to buy the five-acre lot on Greentree Lane and build their dream home eight years earlier. "It was a house they hoped would be a safe haven from all the problems that come with life in the big city," he said. "But we know problems will find us anyway."

The clergyman asked the gathering to avoid allowing the tragedy of the murders to dominate their memories of the couple. Ruth, he said, was a woman who instilled the spark of life into any environment. He described Rick as a man who had insight into others and a knack for always giving the right gifts at Christmas.

The couple were laid to rest at the Glen Haven Memorial Park & Mausoleum on Temple Drive in Winter Park, where two freshly opened graves were already prepared. A friend drove Jennifer to the cemetery, trailing slowly behind the black hearses in the shiny red convertible that her parents had presented to her as an early high school graduation gift. Jennifer's boyfriend stood at her side, holding an arm comfortingly around her waist during the brief graveside service. Other friends also approached her as she stood by the twin caskets, hugging or kissing her while tears streamed down their faces.

Although the teenager who called herself "Zoe" and ran away with her friends to Louisiana was missing from the services, three other daughters and three grandchildren of her mother were in attendance. One of the family secrets uncovered by investigators was that Naoma and Richard Wendorf were never married and lived together in a common-law relationship. Naoma Queen was in fact still married to Joseph William Queen in Dallas, Texas, and they had two grown daughters, Paula Queen and Sandra Queen. Both the Queen sisters lived in Dallas. And, according to information later disclosed on his death certificate, Richard Wendorf had ended a previous marriage by divorce.

Jennifer was interviewed in more detail a few days after the tragedy by Sheriff's Detectives Ken Adams and Alvey Gussler. Shocked at the savagery and suddenness of her parents' deaths, she also appeared alarmed at the fragility of her own mortality and the frightening possibility that she may have escaped sharing their fate by only a few minutes. There seemed to be a distinct possibility that if she hadn't stopped at her boyfriend's apartment after work, she might have walked in on the killers and become a third victim.

"If they're bossy enough to take two people's lives, then they could've just as easily taken my little old life. . . . I would have had no defense against a crowbar or whatever it was," she shuddered.

While the experienced homicide investigators gently prodded her for information, she said she had believed at first that Rod was simply someone her younger sister felt she could talk to. "And then they just got too serious about something stupid," she said in what appeared to be a reference to the shared interest in vampires.

Jennifer recounted the disturbing story of an incident that had occurred about a year earlier while the family was gathered in their home, talking and laughing. Jennifer was dating a different boy then, and he told her that while her parents were enjoying themselves, Heather stood behind a door where no one could see her but him ". . . and she acted like she was cocking a gun, like cocking a rifle and blowing away everyone in the living room," Jennifer quoted the boy as saying.

One of the first things Heather did after she was locked up at the juvenile detention center in Baton Rouge was to write a letter to her sister and deny that she had anything to do with the murder of their parents. The frightened teenager blamed the murders on Rod. While sharing the information with the homicide detectives, Jennifer revealed the emotional tug-of-war she was undergoing. She said she didn't want to believe anything, even if it came straight from her sister. "Even if she swears that that's her word, I don't wanna believe anything until I've got all the evidence laid out in front of me," she said. "So I don't really take that letter to heart."

At another point in the interview, however, Jennifer said that she wanted to believe Heather "because she's my little sister, and I love her to death." Then she turned to the doubts that had gnawed at her since the terrible night her world was turned topsy-turvy. "Maybe she's just putting all the blame on Rod just so she . . . won't get in trouble," Jennifer suggested, as much to herself as to her interviewer. "She could just be saying this just to get my support, and it could all be a lie."

7. OPENING THE GATES OF HELL

The frightened runaways, along with some of their teenage friends and a few adults in Florida, helped police and the public reconstruct the grisly events in the final hours leading up to the murder of Richard and Naoma Wendorf. The story unfolded in bits and pieces, in interviews and depositions patiently collected by law enforcement officers in three states—and by news reporters who sought out everyone they could find who had even the most remote connection to the case.

Dana's return to Lake County triggered the release of a shower of documents that for the first time provided the public a close-up look at some of the evidence detectives had been industriously piecing together. The most productive accounts, disclosed in court hearings and in documents released to the public a few at a time, however, came from the lengthy videotaped statements taken from Rod, Heather and other members of the fledgling Vampire Clan in Baton Rouge shortly after their arrests. The suspects were submitted to two different sets of interviews—one set by Baton Rouge Police Department detectives, and another session of interrogations by Longo and Gussler. The LCSD detectives arrived in Baton Rouge at 8:45 Friday morning after the arrests, and spent the rest of the day interrogating the prisoners.

None of the adolescents were seasoned criminals, and the most serious trouble any of them had been in before was Rod's reputed involvement in the ritualistic slaughter of the puppies. So it wasn't surprising that, under the skillful prompting and prodding of veteran homicide investigators, the teenagers were quickly spilling their guts. Rod and his clutch of pseudo-vampires simply weren't in the same league with some of the hardened criminals the veteran interrogators were used to questioning.

The young suspects were grilled separately in each of the sessions, and the lengthy interrogations later led to some questions by defense attorneys. The lawyers indicated that the length of time the teenagers were held without legal representation, and questioning of the four juveniles without either attorneys or their parents present might lead to challenges to the use of the statements as evidence at some time during pre-trial proceedings. Judge Johnson expressed similar doubts about their handling immediately after the arrests.

Baton Rouge police denied there was any improper handling of the youths, and said Florida laws were followed in carrying out the interrogations because the alleged crimes occurred in that state. Florida statutes permit police questioning of juveniles in situations like the detectives were facing after the arrests in Baton Rouge, as long as reasonable efforts are made to locate parents. But the parents of Rod and his friends from Kentucky were hundreds of miles away. Heather's parents were dead, and other close relatives who might have stood in for them were also hundreds of miles from the police department headquarters in Baton Rouge when she and her friends were interrogated.

Some of the most chillingly damning statements were made by Rod, when he described the murders during questioning by Sergeant Odom. Heather's mother was taking a shower and her father was asleep on the couch when he walked into the house, he said. "I went over to Dad and hit him with a crowbar until he stopped breathing." The skinny youth said that he rummaged through Richard Wendorf's pockets and took his Discover card, then hid the body. Referring to Naoma as "Mother," he said that when she first saw him she asked what he wanted. Then she lunged at him and he stabbed her in the skull. After the murders, he rummaged around until he found the keys to the Explorer, and left.

The story related by Rod to the Louisiana homicide detectives wasn't an exact fit with other information being developed by investigators in Eustis, but it placed him in the house at the time of the murders—and by his own admission identified him as the killer of both victims. There were certain conflicts in other elements of his statement that puzzled investigators and didn't mesh perfectly with information being collected from other individuals and sources. That's the way it is with many homicide investigations. Detectives, technicians and scientists take things one step at a time, trimming away inaccuracies and patiently building a believable picture of what really happened. Rod's recollections, as reflected in various statements to legal authorities involved with the case, and to outside sources, would change and mutate over time.

While he was being questioned by Odom, and later by Lake County homicide investigators, he alternately sobbed, smirked or treated the deadly serious inquiry like a casual conversation. At times he veered off into wildly fanciful spiels about exposure to sinister blood cults during his early childhood. Other elements of the interviews, when he was talking about the trip to Florida and the murder of the Wendorfs, fit closely with the accounts related by his companions. He showed more emotion when the conversation turned to Charity than he did when the murders were being discussed. She was his fiancee and they planned to get married, even though her father called him an "A-class freak," he told Gussler and Longo. The Kentucky youth also told his interrogators that Charity was pregnant with his child, and she confirmed the statement during her own interview. Rod said that he was glad he was finally captured because he had been awake for almost seven consecutive days.

The veteran investigators listened patiently while the scraggly youth launched into an outlandish story about being initiated by his grandfather Gibson into a cult in Murray when he was five years old. Rod said that a woman was sacrificed during the devilish ceremony. Eventually he became "guardian" of the cult. Rod explained the scars on his arms by blaming things that had happened to him when he was younger. He said the experiences triggered his memories at times, causing him to freak out. "I cut myself because I override my pain," he said.

Charity also blamed her scars on cuts she inflicted on herself when she became upset, and showed a flare of temper because detectives continued to ask about the injuries. "Why, why is everybody so messed up about that?" she demanded. "It's just how I, if I get mad, I cut myself. . . . Because the anger goes away if I cut myself." Charity said she never underwent the blood-drinking initiation ritual to "cross over" from mortal to vampire. Rod wanted to initiate her, but she never let him do it.

Rod said that he was unable to explain the scars of lacerations on the bodies of his companions. "I don't know about the others, because Zoe is kind of a freak chick, and Dana, she's just Dana. I don't know." When Dana was asked about her scars, she responded that she slashed herself so she could feed vampire friends who were weakened and needed sustenance.

At one point in Rod's interviews, he broke down in tears and said he was sorry and had to cry because what was happening to him was like a big joke. "My life seems like a dream. So, my childhood was taken away at five. I don't know whether I'm asleep or dreaming anymore, so whatever, where I know I could wake up in five minutes."

"Rod, I can assure you it's not a dream," one of the Baton Rouge detectives interjected.

The yarn about Rod's grandfather sounded about as freaky as could be, but it was that kind of a case—and the officers were grilling that kind of a suspect. Everything about the affair was about as wild and grotesque as a 1960s Hammer Films horror flick.

Harrell Gibson, who had steadfastly professed his love for his grandson ever since members of the Vampire Clan were publicly linked to the Florida slayings, was shocked when reporters telephoned him at his home in Murray and told him about the cockeyed story. The stunned grandparent declared that he had never known about any such thing. He was a church-going man who loved Jesus Christ and didn't have any truck with Satan.

After Longo and Gussler questioned Rod and Charity in separate sessions, the teenage sweethearts were permitted to meet briefly in one of the stark interview rooms. Neither of the teenagers was aware that their words and movements during the bittersweet reunion were being recorded on videotape.

Rod told his girlfriend that the meeting was part of a tradeoff with police. He agreed to tell them whatever they wanted to know, if they would give the sweethearts a few minutes together in return. The videotape revealed the Vampire Clan leader as alternately comforting and threatening toward the frightened girl. At one point Rod consoled Charity and reassured her that she would be freed because he had taken all the blame for the murders.

"It's pretty simple. I either get seventy-eight years or they give me the death penalty. They pretty much said that," he told her during the Friday encounter. "It's all my fault. You guys didn't have anything to do with it." He said he expected to be put on trial as an adult, and that would mean he would probably face the death penalty. Seventy-eight years would be the best sentence he could hope for, he said.

Rod urged Charity to take care of the child they both believed she was pregnant with, and asked her to visit his grave once a year. For a while he considered the possibility that he might someday get out of prison, and said that if that happened he would "hit the street. I have no destination in mind, but wherever you are, I'll find you. You should know by now, I'm a good hunter."

At another point during the reunion, he lapsed into self-pity, and rambled on about committing suicide. While Charity begged him not to take his own life, he ran through twenty different ways he could kill himself in the interview room. He responded to her pleas not to kill himself by assuring her that even if he didn't, he didn't expect to die a natural death. "It's just going to be by the electric chair," he said. "Old Sparky." Rod also asked his girlfriend to "take care of Zoe," and see to it that she was reunited with her older sister, Jennifer.

Amid the hugs, reassurances, tears and whispers, Rod revealed a glimpse of his darker side and warned his girlfriend not to cheat on him while they were separated. "If I find out you've had anyone while I've been gone, I'll beat the . . . out of you," he threatened. "Then I'll have no remorse for you." Charity interrupted her sniffling with a girlish giggle, then reached out and gave him another hug.

The teenage lovers exchanged a litany of petty complaints about their treatment by their interrogators. Rod griped that police persisted in asking him "the stupidest questions," and said the officers wanted to know if he felt remorse for killing the Wendorfs. He complained bitterly during one of his interviews about being shackled, and described himself as being congenial and cooperative. Charity was upset because an officer didn't permit her as much privacy as she desired during a bathroom break. "He, like, made me use the boys' bathroom so he could stand in the doorway so he could know I wouldn't try to crawl out a window, which there is no window to crawl out," she whined in classically fractured teenage grammar.

During her own interview, Charity turned the tables on the detectives by asking if they thought her companions were vampires. The officers said they didn't. "Well, I don't either," she responded. The fifteen-year-old was clearly in over her head trying to deal with two experienced police interrogators and there were times when her account simply didn't add up. They accused her of inconsistencies and of digging herself into a hole by trying to protect her boyfriend.

She was jumpy and at one point became so upset that her interrogator told her to calm down. "I can't. I'm scared," she said.

"Take a deep breath," he recommended. "Why are you scared?"

"Because I don't want to lose Rod. And I don't want to get in trouble with all of this stuff," she said. Charity told the detectives that she was afraid she would end up in jail for something she didn't do, and she was worried about her boyfriend. She wasn't scared of him, but was afraid of what would happen to him. "You've got to realize I love Rod more than anything," she pleaded.

Heather wasn't in love with Rod, but she clowned around with him during a display of teenage silliness that defied the seriousness of the situation they had gotten themselves into. She made faces at him in the hallway shortly before she was led into the interrogation room to be questioned. One of the detectives asked her why she made the faces, and she said she was merely "bringing a little levity" to the situation to avoid going crazy.

On a more serious note, Heather told the detectives about being en route to Louisiana when she was informed by the other girls of the murders of her parents. She said she didn't flee from her companions after learning of the slayings because she was afraid that if she tried to leave, Rod would hurt her. Interviewing the girl was a challenge. At times she clammed up, or sobbed. At other times she chatted matter-of-factly about her fascination with vampirism, about blood-drinking and about Rod.

Peering at scars of cuts on one of Heather's arms, one of the officers apologized and said he and his partner weren't making fun of her, but they needed help understanding the mutilation. "I mean," he asked, lapsing into jargon sounding a bit like one of the girl's teenage friends back in Eustis, "they just drink from your arm?"

The police officer's concept of the grisly process was slightly askew, so Heather corrected his misassumption. "Just, no, just suck on it, you know, just drink the blood off, lick the blood off as much as they need, and then you do the same to someone else.'' With that explained, her inquisitor asked if she could fly like a bat. "Yeah, yeah. They say you can see and hear and smell things differently, more acute—that's just the beginning,'' she replied.

The detectives also did their best to destroy whatever mystique Rod might still retain in the eyes of the Eustis teenager. One of the interrogators told her that Rod had "laid a big line'' on her, but he was "a little scared boy . . with big tears in his eyes.'' Heather was apparently already having serious doubts about the self-appointed vampire lord who had shown up to rescue her from the "hell'' of life in rural Lake County and spirit her away to more exciting locales. She said at one point in the interview that she didn't want to look at him again.

The teenager also told the deputies that she had made it clear to Rod hours before the murders that she didn't want her parents hurt. "I said straight out I wanted them alive.'' According to her account, the subject came up shortly after Rod arrived back in Lake County and they had driven to a cemetery near Eustis High School to conduct her crossing-over ceremony. During the eerie ritual, conducted among the darkly shadowed tombstones and moss-covered oaks of the quiet graveyard, Rod shared his blood with her so that she could become a vampire.

They were going over details of their plans for her to run away from home when she laid down the law to him, she told the detectives. "I don't want you messing with my parents. I don't. Just leave them alone. I want them alive,'' she recounted saying. One of the wildly imaginative schemes concocted to cover her absence called for Clan members to stage her abduction by tying up her parents and knocking them unconscious. Heather told investigators that her response to that was a firm, "No, no.''

She said she didn't know that Rod was going to kill her parents, and believed he was merely helping her run away to New Orleans where they could have a good time.

"Are you afraid to admit that you knew what he was

gonna do and you couldn't stop him?'' Longo asked.

"I didn't know what he was gonna do," she replied. "I didn't know he was gonna kill my parents. I thought what he meant when, when we were gonna break the ties, I thought that just means to leave, just go, not actually kill them."

"You told him 'no' but he was gonna do it anyway, wasn't he?" Longo observed.

"Yeah," she agreed. "He wasn't gonna listen to me 'cause I was telling him 'no,' and he likes to kill people."

During her videotaped interrogation by Longo and Gussler, Dana also talked about Rod's intent to murder the couple. When Longo said he understood that the four Kentucky youths came to Florida "to pick up Zoe," she replied with a one-word answer: "Correct."

"And to take another vehicle back?"

"Correct."

"And to kill Zoe's parents, is that correct?"

Dana nodded her head up-and-down in affirmation.

During an interview with LCSD detectives in Murray a few days after Rod and his companions were returned to Lake County, John Goodman, formerly known as "Damion," told a chilling story about his erstwhile boyhood pal. In their written report of the interview, the homicide detectives wrote that Goodman had said that for the last few months immediately preceding the murders, Rod was "possessed [sic] with the idea of opening the gates to Hell, which meant he would have to kill a large, large number of people in order to consume their souls. By doing this, Ferrell believed he would obtain super powers."

Goodman also described the symbolism behind the letter "V's" and the dots found burned on the bodies of the Wendorfs. The five dots that were connected to form the "V" symbolized Rod, and the two pairs of dots on either side represented the members of his Vampire Clan: Scott, Dana, Charity and Heather.

The Kentucky youth also told Gussler and LCSD Detective C.J. Thompson during the interview that Heather had wanted to run away from home for seven months before the plan was finally put into action on the night her parents were killed. She begged him (Goodman) to come to Florida and deliver her from "hell," he said.

Goodman recalled his long friendship with Rod, and told about joining him in role-playing games since they were in elementary school together. He composed a few of his own, including some that were based on games such as "Dungeons & Dragons," and others calling for the players to assume the roles of vampires. One of the games he created was named "Dark Strangers," and he assumed the job of gamemaster, assigning roles to the participants. The only part in "Dark Strangers" that Rod ever agreed to act out was the role of a paid killer, Goodman said. He described his former chum as a "master of mind control" and martial arts.

Gussler and Thompson kept busy conducting interviews and collecting other evidence while they were in Calloway County. A thick stack of letters written to Damion by Heather was among the material they carried back to Lake County with them. From another source, not immediately disclosed, they located a reasonably accurate sketch of the layout of the Wendorf house.

The detectives also interviewed James Elkins, who said that Rod often talked about killing someone "to see what the rush would feel like." He told the investigators about his telephone conversations with Heather, and said she'd complained that she hated her parents because they didn't treat her right. She wanted to run away from home.

The case file grew rapidly, and was bulging with grotesqueries and lunatic schemes so outlandish that no one, adult or adolescent, could take them seriously. But someone did, and it was becoming increasingly evident that because he did, two innocent people had died horribly.

When Rod was drifting through Murray as silent and gray as a fog bank or a Kentucky mountain mist, stirring up trouble with his friends and reputedly mutilating the puppies at the shelter, he may have been warming up and making preliminary preparations to rip open "the gates of Hell." He provided investigators with a vivid glimpse of the horror that lay behind those gates during his videotaped interrogations in Baton Rouge.

Neither Dana nor Charity added much more solid information to the stories told by Rod, Scott and Heather during their interrogations. None of the girls, including Heather, were at the house on Greentree Lane when Richard and Naoma Wendorf were killed. Charity was running away with her boyfriend, and Dana was sticking with her friends.

The Andersons' exhausted old Skylark was wheezing and rattling like a retired coal miner with black lung disease, the engine was making strange noises, and it was belching smoke after the five-hundred-mile drive. The four teenagers who were packed inside were hungry and nearly broke when they arrived in central Florida. Rod planned to pick up Heather and expected to recruit his former girlfriend, Jeanine LeClaire, and possibly some other teenagers, into running away with the Vampire Clan.

Jeanine had "crossed over" the previous year during a ritual on her fifteenth birthday, but her parents and her own good sense had been weaning her away from the vampire-obsessed boy. She and Heather were still close friends, but they were developing separate interests and Jeanine was involving herself in more wholesome teenage activities at her school and church. Vampires represented death and horror—and they weren't even real.

Jeanine was surprised when Rod showed up outside her house on East Lake Seneca Road in Eustis on Sunday, November 24. Her home was one of the first places he stopped after the battered old Skylark limped into town. It was the day before the girl's sixteenth birthday, but Rod didn't arrive with a present. He asked her if she wanted him to kill her parents. The teenage girl was horrified, and her shocked response was impossible to misconstrue: "No. Stay away from my family. Get away from my house." Jeanine's mother later told homicide investigators about the chilling confron-

tation during a formal statement. She believed that Rod
wanted to steal their property because he needed money.

The gaunt, menacing boy from Kentucky wasn't Jeanine's
only visitor that day. Heather also showed up, and according
to Mrs. LeClaire, she looked sad, depressed and worried.
When Mrs. LeClaire asked what was wrong, Heather
shrugged. "Teenage stuff," she replied.

Rod's sights were set on driving to New Orleans, where
he and his companions expected to participate in the Mardi
Gras. Neither Rod nor the other teenagers were aware that
the merry-making didn't begin until early the following year.
The annual celebration traditionally extends for several days
of non-stop partying before finally winding down on Shrove
Tuesday—or Fat Tuesday—the last day before the beginning of Lent. The small Vampire Clan from Murray arrived
in Eustis about ten months too late for the 1996 Mardi Gras
and a couple of months early for the next one.

The runaways, who didn't even know when the Mardi
Gras was celebrated, had formulated sketchy plans to follow
up their tour of New Orleans by going to France. None of
the Kentucky teens spoke French, had passports or visas, or
had ever traveled in Europe. They were also so seriously
short of cash that they were hardly able to buy fuel and food,
but somehow they expected to travel—and presumably visit
some of the vampire hotspots of the world. Dana provided
most of the group's finances for the trip with $100 from her
work at Wal-Mart.

After arriving in Eustis, the teenagers twice visited Shannon Yohe's house in the Pine Lakes neighborhood.
Coincidentally, the pert sixteen-year-old blonde was a distant cousin of Jim Yohe in Murray, although they didn't
know each other. Shannon was also a classmate of Heather's
and had been a close friend of Rod's when he attended Eustis High School. During the visits on Sunday and on Monday night, Rod and his friends proved to be distressingly
freaky houseguests, according to Shannon's accounts. She
talked with reporters, and gave a formal statement to Sher-

iff's Detective Ronald S. Patton and Assistant State Attorney William Gross the day after Thanksgiving.

Before Rod moved to Kentucky, Shannon considered him to be a little bit weird, but she thought he was nice. When he showed up at her house with his friends, she realized he had changed. He was more than merely a little weird. His scrawny arms were scarred by knife or razor slashes, and on Monday evening, after they'd talked awhile, he walked into the kitchen and began rummaging around through cabinet drawers. He finally found a sharp knife, and announced, "Watch this." Then he drew the blade across his arm. As blood oozed from the cut, the chunky, big-hipped girl he'd brought with him from Kentucky murmured, "Oh, I want some." Leaning forward, Dana pressed her mouth to the cut and sucked up the blood. Then the visitors began talking about which parts of the body were the best places to cut, and which parts tasted the best.

"I was like, 'Get out of my house,'" the Eustis schoolgirl later told reporters.

Shannon was grossed out by the blood-sucking demonstration, but it wasn't the only outrageous behavior, or even the most ominous, during the disturbing visits. Rod's conversation was speckled with references to violence; once while he was fooling around acting like he was swimming on a dishwasher he began talking about "cracking" necks. After a while, Rod, Scott and Dana announced their intention to kill the Wendorfs and steal the Ford Explorer. Rod had seen the vehicle and figured it would make a dependable replacement for Scott's ailing Buick. Charity didn't participate in the talk about murder, but Shannon asked if Heather was in on the plans to kill her parents. Rod's reply was cryptically indirect: "She doesn't like them," he said.

An animated girl with a sunny smile and an explosion of long, frizzy blonde hair, Shannon was disgusted by the talk. She didn't understand why Rod or any of his friends would want to kill the Wendorfs, so she didn't believe it. Rod didn't go into detail about the absurd scheme, but while he chattered about murder as casually as if he were selecting a pizza topping, Dana and Scott sat across from him nodding their heads. Charity was the only one of Rod's companions from Kentucky who didn't nod in assent. The quiet girl, whom she knew as "Sarah" or "Shea," "didn't really seem like she was into it," Shannon said.

The talk about murder was shocking, but the teenage hostess wasn't as concerned as she might have been if it had come from someone else. Rod claimed to be a vampire, but he said a lot of goofy things. He had a reputation for telling outrageous whoppers, like the story that a computer at Eustis High had malfunctioned and graduated him. All his friends at EHS knew he'd left town after his freshman year. When he was spouting off, whoever he was talking to had to consider the source and take his statements with a grain of salt. Even before he got into all the trouble, other teenagers told their own story about him. It was easy to tell when he was lying, they joked. Just watch to see if his lips were moving.

Before leaving Shannon's home Monday night, Rod telephoned Heather to ask for directions to her house. After the Kentuckians left, Shannon telephoned a friend who knew Rod and recounted some of the conversation about murder and thievery. Her friend said not to worry about it. Everyone knew Rod Ferrell was a windbag who had trouble telling the truth. It was surely just more of his silly talk, and there was nothing to worry about. Shannon apparently took the advice, and didn't bother to pass on the information to any responsible adults.

Heather was at home while the talk about murder was going on at the Yohe house, and she telephoned her best friend, Jeanine. Mrs. LeClaire listened in on part of the conversation, and heard her daughter's firm, uncompromising and uncharacteristically angry tone when she told Heather: "No, I can't do that."

Heather had a busy night on the telephone. She also called her boyfriend, Jeremy Hueber, at his house and after talking once more with Rod by telephone, called Jeremy again. Jeremy thought his girlfriend sounded nervous. According to his later account to police, she told him that Rod was at her house and was thinking about killing her parents so the Clan could go to New Orleans. After concluding her call, while her unsuspecting parents were elsewhere in the house relaxing and settling in for the evening, she gathered up a few of her most prized possessions, stuffed them into two backpacks and crawled out of a window.

Heather had slipped into a denim skirt, black leather jacket and a prize pair of dark fishnet stockings that looked like they were fashioned from a cargo net. She joined the Kentucky teens a few yards down the road from her house. Then she drove away with the other two girls while Rod and Scott remained behind. Heather later said that the boys were supposed to walk five miles to Jeanine's home, where the teenagers planned to meet after she (Heather) had talked with Jeremy.

Around 9 p.m., Heather tapped on the window of Jeanine's room. She said it was time to go. Jeanine replied that she wasn't ready, so Heather said she would return after stopping at Jeremy's house to say goodbye. As soon as Heather left, Jeanine slipped outside and hid in a stand of woods across from the house.

Mrs. LeClaire had fixed a special dinner for her daughter's birthday, and after cleaning up the dishes she went to Jeanine's room to check on her. No one was there. It was an alarming discovery. Far too much teenage intrigue had been occurring in the last couple of days, and the worried mother hurried to her car and began driving down the dirt road that ran in front of the house, looking for her daughter. She proceeded only a few miles, however, before a strange feeling swept over her that she should turn around.

She had barely pulled back into the driveway before Jeanine stepped out from the stand of trees. The girl told her mother that Heather was running away. After taking her daughter back inside the house, Mrs. LeClaire went straight to the telephone to call the Wendorfs. But the line was busy. Jeanine returned to her room and went to bed. Her mother got back into her car and began driving the approximately four miles to Greentree Lane to warn Heather's parents about the scheme to run away.

At about 9:30 p.m., Heather stopped at Jeremy's house with the two Kentucky girls to say goodbye. Jeremy had been dating Heather for about six weeks, and he knew about her obsession with vampires—and with Rod Ferrell. He later told authorities that both of his girlfriend's arms were scarred with cuts, and that she believed she had lived before as an evil demon. She claimed to enjoy drinking her own blood and the blood of other people. One time Jeremy asked Heather how old her strange familiar from Kentucky was, and she replied that he was as old as he wanted to be. Jeremy asked what that meant, and Heather replied that Rod was centuries old.

When Heather showed up at Jeremy's house, she told him that Rod had gone to pick up Jeanine, and invited him to run away with them to New Orleans. She explained that they were in a hurry because of an incident that had occurred earlier that day. Rod was driving the old Buick in Mount Dora, when one of the tires went flat. A policeman stopped while they were changing the tire, looked over the carload of teenagers and wrote down Rod's name. The teens were unaware that the tire had deflated in front of the home of Sheriff Knupp.

Jeremy wasn't interested in accompanying Heather and the other runaways in the big adventure. There was a host of good reasons for the boy's refusal to join in the hare-brained scheme, and one of them was the disturbing talk of murder. Heather told him that Rod had suggested killing her parents because it would make it easier to run away. But she said she would try to stop him if he tried to carry out the plan. Jeremy wasn't having any trouble at home, he was a popular boy at school and he had no reason to consider running away to New Orleans with Heather and her strange friends. He told her the whole idea was crazy and urged her to forget about it. She said she had to go, but she wouldn't say why.

A couple of days later, LCSD Detective Ronald S. Patton

showed some of the photographs he had taken of the abandoned Buick Skylark to the curly-haired schoolboy. Jeremy identified it as the car that Heather and the two other girls were riding in when she arrived at his house to say goodbye.

The girls were surprised when they showed up for their rendezvous with Rod and Scott after leaving Jeremy's house. The boys weren't at Jeanine's house, where they had said they would be. A short time later, they found the boys in Richard Wendorf's Ford Explorer. Charity later told police that blood was smeared on Rod's face and shirt.

Heather hadn't known that stealing the car was part of the runaway scheme and, according to her accounts to investigators, she didn't learn until after the slayings that her parents were being battered to death while she was on her way to say goodbye to Jeremy. Details surrounding the approximate time Heather learned about the murders of her parents, and her reaction to the news, were subsequently a bit blurred, depending on who was recalling the event.

Rod told Sergeant Odom in Baton Rouge that Heather was still at Jeanine's home when she was told. "Heather flipped out about her parents and said, finally, 'OK, they're dead,'" he said. But investigators determined that Dana and Charity told her about the murders while the three girls were in the old Buick driving to Sanford to meet the boys before embarking on the long drive out of central Florida to New Orleans.

James Hope, a criminal defense lawyer in Tavares, who was later appointed to represent Heather, said that she didn't have any idea before the murders that her parents were going to be killed. She was also so traumatized after learning about the murders that she went into a deep state of shock and didn't speak for twenty-four hours. "At one point, she was being held down in the car by one of the others—whether this is consoling or controlling—so she wouldn't go berserk," he added.

Regardless of who was telling the stories, it seemed plain that it was a night of many surprises for the headstrong high school girl. The unexpected appearance of the sports utility vehicle was just one more incident in a series of events that hadn't gone the way she'd expected them to go since the plan to run away was set in motion. None of her friends from Eustis would be going along with her and the Kentucky contingent. Jeremy flatly refused to have anything to do with the scheme, and Jeanine had also become a no-show. No one asked Shannon to go.

It had been a long and eventful day for Jeanine LeClaire, and she was sleeping soundly when her mother walked into the girl's bedroom and woke her up. Mrs. LeClaire told her daughter that something horrible had happened. Police were already at the Wendorf home when Mrs. LeClaire had driven up.

In Baton Rouge, three days after Dana waived extradition, the remaining teenagers were cleared to be returned to Florida. Rod was the first to waive extradition, and the next day Charity consented to return. Scott and Heather continued to oppose the process, but at the conclusion of an extradition hearing that extended through two days, Judge Johnson approved their release to the custody of Lake County sheriff's deputies. Once they moved out of her jurisdiction, the questions that hung over their initial handling by police in the early hours after their arrest would be a matter to be dealt with in the Florida courts.

The Florida officers were outspokenly relieved by the developments. "It's been a frustrating process," Longo told reporters in Baton Rouge. "We were not familiar with Louisiana's laws on extradition."

Leon Harrell, Charity's court-appointed lawyer in Baton Rouge, also took advantage of the opportunity to talk to reporters about the troubling public image of the runaways as members of a vampire cult. He said that he hadn't seen any documentation during the closed hearing to indicate that the case was cult-related. "Charity is an innocent, naive and frightened sixteen-year-old," Harrell declared. "I don't think that cult stuff has any merit."

That was the type of thing authorities in Florida had been

saying for days, but the protestations were taking on an increasingly hollow ring. As far as most of the media were concerned, they were dealing with a case about a deadly killer vampire cult. There wasn't much that police, prosecutors or defense attorneys could do to convince the press and the public that it was anything less than teenagers run amok after they confused reality with dark vampire fantasy.

In Murray, Sheriff Scott didn't show the same reticence that his counterpart in Tavares did about talking publicly of the apparent role played by vampire cultists in the tragedy. He told Jim Mahanes, a tall, lanky Louisville native who worked as a reporter for the *Ledger & Times* when he wasn't performing on stage as lead singer for "Trippin' Lizard," that he had been troubled by an uneasy feeling that something bad like the Wendorf murders was going to happen. The sheriff added that he figured about thirty teenagers were involved in the local vampire scene.

But Murray's vampires were clearly on the run and in disarray. The local vampire underground had become exceedingly unpopular almost overnight. CCHS Principal Jerry F. Ainley held a press conference and issued a typewritten statement stressing the positive by pointing to the ninety-five percent of students who neither made headlines nor caused major problems at the school. In other remarks in the statement, he referred to "the unfortunate incident," and said that he felt the relationship between that incident and the school population was minimal. Ainley added that students were informed that counseling would be available to anyone who wished for help dealing with the problem. Information was also being made available to faculty about warning signs that might indicate possible association with a cult, he said. Ainley added that most of the students identified with what he referred to as "this group" were not enrolled at CCHS.

Alarmed clergy also got together with civic leaders and organized a community prayer service that was conducted a few days after the story broke linking Murray's Vampire Clan to the murders. They scheduled another prayer service

for the following September, and announced that Sheriff
Scott would be one of the speakers. People were seriously
spooked, and worried about the spiritual and secular future
of Calloway County's young people.

Even the Vampire Hotel was affected by the wave of
shock and outrage that swept through western Kentucky in
the wake of the grisly slayings more than five hundred miles
away. Some anonymous hikers armed themselves with cans
of spray paint and trudged up the bramble- and poison-ivy-
choked hill to the silent ruins to make a few alterations. The
new graffiti artists painted over some of the most overtly
ominous vampiric and occult slogans, signs and obscenities
with freshly sprayed references to Jesus and the Savior's
love. A huge slogan advising "CHAOS NEVER DIED," was
painted over with the classic Christian message, "JESUS
SAVES." Just above both messages someone else had
sprayed a more secular announcement: "JESSIE LOVES
AARON."

Another visitor, who signed his name to his work, left a
crudely written Christian message in white paint on a flap
from a heavy corrugated cardboard box. It read:

> John 14:6
> Jesus saith unto him I am
> the way the truth
> the life no man come
> unto the Father but by
> me.

There was evidence that not all the vampire-haters shared
the strong religious convictions of the individuals who
spray-painted Christian slogans. One anonymous graffiti artist sprayed over the word "Vampire" on a section of
cinderblock wall with a huge blue-painted "X," then
scrawled an obscenity immediately underneath in the same
blue paint.

Unsurprisingly, "Vampire: The Masquerade," its publisher, White Wolf, and devotees of "Vampire" and other

role-playing games were caught in the fallout from the hideous act in rural Eustis. The unfortunate connection and sudden negative attention to "Vampire" was a reprise of the furor that erupted a few years earlier when several teenagers known to play D & D were tied to Satanic murders and other ritualistic bloodlettings, including suicides, that were blamed on the game by detractors. The commotion over D & D continued for years and was debated in church pulpits, the media and government circles before it finally died down. The tumult over "Vampire" was shorter-lived, possibly because company executives at White Wolf had learned valuable lessons from the tribulations of their predecessors, and were ready with the correct answers when critics and the media called.

The tenuous tie that seemed to link the hideous blood feast on Greentree Lane and the young vampire-fancier blamed as its principal architect with "Vampire: The Masquerade," nevertheless took its toll on gamesters. VAMPS was one of the most immediate casualties, and was never revived at the MSU campus after the slayings.

Steven Murphy and other gamesters defended the role-playing game, and Rod's former friend placed the blame for the tragedy squarely on the tiny minority of enthusiasts who failed to separate the fantasy vampire world from reality. "People always degrade games like this," he told Mahanes. "It's not the game that messes people's heads up. The person is already messed up before they play or it wouldn't get to them like that." Everything had become twisted around, he complained.

At last, before the end of the first week in December, while the fear and the fallout from the murders continued to swirl around them, the four teens suspected of being core members of the murderous blood cult began the long trek back to Florida. They left Baton Rouge a few minutes after 7 o'clock Friday morning, riding in two green-and-white LCSD vans. Heather and Charity occupied the back of one van, and Rod and Scott rode in the other. The runaways were transported in handcuffs, leg chains and two-piece suits that were as brightly orange as the ripe fruit plucked from Lake County citrus orchards.

As news of Judge Johnson's decision flashed through central Florida and western Kentucky, fact mixed with a toxic melange of rumor, misinformation and fear. Some central Florida radio stations reported on Thursday afternoon broadcasts that Rod was expected to arrive in Tavares on Friday morning. The radio announcers were a few hours early.

The alarm that swept through the two communities most keenly touched by the vampire-obsessed teens was also mixed with other emotions, including disgust and anger. An ill-humored remark by a woman who had told a friend in a Tavares restaurant that she felt like shooting the teenagers when they arrived in town set off a brief flurry of activity after it was reported to the sheriff's department. An alert was issued, then called off after officers checked out the report and confirmed that the statement was nothing more than a casual comment that was never meant to be taken literally. No one was waiting to gun down the teens the moment they were ferried into town—or later.

The woman's offhand comment and the reaction to it, however, provided a vivid example of the anger, shock, frustration and sincere feeling of loss among many residents of the close-knit central Lake County towns. The sense of privacy, safety and community had been grossly invaded. All manner of strange, frightening stories were making the rounds. Emotions soared, and some scare stories were so wildly dramatic they might have been lifted right out of the more imaginative supermarket tabloids such as the *Sun* and the *Weekly World News*.

In Eustis, some mothers of young children shuddered when they heard that Heather had accompanied a girlfriend who was helping out at a pre-school program at one of the local churches. For months, Lake County had been suffering through one shocking incident after another involving local teenagers, and the murder of the Wendorfs, with the search for and capture of the runaways, was only the latest staggering blow to land.

Classes had resumed for only a few days the previous September, barely two months before the Wendorf tragedy, when a fourteen-year-old student at Tavares Middle School shot a thirteen-year-old classmate to death. Keith Johnson, a bespectacled, tow-headed, baby-faced eighth-grader was subsequently convicted of first-degree murder and sentenced to life in prison for the campus slaying of Joey Summerall. Keith confided to a few of his schoolmates that he had a gun and was going to blow Joey away, but they either didn't believe him—or they didn't care. Then Keith pulled a semi-automatic on a crowded sidewalk in front of the school and emptied the clip into the boy while horrified classmates scattered in terror.*

Lake County schools were suddenly developing a nasty reputation. The month that Keith gunned down his classmate, a report based on a study by the Florida Department of Education was issued pointing the finger at Lake County schools for having the highest rate of violence in the state. Considering the grim reputation for violence of cities like Miami, Fort Lauderdale and Jacksonville, it was a shocking report. Obviously, Keith Johnson wasn't the only dangerous troublemaker.

About a dozen students were expelled from middle schools and high schools in Tavares, Umatilla, South Lake and Eustis in the early months of the same school year. Two students were kicked out of Eustis High for carrying pistols, and a student at Clearmont Middle School was expelled for carrying a pellet gun on campus. Other Lake County students got into trouble during the same period for making bomb threats, peddling drugs, carrying knives on campus, threatening to murder teachers as part of a gang initiation, and attacking other students with knives or razors.

The perplexing outbreak of violence and other crime was deeply frightening to Lake County residents, including a

---

*Keith Johnson was sent to the Apalachee Correctional Institution to begin serving his prison term. In pronouncing sentence, Circuit Judge Don F. Briggs admonished the boy: "You have robbed this community of its innocence."

large number of families who—like the Wendorfs—had moved to the smalltown Florida communities to escape the stresses and dangers of big cities. But none of the infractions or incidents of violence was as traumatizing for the community as the savage murder of the Wendorfs and the accompanying indications of macabre vampire cult activities.

A strong feeling of sympathy and support for Heather existed among many Lake County residents who knew her or other members of her family. At Eustis High, a fellow freshman student who was a friend of Heather's described her to reporters as a nice girl who had started hanging around with a different crowd and went from being nice to being really quiet, dyeing her hair purple, wearing black and talking about being a vampire.

Some of her friends believed that Rod had been infatuated with Heather for a long time, and when she refused to run away with him, he murdered the Wendorfs and kidnapped her.

Jerry Smith, superintendent of the Lake County School District, learned about the murders in a telephone call at 5 o'clock Tuesday morning. When students began arriving on campus a couple of hours later, eight counselors with the district crisis team were waiting. They comforted a steady stream of students throughout the day. The beginning of the long Thanksgiving weekend was only a couple of days away and students were advised where they could go during the holiday if they needed additional counseling or simply wanted a sympathetic adult shoulder to cry on. Under normal circumstances, with a holiday and an important football game for the Panthers coming up over the weekend, a festive air could have been expected to have existed on campus. The mood in the hallways, however, was somber, and many of the students were plainly having a difficult time getting into the holiday spirit.

Clergymen from throughout the city contacted school officials and offered their guidance, and members of the Fellowship of Christian Athletes added their support. Like any small town, Eustis had its share of problems, but a strong sense of community existed among the residents that was especially visible in times of crisis.

After school, about two hundred students gathered together in the auditorium for a huge prayer meeting. Senior Erica Nolle, who remembered Mrs. Wendorf as the last person she saw before leaving the campus Monday afternoon, led one of the prayer groups. Some prayed that Jennifer and Heather would feel their love and know that they had the support of their fellow students. Another group prayed for understanding, and for an end to the frightening rumors. Clark Blake, one of the teachers, led a prayer asking God to give them the courage to deal with the tragic event that had touched their lives.

In these days of heightened sensitivities and constant vigilance by the American Civil Liberties Union, Principal Jim Hollins might have been sticking his neck out by allowing the prayers. Hollins, however, worked in Eustis, a community with a long history of religious fealty and a strong sense of spirituality. Several students asked the principal for permission to hold the volunteer assembly after class, and he figured it was the right thing to do. There was no backlash or any lawsuits challenging the use of school property for the prayer meeting.

Heather's heartbroken seventy-five-year-old grandfather was one of her most outspoken defenders. He described her to reporters as a quiet, demure little girl, and said he never saw any evidence to indicate that she was dabbling in darkling activities.

Not everyone shared his empathy for the orphan. Another girl from Orlando who had previously lived in eastern Lake County telephoned the local CrimeLine and reported that Heather had told her that she'd helped plan the fatal bludgeoning of her parents. The tipster was a fifteen-year-old with the strangely congruous name, Amber Blood.

The exhausted teenagers were driven into the sally port at the detention center in Tavares at almost exactly 6:30 p.m., eleven hours after the trip began in Baton Rouge. A welcoming committee of television and still photographers was on hand for their arrival, and Rod didn't disappoint them. As he was led inside the booking area, he spotted the photographers and pressed his face against a glass partition. Then he leered, stuck his tongue against the glass and blew a kiss to them. They were delighted. It was a performance worthy of a Charles Manson, notorious as the leader of a killer cult, or a Richard Ramirez, who became known as the "Night Stalker" while terrorizing suburban Los Angeles for two years in the mid-1980s by committing a series of particularly vicious rapes and Satanic murders. Both loved to make faces and clown for the press.

Rod's companions were more subdued and showed little emotion during or after the long journey from Baton Rouge. Scott appeared bored, or simply worn out, while he waited for his companion's juvenile antics to run their course. Heather's long hair hung loose over her shoulders and she shuffled slowly forward in her leg chains while a female officer steadied her with one hand around her elbow. Both Heather and Charity kept their heads down while they were led past the press gauntlet, just as they had done in Baton Rouge.

After the photographers were ushered out, the attention of the youthful prisoners was taken over by booking officers and other corrections authorities who conducted the intake interviews, shot video pictures and rolled the young suspect's fingerprints onto new cards. Even though Rod had been in police custody for several days, corrections officers ordered him to remove his socks and lift his long hair so they could search for weapons. Rod's vampire name, "Vassago," was listed in the square for aliases on his booking form, as "Vesago", along with "Dude Man" (misspelled as "Dood Man") and a couple of others that seemed glaringly inappropriate for someone who was suspected of such horrid crimes—"Bunny Foot," and "Patty Wack." The quartet didn't tarry long at the jail, having been given just sufficient time to be booked and advised of the formal charges. Rod, Scott and Heather were accused of murder, and Charity was booked as a suspected accomplice. There were no reunions at the jail with Dana.

At 9:15, they were loaded back into the vans and driven to Ocala in adjacent Marion County, where they were locked up in the Florida Department of Juvenile Justice's sixty-eight-bed Regional Juvenile Detention Center. A strong movement was already underfoot by some local politicians, business leaders and movers and shakers in the juvenile justice system to win state approval and funding for construction of Lake County's own juvenile detention center. More than a thousand juvenile arrests were eventually recorded before the end of the year, more than fifteen percent of the total 1996 arrests in Lake County, and dealing with criminal behavior by adolescents was a rapidly growing problem. Overall, Florida had one of the highest juvenile crime rates in the country.

A local task force was studying the problem, including the possibility of adding a screening and evaluation center to the proposed project, but for the time being the little band of would-be vampires, like other suspected juvenile offenders who got into trouble in Lake County, would continue to be shuttled back and forth on an exhausting one-hundred-mile round trip between Tavares and Ocala.

Serious crime historians recognize Marion County as the site of a furious one-sided shootout in January 1935 that shattered one of the most vicious gangs of bank robbers, kidnappers and cold-blooded killers in the country. Kate "Ma" Barker and her youngest son, Freddie, lost a four-hour submachine-gun battle with an army of FBI men and local police while they were holed up in a cottage at Lake Weir near Oklawaha, seventeen miles south of Ocala. The firefight ended with 1,500 bullet-holes in the wood-frame cottage with the screened-in front porch, Ma dead with one to three bullet wounds, depending on which version of the epic confrontation is believed, and Freddie dead with fourteen. Freddie was still clutching his Thompson submachine-gun, and Ma had more than $10,000 in her handbag, a huge amount of money for the middle years of the Great Depression.

Now Marion County was host to a newly notorious group of suspected desperadoes, but they had none of the wild daring or panache of the old-time bank robbery gang. The exhausted teenagers had spent more than twelve hours on the road and another three hours being booked into the detention center before they were signed in at the juvenile justice facility. At last they were permitted, tired out and appreciative, to flop onto their bunks and close their eyes.

8. HEATHER'S SURPRISE

Heather occupied center stage during a fifteen-minute hearing in the Marion County Jail in Ocala when a judge ordered her and her three companions held without bail.

The listless schoolgirl with shackles on her hands and feet shuffled awkwardly with her shoulders slumped and her head down while a deputy led her into the small hearing room at the jail around 11 a.m. She and Charity were dressed in hot-pink sweatshirts, blue pants and purple shoes. The boys wore jailhouse shirts and pants with sneakers. All four of the youths wore belts around their waists that were threaded through single large metal rings attached to the small chains linking the cuffs around their wrists.

When Judge Frances S. King asked Heather if she needed a court-appointed attorney, she replied in a barely perceptible voice, "Yes, ma'am."

Heather's demeanor never changed during the brief appearance, and she spent most of her time in the courtroom looking down at the floor, while nervously twirling a single pigtail she had braided in her long hair. Heather's nervous habit of twirling the pigtail with her manacled hands would become a trademark of her appearances at court hearings.

The Kentucky teens were also subdued during the hearing, and for the most part replied to questions from the judge with polite monotone one-word answers. Rod showed no trace of the cockiness he had displayed when he was booked at the Lake County Detention Center the previous evening, and his long, stringy hair was still dark and flopped across his face while he stared vacantly in front of him. A glimpse of the bottom edge of the dragon tattoo on his left arm was visible under the fringe of his short-sleeved prison shirt. In response to questioning by the judge, he said his mother and grandparents were in the process of moving to Florida from Kentucky.

Judge King designated Bill Stone, of Florida's Fifth Judicial District Public Defender's Office, to represent Rod. In order to avoid conflicts of interest between lawyers, it was common practice for the Public Defender to represent the defendant who appeared to be in the most serious trouble or peril in cases when more than one individual was charged with the same crime. In the Wendorf murder case, it was already clear that that defendant was Rod.

Private attorneys were appointed for the other prisoners. Michael Graves was named to represent Scott and James Hope was assigned to Heather's case. Charity told Judge King that her parents might hire a lawyer for her. Attorney R. Thomas Carle was eventually named to defend her—at taxpayer expense.

The judge ordered Rod, Scott and Heather held on first-degree murder charges, and Charity held on a charge of accessory to murder—all without bail. At the conclusion of the no-frills fifteen-minute proceeding, the two girls and two boys were led back to waiting police vans and returned to the juvenile lockup where they were isolated from each other.

The selection process for assigning attorneys to be paid at public expense had an element to it that was reminiscent of the draft for college athletes moving up to professional sports teams. Local lawyers were moved onto pauper defense cases when their numbers came up, or so it seemed. But it wasn't that cut-and-dried. Individual lawyers have widely varying specialties, abilities and skills, and judges take great care in serious cases such as anticipated capital murder trials to appoint defense counsel who are up to the demands. The suspects in the Wendorf slayings didn't possess the personal fortunes of an O.J. Simpson and couldn't pay a multi-million-dollar "Dream Team," but judicial authorities in Lake County were determined to see to it that they got the best defense possible. The lawyers assigned to the teenagers were experienced in criminal defense and were expected to be formidible advocates for their clients.

Attorneys handpicked by the court to defend the teenagers may very well have had conflicting emotions about their selection. They were taking on a challenging, high-profile case that would offer them an opportunity to enhance their professional reputations as criminal defense attorneys by showing off their investigative, organizational and courtroom skills to a large audience.

On the downside, the attorneys were faced with the staggering responsibility of defending clients who were charged with terrible crimes that could possibly lead to the death penalty or lifetimes behind bars. And the job had to be done on relatively modest budgets that were restricted because they were being paid for their work with taxpayer money. People close to the case were already estimating that Lake County taxpayers might eventually be handed the tab for as much as $250,000 to defend the accused Vampire Clan killers. Attorneys' fees would account for a large portion of the expense, but the costs for police and prosecutor salaries, expert witnesses, depositions, laboratory analyses, transportation, lodging and meals for witnesses and myriad other necessities were certain to add significantly to the drain on available funds. The estimated $50,000 per defendant was a staggering amount of money to siphon off from public funds but, based on costs of many other complicated murder trials, it was relatively modest.

The job of defending the wannabe vampires would also be taxing on the lawyers' personal finances. The hourly rate paid to court-appointed defense attorneys was established at

$60 by administrative order. The same rate applied whether attorneys were defending someone who was arrested on misdemeanor charges of assault after getting into a fight in a bar, someone who was accused of selling a couple of ounces of marijuana—or a would-be vampire charged with two counts of capital murder and other felony offenses.

The $60 hourly rate may have looked good to a warehouse worker at Crown Cork & Seal, a hamburger cook at McDonald's, or a cashier at the local Wal-Mart, but it was a far cry from the $125 hourly rate or flat fees of many thousands of dollars that savvy criminal defense lawyers commonly commanded for their work. Capital murder cases can tie attorneys up for hundreds of hours, and there was no indication that this one was going to be an exception. And while they were toiling on the vampire murder defense for half their normal rate, the time would be lost for work on other more financially rewarding cases.

Judging from all appearances, the attorneys for the vampire cultists were assuming obligations that would keep their legal noses to the grindstone and have them burning the midnight oil for a year or more.

In Florida, state attorneys can file most felony charges, but according to the criminal statutes only grand juries may hand down first-degree murder indictments. Any of the juveniles indicted for first-degree murder would automatically be moved into adult court.

State Attorney Bradley E. "Brad" King and Assistant State Attorney William Gross began selecting the eighteen-member panel from a pool of thirty-five prospects early on a mid-December Monday morning, and before noon they had settled on twelve women and six men. Several prospective jurors were rejected, including a woman who broke into tears as she confessed she couldn't make a decision that might lead to sending one or more of the teenage defendants to the electric chair. Circuit Judge Jerry T. Lockett presided, but left the room after giving the jury detailed instructions. He wouldn't speak to the panel again until the jurors were ready to report a decision. Defense attorneys, who were permitted inside the room during the jury selection process, were also required to leave prior to presentation of evidence and testimony of witnesses. The newly impaneled jury spent a long Monday afternoon listening to witnesses in the sensational case. Testimony continued through most of the following morning.

Although grand jury testimony is secret, anyone stationed in the first-floor lobby of the judicial building outside the courtroom of Judge G. Richard Singletary, where the proceeding was underway, could easily keep track of witnesses moving in and out. Homicide detectives, friends and classmates of Heather and Rod, and various other witnesses—including Jennifer—trooped in and out of the courtroom one at a time. Shannon Yohe and Jeremy Hueber were among the teenage chums of the defendants who responded to questioning from King and Gross. Another of the witnesses was Amber Blood, the Orlando girl who volunteered the CrimeLine report about Heather.

Forensics technicians and homicide detectives who worked on the case, including Gussler, Adams and Longo, also contributed to the seven hours of closed-door testimony. Depositions were also heard regarding the story Sondra Gibson told to the Orlando newspaper about Heather saying she wanted her parents killed.

Grand juries are valuable investigative tools, whether the subject being probed is political corruption like White House fund-raising scandals, or shocking murders like the barbaric bludgeoning of two loving parents within the violated sanctity of their home. It is not the job of the panelists to decide that a defendant is guilty and can be convicted, but to determine if the accusations are based on evidence that is so persuasive that indictments should be returned in order to see that justice is done. Guilt and convictions, or findings of innocence, are the job of trial juries—and sometimes of judges.

On Tuesday, December 17, barely three weeks after the bloodbath on Greentree Lane, the grand jury, after less than

a full hour of deliberation, returned felony murder indictments against the four Kentucky teenagers. In the report,
Rod was indicted for first-degree murder, armed robbery and
armed burglary. Scott was indicted for being a principal accessory aiding or assisting in first-degree murder, and for
armed robbery and armed burglary. Charity and Dana were
indicted for being principal accessories aiding or assisting in
first-degree murder, aiding or assisting in armed robbery and
aiding or assisting in burglary.

The jurors reported that they found compelling evidence
that Rod killed the Wendorfs by striking them ''repeatedly
with a blunt, hard object similar to a crowbar or a pry bar.''
Both boys were also accused in the indictment of stealing
money, credit cards, keys and Richard Wendorf's Ford Explorer. The jury added that evidence was established indicating that Scott, Dana and Charity helped plan and execute
the slayings. King dismissed the juvenile charges the youths
were previously held under.

Although not unexpected, the indictments and the new
charges filed in adult court against the four teenagers were
a stunning and sobering development. The grand jury's action may have been especially disappointing for Scott and
the two girls. In Florida, the penalties for aiding or assisting
a crime are identical to those for committing the crime itself.
There is no legal distinction between committing the crime
or assisting in a crime, once a defendant has been convicted.

The lives of the Kentucky teenagers were in freefall, and
there was every indication that at the very least they would
remain behind bars throughout the next year while the criminal proceedings were making their slow way through the
courts. That was the best they could hope for. The worst
would be convictions and sentences ordering execution in
the electric chair. In his immediate post-indictment statements, King refused to say if he planned to seek the death
penalty. But speculation in the halls of the handsome Lake
County Hall of Justice, where the work of the courts was
carried out, swung heavily toward a later announcement that

the prosecutor would seek the electric chair at least for Rod and very possibly for both boys.

The panelists reported that they wanted more time and more information before making up their minds about Heather. The grand jurors had carefully weighed the evidence presented by King, but they weren't satisfied with the testimony of two witnesses whose accusations about Heather appeared to be the most damning. Lake County authorities announced that the grand jury would reconvene a few days after the beginning of the new year to determine if there was sufficient evidence to justify returning an indictment against Heather, or if she should be freed. King, who worked out of offices in Ocala and was head of the prosecution team, was predictably pleased with the indictments. "I think their decision was wholly appropriate given what we know," he told reporters.

While Heather remained in the Regional Juvenile Detention Center in Ocala held on scaled-down juvenile charges of second-degree murder and a single count of robbery, her former companions were cuffed and shackled at the wrists, ankles and bellies, then transported back to Lake County. Since they were to be put on trial as adults, they were locked in the same jail where Dana had been held since her transfer from Baton Rouge. Again, however, there were no reunions. According to standard practice, three of the Kentucky teenagers were assigned cells in a special juvenile section of the jail, and further isolated from each other in separate pods. Rod was the exception, and was assigned a separate cell in an even more restrictive area of the jail in order to isolate him and Scott from each other. The day after the indictments Scott turned seventeen and spent his first full day behind bars at the securely modern jail.

As part of their welcome to life at the county lockup, the new inmates were tested for syphilis. It was standard procedure for all newcomers, and samples of blood were taken from the three reputed members of the Vampire Clan. There was no slashing, licking or sucking involved in the collection process. The samples were collected according to the normal procedure used at the jail: with a hypodermic needle.

Every new inmate in the facility is medically screened, and as juveniles, even though they were charged as adults, Rod and his companions were also put on a temporary suicide watch. Rod, Scott and Charity were asked if they had ever tried to commit suicide in the past and quizzed about their medical backgrounds and family histories, along with other matters aimed at providing jailers and other professionals with a good idea of their physical and emotional health. A psychiatrist whose services were contracted for from a local mental health agency called Lifestreams visited the jail twice a week and was on call for emergencies.

The LCDC was unlike many other city and county jails and state and federal prisons where officials believe the easiest way to keep convicts quiet and avoid stirring up trouble is to provide them with top-notch recreational facilities and educational opportunities. There were no weight piles, inhouse college classrooms, word processors or organized group therapy sessions for inmates held at the jail in Tavares. Security has priority there, and the prevailing attitude among the corrections staff leans toward avoiding anything that will make prisoners overly comfortable.

Captain Christopher Drinan, a no-nonsense college-educated corrections professional who is tall, athletically built and looks like a young Burt Reynolds, proudly agrees that the LCDC is tougher than most prisons. The jail experience shouldn't be made into something that inmates look at as an opportunity to take a little time off, or as no big deal, he says. Drinan believes firmly in making jail a place inmates hate to be, and one way of doing that is by cutting out all unnecessary frills. "This is jail, not Yale," is one of the former Bostonian's favorite expressions.

At the LCDC, Rod and his former followers would have no coffee, no cigarettes or chewing tobacco, and no cable television. When the jail was first opened, inmates were provided with cable TV. "So all they did was watch this MTV garbage—that's my personal opinion," Drinan says. Sheriff

Knupp changed that by removing the cable and installing an antenna on the roof. By the time the Kentucky teenagers were booked in, they had a choice of the three basic channels and could watch game shows, soap operas and other traditional television fare. They were lucky. If Drinan had his way, the cable would be put back in and inmates at the LCDC would be restricted to two channels: one with religious programming and the other with education.

A select group of prisoners are assigned to jobs outside the jail. Outside crews may be called on to clean up after windstorms, cut weeds and perform other manual labor that benefits the community. A special crew, varying at times from four to six inmates, works under the direction of a corrections officer who is a resident farmer in the neighboring community of Astatula, and cultivates a ten-acre vegetable garden. The inmate farmers and other outside crews dress in black-and-white-striped uniforms and are closely guarded. They look like old Southern chain gangs.

The sheriff's farm operation raises tons of food each year, including all the vegetables served with prisoners' meals. During some peak harvest periods the inmate gardeners raise more vegetables than jailers can use or store, and the overproduction is distributed among Lake County schools, church groups and charitable and civic organizations. Even if any of the Kentucky teenagers had wished to join the work crews in order to get outside in the fresh air for a while, however, they wouldn't qualify. The work assignments are restricted to inmates who have already been sentenced and are serving short terms at the jail.

Rod and his friends were stuck inside, confined to their cells or to their individual cellblocks. Scott and the girls lounged in their cells, or wandered around the common areas with little to do but watch television and think about the mess they had made of their lives. The situation was even more restrictive for Rod. He spent almost all of every day and every night in his cell.

The vampire kindred were caught up in a situation that was as dark and dismal as the morbid thoughts of their

leader while he prowled the streets of Murray, allegedly mutilating helpless animals or plotting other dark deeds. The
winter solstice, the shortest day of the year, was only a few
days away, but time and the grim prospects seemed to be
dragging out interminably. The grand jury indictments put
the icing on the cake. There wouldn't be any happy Christmas surprises of no-indictment reports by the panel, or of
trimmed-down charges and decisions by kindly judges
suddenly allowing bail so they could go home to Kentucky,
South Dakota or Montana. They were caught up together in
the same bad dream.

The shock of the grand jury indictments returned against
the Kentucky teenagers also marked the beginning of a defense attorney's nightmare, as reporters from the print and
electronic media converged on the reputed vampire cultists
with requests for interviews. By that time, Assistant Public
Defender Bill Stone had moved out of the picture and a
colleague with the agency, Candace Hawthorne, had assumed the role as Rod's lead attorney. Among all the defense lawyers for the reputed Vampire Clan members,
Hawthorne had the heaviest immediate burden. Her client
was the focus of a local media frenzy, and he had never
been especially good at keeping his mouth shut.

The media rush was sparked in part by a series of scoops
by the *Orlando Sentinel* and its Lake County edition, the
Lake Sentinel. Reporter Frank Stanfield, who worked out of
the Lake County bureau, and his colleagues at the newspaper
were digging out one dramatic new development after another. The big city newspaper's local competitor, the
Leesburg-based *Daily Commercial*, was also staying on top
of the story. But it was a pair of exclusive back-to-back
telephone interviews with Rod from the Lake County Jail
that appeared in the *Lake Sentinel* that really shook up the
troops.

Stanfield wrote to Rod, identifying himself as a court reporter, and offered him an opportunity to give his version
of the events. Unfortunately, much of the information previously available originated from a single source—the po-

lice, he wrote in the neatly typewritten note. Rod was the only one of the imprisoned teenagers who agreed to an interview, although the others were also approached by reporters.

Using a telephone was one of the few privileges extended to inmates at the jail. Along with the lone television set, each cellblock at the LCDC is equipped with four wall-mounted pay telephones. Since inmates are not permitted to handle money, which could be used for gambling or other forbidden activities, the phones are operated on a collect-call basis. Rod and his fellow inmates were permitted to use the telephones during normal waking hours, and ten-minute limits were established for each call. If no one was waiting in line for the telephone at the conclusion of a call, the same inmate was permitted to dial again and continue the conversation.

The day after his indictment by the grand jury, Rod talked with *Sentinel* reporters and confided that the Wendorf murders were carried out by members of a rival vampire clan from Murray headed by Steven Murphy. Steven's group framed him and his friends for the crime, and four vampires were dispatched from Murray to commit the murders as part of a plot to get him out of the way, he claimed. According to Rod's account, he and his friends spent the Monday of the murders at the Lake Square Mall and generally roaming around.

Rod claimed that his adversary asked him to contact people in Florida who might make good vampires, and arranged the Wendorf murders because he figured the Kentuckians would get together with Heather. He indicated that bad blood existed between the clans because the rival vampire lord had attempted to get him to do things that were immoral, such as killing animals. Rod said that he had witnesses who knew about the hit team from the rival clan, and planned to talk to his lawyers about them.

He denied that he hurt animals and described himself as "very gentle natured." Rod said he was the kind of person who would stop at the side of a road to pet a stray puppy.

The evil vampire lord in Murray who really ordered the killings was getting revenge because Rod refused to knuckle under to him, he told the reporters. He knew that members of the rival clique were the killers, and they had taken advantage of his decision to drive his fiancee to Florida and show her around the Sunshine State, Rod declared. Initially he planned the trip as an adventure that only he and Charity would share. Then Scott, followed by Dana, decided they wanted to go along, he said. At the conclusion of the Florida trip, Scott had planned to take Heather back with him to Kentucky.

In other remarks, the chatterbox set up an alternate scenario that appeared designed to point the finger at Scott, whom he referred to as his "best friend," just in case the story about the evil maneuverings of a rival vampire lord in Murray didn't stand up. Rod said that he was never in the Wendorf house, and that he and his friends met Heather at the end of the road after she slipped out a window carrying a packed bag. The only reason they were on Greentree Lane was to pick up Heather, but moments after she joined up with them, Scott announced that he "had an idea." Then he told Dana and Charity to take Heather to her friend's house, and the girls drove away in the Skylark.

It was just after sundown and the boys were left standing alongside the road when Scott borrowed Rod's combat boots and walked off down Greentree Lane, Rod continued. Rod was exhausted and after sitting down to rest was just about to doze off when Scott showed up driving the Ford Explorer. Scott honked the horn and told his friend to climb inside. Rod said that Scott assured him the Wendorfs were unharmed. "I don't think he is capable of killing anyone any more than I am," he told the reporters.

Rod's self-serving remark about Scott's non-violent nature may have been true, but he had nevertheless done a neat job of casting suspicion on the Mayfield boy for committing the murders. He even thought to add the combat boots, with their distinctive worn soles, to the story as handy props.

Rod also asserted that he had multiple personalities, and

experienced brief blackouts that left him without any memory of his behavior during the episodes. A psychiatrist he had met with counted off at least ten separate personalities, the boy said. He identified one of the intruding personalities as "a knowledge freak" named Valius. Rod cited the shenanigans for the press in the booking area of the jail following the trip from Baton Rouge as an example of one of the blackout periods. He didn't remember anything about sticking his tongue against the glass partition or grimacing for the photographers, he said. Stress brought on the personality changes.

Turning to his obsession with vampirism, he said his interest was initially sparked by a minor mishap when he accidentally pricked his finger during a ninth-grade biology class at Eustis High School. He reacted automatically, pressing his lips to the cut and sucking the blood, and that led other students to begin calling him a vampire. There were times when he thought they were right: that he really was a vampire.

Rod also had an explanation for the blood-smeared bedsheet and paper towel that evidence technicians found in Richard Wendorf's Ford Explorer when it was searched in Baton Rouge. Rod said it was his own blood, shed after he accidentally slashed himself with a knife while he was cutting a tree limb. He cut to the bone, and that was why there was so much blood.

Rod added that he wanted to set the record straight about another matter, as well. Despite some news reports that he and Heather formerly dated each other, they were never boyfriend and girlfriend. Some of the reports surfaced after it was disclosed that investigators had found a packet of letters from him in Heather's bedroom, but he explained that they were written to another girl. Heather stored the letters in her room because the parents of the girl he wrote them to disapproved of him and she couldn't keep them at home.

Earlier statements by Rod's mother seemed to add some support to his mention of another vampire known as the Prince of the City, but she was mired in troubles of her own that had authorities taking an unusually close look at anything she had to say. There was no getting away from it, Rod's account of a hit squad sent to Eustis by rival vampires had an unmistakable barnyard odor about it. He hadn't breathed a word about the nefarious plot by his vampire enemies during his interrogation in Baton Rouge, or to prosecutors or representatives of any other law enforcement agency investigating his activities.

King nevertheless checked the story out, making a second trip to Murray and talking with Steven Murphy. Stories circulated around the college town that King also arranged to take hair, tissue or blood samples from the boy that could be used in DNA and other laboratory analyses, but the state's attorney declined to confirm or deny the reports to the local press. Reporters tracked Murphy down in Tennessee, where he was staying with friends for a while, and he pooh-poohed Rod's accusations, describing his former crony as "a delusional little kid." Told about Rod's claim of being gentle-natured, Murphy recounted the cat-killing story, and said the accused murderer had "no morality."

Most people closely linked to the investigation and court procedures wrote off Rod's talk about a rival vampire clan being responsible for the murders as a thinly constructed cock-and-bull story. He had a reputation for blaming other people for his misdeeds when he got into a jam. Sheriff Knupp, a thirty-five-year law-enforcement veteran who had seen it all, didn't give any credence to the yarn. "We've got the right people in jail," he said.

Rod's court-appointed lawyer was predictably horrified by the interview and described her client as a "disturbed child" whose naivete was taken advantage of by the media. He didn't realize the severity of the charges against him, or the effect his statement could have on his defense, she complained. Whatever Rod said to the press, confided to fellow inmates or wrote in letters to strangers, friends or family was fair game for the prosecution and could be used against him to further the investigation, and during his trial. He was playing a dangerous no-win game that was far more likely to hurt his cause than to help in any way.

The newspaper's scoop was impressive, nonetheless, and it set off a stampede by reporters in two states seeking similar exclusive interviews with the reputed Vampire Clan leader. Rod was deluged with telephone calls and letters sent to the jail by eager reporters from television and the print media. In accordance with LCDC regulations, letters mailed to the jail were delivered to him after they were inspected for news clippings or other contraband.

Like Stanfield's plea, most of the requests in the new flood of mail originated from news outlets in central Florida. Kathy Marsh mailed a handwritten note to Rod in care of the Lake County Jail at 551 West Main Street in Tavares identifying herself as a reporter with News Channel 2, WESH-TV in Orlando. She said she had read his statements in the *Sentinel* and asked to do "a phoner."

One of her competitors, Trevor Pettiford, a reporter for WFTV's "Eyewitness News" in Orlando, wrote that it was Channel 9's policy "to bring fairness and clarity to every story we do," and in their efforts to be fair were willing to talk to him by telephone if he wished. Identifying herself as the Lake County reporter for WCPX-6 in Orlando, Jackie Kennum mailed a typewritten letter asking permission to meet with him at the jail and to bring along a cameraman.

Rod also heard from a television journalist closer to his home. In a letter typed on letterhead carrying the slogan "The Spirit of Wave Country WAVE 3" and beginning "Dear Rod," news anchor Julie Nelson from Louisville wrote that she realized he was experiencing "a difficult time of your life, a time when you probably feel very alone and unsure." He was invited to telephone if there was something he wished to pass on to her, anything he wished to "convey back to your part of the world." In the note mailed to him at the jail in care of Captain Drinan, she offered him a chance to tell his side of the story and provided an 800 number.

Suddenly, television reporters and anchors who wanted to

do the right thing by Rod were coming out of the woodwork. They wheedled, cajoled, flattered and held out promises of helping him to set the record straight, but his lead attorney had talked with him herself and put her foot down. The day after his interview with the newspaper, Hawthorne firmly clamped down on any further talks with the press, corrections officers, police or prosecutors.

Hawthorne and her boss, Howard H. "Skip" Babb, Public Defender for the Fifth Judicial Circuit, filed a formal notice with the court demanding that she be present during any questioning of the youth about pending or potential criminal matters. Babb claimed that Rod had talked with the press without the knowledge or permission of his defense attorneys, and also complained that law enforcement officers had tried to interview him and place him in police line-ups. "Defendant demands that the Lake County Jail not allow any law-enforcement officers to interview him or place him in a line-up without his attorney being present," Hawthorne and her client wrote in the notice.

Hawthorne later cited the media's efforts to talk with her client, and attached copies of the letters, in a motion seeking a protective order restricting disclosure of further pre-trial discovery, including but not limited to the videotapes filmed in Baton Rouge during the interrogation of her client and his companions.

The lid had been effectively slammed on nosy reporters and anyone else who might stir up additional trouble for Rod, or his friends, but there was little the defense lawyers could do about another problem their clients were having a difficult time dealing with: The teenagers were bored. Holidays are an especially difficult time for prisoners, even for would-be vampires, and the young runaways from Kentucky were no exceptions. There were no shopping trips to the local mall, presents to wrap, mystery packages under Christmas trees to jiggle and wonder about. There was only the same old routine: nutritious but uninspiring meals slid through bean holes three times a day, the predictable clang of cell doors, the groans, cries or rantings of other inmates, and the occasional dull thud of footsteps as correctional officers made their rounds. Boredom and depression were near-constant companions.

On Christmas Eve, exactly one week after the indictments were returned by the grand jury, guards discovered a noose fashioned from sheets in Rod's cell. A message that appeared to be a suicide note was scrawled on a wall. Rod was moved to another unit where he could be observed more closely and was placed on a suicide watch. On Christmas and New Year's Day, he and his friends spent their second and third straight holidays, following their arrests on Thanksgiving night, behind bars, securely isolated from the outside world.

By early January, Rod was in trouble again. He was decorating the walls of his cell with graffiti. That was not only a violation of jail regulations, but the drawings—and/or writings—also provided more grist for the thick file of evidence and other information the state was collecting for his upcoming trial. Sheriff's investigators snapped photographs of the scrawls and turned them over to the prosecution team. Prosecutors and spokesmen for the jail refused to publicly disclose whether the graffiti was drawing, writing or both. The material was part of King's continuing investigation into the murder case, spokesmen said. Even when he was locked up, Rod was demonstrating that he was capable of coming up with one surprise after another.

Heather was waiting in the wings with her own surprise. At the recommendation of her attorney, she decided to testify before the grand jury. Speaking for his client, Hope said she hadn't had a fair opportunity to tell her story to the panel, and he believed her testimony would lead to her exoneration. He also complained to reporters that Heather had been mistreated in the press and by the sheriff's department. The defense attorney even took a swipe at Heather's older sister, Jennifer. His client wasn't angry at her big sister, Hope told the *Commercial*, but ". . . nearly everything Jennifer has said about Heather, Heather could say about Jennifer. She's just as much of a teenager with problems."

Hope accused the sheriff's department of controlling information about the case in order to make his client look bad and her sister look good. Detectives were "repressing the truth" about Heather, although they knew she played only a small part in the tragedy, he contended.

Suspects being investigated by grand juries are often asked by prosecutors to testify, but can't be compelled to appear. It's rare for someone to exercise the option of testifying before the men and women investigating the possibility that he or she may have been involved in felony crimes, and the surprise move was a calculated risk. When the former Eustis schoolgirl volunteered to appear before the grand jury, it meant she was waiving her Fifth Amendment protection against self-incrimination. Anything she said during her appearance could be used against her if she was indicted and put on trial as an adult. The state attorney's office added its authorization to the request.

It was a big advantage to give up, and none of Heather's co-defendants chose to testify before the grand jury before their indictments were returned the previous month. But ever since the fugitives were rounded up in Baton Rouge, Heather had insisted in statements to police and her own lawyers that she had planned only to run away from home, not to have her parents killed. Although Heather's lawyers were unwilling to volunteer anything about what she might or might not say when she appeared before the panel, speculation in Lake County leaned heavily toward the teenager sticking to that story.

Other factors that would affect the panel's deliberations, which the public knew nothing about at the time, were also at work. During the recess between returning the first set of indictments in December and resuming deliberations in January, Sondra Gibson and Amber Blood, the fifteen-year-old Orlando girl who had called CrimeLine, were given lie-detector tests. During the polygraph test, Amber recanted her story that Heather told her of plans to have her parents robbed and murdered. The volunteer informant didn't even know Heather. When Sondra was asked about her statement to the newspaper that Heather had talked for a long time about killing her parents, she experienced a change of heart. She said that she couldn't remember Heather saying anything like that.

On the Friday before the grand jury was scheduled to reconvene, Rod's lawyer walked through the Wendorf house accompanied by Assistant State Attorney James McCune. Hawthorne took a good, long look through Heather's bedroom and other areas of the house. The visit to 24135 Greentree Lane was a trip designed basically to get the lay of the land, but the defense lawyer's personal investigation of the case would eventually take her much farther afield. She had interviews to conduct and possible evidence to examine in Baton Rouge and in Calloway County.

On Sunday, January 26, James Wendorf visited with his granddaughter at the juvenile detention center in Ocala. Bright and early the next morning, Heather was driven to Tavares and exactly at 9 a.m., she began to tell her story to the men and women on the panel. Accompanied to the justice center by a pair of female guards, she was dressed in a neatly pressed light-colored suit with a high-necked blouse, a pair of handcuffs around her wrists in jarring contrast with the young-ladylike appearance she otherwise projected. The cuffs were removed before Heather was led before the panel. Although only the prosecutors are permitted to ask questions and defense attorneys are rarely even allowed into a grand jury room, Hope accompanied his young client inside.

The grand jury was intent on bringing the ordeal to a conclusion one way or another. Heather looked demure and contrite, and she was fidgety and frightened, but the jurors were also under enormous pressure. A terrible crime had been committed, and a young girl's future was at stake. The situation called for a calm, measured inquiry, cool deliberation and a carefully thought-out decision. It went unspoken, but it was also clearly understood that each of the jurors wanted to return home that night satisfied that he or she had done his or her level best to reach a fair and just conclusion while seeing that justice was done. Heather testified for nearly two hours, breaking down more than once during the grueling ordeal before she was finally led outside and driven back to Ocala. A few days earlier she had quietly observed her sixteenth birthday at the juvenile detention center. There was no present of a shiny, new candy-apple-red Saturn convertible like her sister's.

In Tavares, Amber was also called back into the grand jury chambers, where she admitted not telling the truth during her earlier statements. The next day, in a decision that came as a surprise to many Lake County residents who were closely following the case, the panel officially cleared Heather of active participation in the murder and robbery of her parents. In a formal statement, the panel declared:

We the Grand Jury of Lake County, having been presented the obligation to determine if Heather Wendorf should be charged with any crimes involving the deaths of her parents do hereby report as follows:

At the time of our original consideration of this issue on December 16, 1996, there was testimony presented from a civilian witness (whom we will not name)* that Heather Wendorf had discussed with that witness the fact that Heather Wendorf and Roderick Ferrell had planned not only Heather Wendorf's departure from home, but also stealing the Wendorfs' Ford Explorer and killing the Wendorfs.

In the course of our previous proceedings, we determined that the testimony of this witness was inconsistent with the statements of each and everyone [sic] of those persons indicted by this Grand Jury on December 16, 1996. In their statements to law enforcement, the four co-defendants, as well as Heather Wendorf, consistently stated that Heather Wendorf had no prior

*Amber Blood's name was later disclosed by court authorities as that of the CrimeLine tipster and grand jury witness.

knowledge that the murders, robbery or burglary would take place.

The panel further explained in the statement that testimony by the Orlando girl didn't jibe with statements from other witnesses, and she didn't know certain things she should have been aware of if her claims about Heather were true:

> Because of the concerns about this witness and at the State Attorney's suggestion, we adjourned our session in order to allow for this witness's story to be more fully evaluated and to allow for any other evidence to be brought forth. The other evidence principally concerned alleged statements of Heather Wendorf as overheard by Roderick Ferrell's mother.

The jurors pointed out that both stories, those of Amber and Sondra's statements in the newspaper account, were "re-evaluated" by sheriff's investigators and by the state attorney. After learning of Sondra's sudden memory loss while taking the polygraph test, the panel discounted her story because they considered her to be an unreliable witness. Amber's earlier testimony was also discounted because she recanted the story during her polygraph exam, and during her second appearance before the grand jury she confirmed that she had lied.

Curiously, neither in the grand jury statement nor in later remarks by investigators did anyone attempt to explain the motivation for the lies. According to the talk circulating through Lake County about the strange development in what was already an incredibly bizarre case, most people believed the girl was attracted by the notoriety of the Vampire Cult murders and was merely seeking attention. They let it go at that.

Continuing the formal statement, the panelists observed that the grand jury had an obligation to protect the innocent, as well as to "pursue those who may have violated the law.

In this regard," they wrote, "we must find that there is NO LONGER PROBABLE CAUSE to believe that Heather Wendorf was a knowing participant in the terrible acts that occurred at her home." Then the panel delivered a verbal spanking to the girl:

> While she certainly acted inappropriately in planning to leave home and arguable [sic] so in remaining with the others after learning what had been done, we acknowledge that these acts are not crimes. We also wish to unequivocally state that these actions were wrong. Heather Wendorf, her sister and the families of both Richard Wendorf and Naoma Ruth Queen will live the rest of their lives with the consequences of Heather's choices of associates and activities. Nothing that anyone can say or do will change the loss they have suffered; we wish them God's mercy and grace in the recovery that must follow.

Her defense lawyer telephoned Ocala to give her the good news while the grand jury was still working on the formal statement. "I don't know if she dropped the phone or what," Hope later said of the teenager's reaction. "She was near hysterical, crying."

It was late Tuesday afternoon, January 28, and Heather had been under an official cloud of mistrust for two months, suspected of willingly participating in the brutal murder of her parents. During most of that time she was locked up. Newspapers wrote about her, pictures of her appeared on television, and she was paraded before the world shackled in handcuffs and chains. In the public eye, she was firmly linked with one of the worst crimes imaginable—parricide. That part of the former Eustis High School girl's ordeal was at last officially over.

The state attorney said that he agreed with the grand jury decision. As he had done after the indictments of Heather's former companions, King dismissed the juvenile charges of second-degree murder and robbery on which she was previously held.

Heather packed up her clothes and a small trove of other personal possessions, then rode away from the detention center for the last time. Law enforcement authorities and family members quickly closed a protective shield around the girl, and refused to disclose her exact whereabouts. Relatives said only that she was with family members. They declined to specify whether or not she and Jennifer were reunited at their uncle's home or if Heather was with other relatives.

Her lawyer told reporters that Heather needed time to "decompress," and added the painfully obvious observation that she had been orphaned by the slaying of her parents. "For sixty days," he said, "the world thought she was a murderess."

Replying to reporters' questions asking if Heather was a hostage during the dash to Louisiana, Hope said that that was too strong a word. Heather was never by herself, there were knives and other weapons present and although she wasn't threatened "there was a pervasive sense of fear," he said. She had feared for her safety after hearing about the murders of her parents.

Paula Queen, one of Heather's half-sisters, told reporters that the family had known Heather was innocent. The family never had any doubts, she said.

"She has no more handcuffs, no more chains," Heather's ecstatic grandfather, James Wendorf, told the *Sentinel*. "She's a free girl." The elder Wendorf also shared his joy with the *Commercial*. "I never lost faith in that little girl," he declared. "I'm very, very pleased and blessed." With Heather free at last, it was time for the family to concentrate on healing the rift between her and her sister, Jennifer, he said. "There were things said that shouldn't have been said."

Heather's exoneration raised the hopes of Harrell Gibson, another grandfather, that it might be an indication of good news in the future for Rod and the other Kentucky teenagers.

He suggested that the grand jury decision may have meant the state didn't have a rock-solid case against any of the youths. "I figure what's good for her is good for the rest of them," he told the *Sentinel*.

Not everyone shared in the jubilation, sense of relief or high hopes that the other teenagers would eventually share Heather's good fortune. David Keesee reacted with skepticism when he was asked about the panel's decision to indict his daughter, then exonerate the Florida girl. "That figures. That's American justice," he responded. "That's all a lie."

One of Heather's fellow travelers in the grand adventure that led them to New Orleans and Baton Rouge, then back to detention centers and courtrooms in Lake County, also indicated that she didn't share in the rejoicing over the sixteen-year-old girl's exoneration. Dana didn't think it was fair that she was still behind bars facing the very real possibility of spending much of the rest of her life locked up, while Heather was set free and treated by a large segment of the local public as a victim. No one believed that Dana, or Charity, had bludgeoned the Wendorfs to death, or were even present when they were killed, any more than they believed that Heather was in the house at the time. But while Heather would be returning to a loving, nurturing family and presumably would soon be registering at a new school, Dana and Charity were still locked up in a maximum-security county jail with hard-core prostitutes, drug dealers, stick-up artists, baby rapers and vicious killers.

Lou Tally, a Mount Dora lawyer, had been appointed as Heather's legal guardian, and her defense attorney hired a special agent to deal with offers from authors, television producers and movie studios for her story. Greg Galloway, an Orlando-based entertainment lawyer who once represented a Lake County boy in a successful court battle for the right to divorce his biological parents in order to live with his adoptive family, joined Heather's legal team. It was Galloway's job to help her handle the media, and to see to it that she made the best possible deals if she decided to peddle her story for books or films. Tally told reporters that she might wish to make money from the affair at some time in the future.

Life prospects were brightening considerably for the teenage orphan from Eustis, but Dana's immediate future—and that of her vampire-obsessed friends from Kentucky—was as darkly foreboding as a visit from Dracula's fictional nemesis, Dr. Abraham Van Helsing, lugging a sackful of wooden stakes.

Heather's exoneration by the grand jury also led to widespread speculation that the state attorney may have offered a deal: Heather would be cleared of any involvement in planning the slayings, and freed. In return she would be expected to testify against her former companions during their trials. Heather either knew things about events surrounding the murder that were unavailable from alternate sources, or possessed information that could corroborate the statements and testimony of other witnesses and players in the drama. It was an intriguing theory, but one that Hope quickly squelched. He and his client didn't ask for any deals, and the state attorney didn't offer any, the Tavares lawyer said. That was the kind of thing King had been saying about the defendants all along.

Heather's decision to testify hadn't been a gamble only on her own future, but could potentially affect the fate of her former fellow runaways. The testimony she provided to the grand jury could be used against Rod and the other Kentucky youths. One of the first moves Candace Hawthorne had made after the indictments against her client were returned in December was to file a motion asking for transcripts of the closed-door grand jury proceedings. Since defense attorneys were not allowed inside the grand jury room, how could anyone know if the process was conducted in a legal manner, she asked, or if some of the witnesses could be impeached? "The accused's right to confrontation provided by the . . . Constitution . . . outweighs the public interest in maintaining the secrecy of the testimony of a co-defendant," Hawthorne contended in the motion. In other remarks, Hawthorne said that she had information indicating that Heather had played a "significant role" in the slaying of her parents.

The day after the grand jury decision, Scott's lawyer disclosed that he also planned to ask for copies of the transcripts of the girl's testimony. ". . . no one in the world" knows more than Heather about the reasons Rod and his entourage drove from their homes in Kentucky to Eustis, Michael Graves said in defense of the unusual request.

Based on historical precedent of grand jury proceedings, the lawyers were facing an uphill battle to pry loose the information. Disclosure of grand jury testimony is not a matter that judges take lightly, and disclosure requests are rejected far more often than they are granted. While the defense lawyers were embarking on a long, complicated process, the trial judge who had originally been expected to preside in the case passed the gavel to one of his colleagues. Judge Don F. Briggs stepped out of the case and was replaced by Judge Lockett, in order to comply with a spanking-new Florida Supreme Court requirement for judges presiding over capital murder cases. According to the new ruling, jurists in cases which could involve the death penalty were required to have attended a three-day course titled "Handling Capital Cases" during the previous five-year period. Judges were also required to have been on the bench for at least six months, according to the new stipulation.

Briggs was an experienced jurist who was the administrative judge for the Lake County Circuit Court. He had been on the bench for seven years and attended various refresher courses and other classes and lectures provided by the Florida College of Advanced Judicial Studies (FCAJS) at twice-yearly judicial conferences in Orlando. But he hadn't taken the capital cases course, which was also offered by the FCAJS, and was made available on a limited basis to only thirty jurists at a time, who were selected by lottery.

Ironically, at the time the complication was disclosed, the state attorney hadn't even decided whether he would ask for the death penalty against any of the defendants. If it turned out that the death penalty wasn't a factor in the case, there would be no question about Briggs' qualification to preside. At the moment, however, the prospect of the death penalty becoming a factor in the trial was an unknown, so Briggs chose the safest option available to him and stepped aside.

Judge Lockett, who cultivated a salt-and-pepper beard and mustache, looked judicial—and he had experience. There was no question the solidly built jurist was up to the job and had the grit to deal with the grueling demands of presiding over a capital murder trial—or two, three or four at the same time. He was already occupied as the trial judge in the case of Terry Lee Woods, a twenty-four-year-old Leesburg resident charged with first-degree murder in the shooting of an older man in a dispute over purchase of a vintage car. The victim's wife was also shot, but survived.*

Lockett was as familiar as any judge in Lake County with Florida's capital murder statutes, and the intricate ins and outs of court procedures that were so important when the life of a defendant was at stake. He had a reputation among local trial lawyers as a fair, professional jurist with a keen knowledge of the law, whose rulings and decisions were well researched and thought out.

The judge didn't believe in molly coddling dangerous criminals, and he was known for imposing long sentences when the occasion called for it. Lockett's stern action on the bench made him unpopular with many criminals, and a few months before he was named to the Wendorf murder case, a woman was sentenced to a fifty-year prison term for trying to hire a hit man to kill him. She was scheduled to appear before him on a cocaine-trafficking charge, and believed that if she could get Lockett out of the way she would have a better chance of bribing whoever was picked to replace him in the case.

Another wrongdoer who ran afoul of the judge's no-nonsense courtroom dealings was sentenced in early January. The man broke into his ex-girlfriend's apartment in

*Woods was convicted in March 1997 of first-degree murder in the slaying of sixty-five-year-old Clarence Langford, and of the attempted first-degree murder of Langford's sixty-three-year-old wife, Pamela. Woods' jury recommended the death sentence, and on April 24 Judge Lockett ordered his execution.

Leesburg while she was inside, and Lockett gave him thirty years. The stunned defendant said that he didn't think the incident was any more serious than a misdemeanor, but the judge pointed out that he had a long criminal history and the woman was "scared to death" of him.

Lockett was not a judge whom attorneys defending a serious felony case were about to take lightly, and he ran his courtroom like it was a ship and he was the captain. When court was in session, he was firmly in charge.

The newly designated Vampire Clan trial judge worked in one of a row of eight courtrooms that stretch along the far wall directly across from the lobby and security areas on the ground floor of the judicial building. The jury assembly room is at the far end of the hallway, and Courtroom Number One is next to it on the right side. Lockett presided in Courtroom Number Four. Officers of the court, other court employees and visitors enter the building through an entrance off the parking lot and, after walking through a spacious lobby, move through the security-check area. The central area between the security check and the courtrooms has a bit of the appearance of a courtyard where office workers snack on brown-bag lunches and gossip about their friends. A row of padded straight chairs runs down the center between the courtrooms and cubicle offices marked for "TRAFFIC COURT," "DEPOSITIONS" and other supporting staff and services. Skylights and floor-to-ceiling windows along the front of the long room take advantage of the Florida sunshine, and contribute to the feeling of spaciousness and freedom. Inside the snug little paneled courtrooms, however, the sense of airiness and light is shut out and the business carried out there often leads to a loss of freedom for the hapless men and women seated beside their lawyers at the defense tables. The courtrooms, like other areas of the judicial center, are clean, modern and utilitarian.

The judicial building, along with the detention center directly across West Main Street, are part of a modern criminal justice complex that comprises a downtown showpiece. The four-story building with a tower at the entrance, which many people insist on referring to as the courthouse, is a handsome, utilitarian building that was opened in 1992; the real courthouse is a five-story structure, built in 1923, that still stands a few blocks down Main Street where it was refurbished as a museum.

A sculpture of a police officer holding the hand of a small child stands just to the left of the entrance and is identified as a "Lake County Law Enforcement Memorial." Dedicated on May 7, 1994, the battleship-gray memorial is engraved with the names of five law enforcement officers, including two sheriff's deputies, who died in the line of duty. The first to die was James Lee Hux in 1924, and the last was Deputy William J. Marie in 1994. Deputy Jean Daugharty, who was killed in 1993, is the only female.

Although Rod and his friends would be led into the judicial building dozens of times before their trials, they wouldn't even get close to the front entrance. After inmates are led in groups through the tunnel from the jail, they are locked up again in a holding area just off the tunnel entrance, which has a capacity of 120 inmates and enough individual cells so that adult males, women and juveniles can be held separately until they are called into courtrooms.

Graves and Hawthorne continued oral and written arguments with the new judge in the case, outlining some of the reasons they believed they should be given access to Heather's grand jury testimony. Graves contended significant discrepancies existed in some of the girl's statements about her whereabouts on the night of the murders. The defense attorneys indicated there were areas of conflict between her account and the story told to investigators by Jeanine LeClaire. Heather's testimony was especially important, they said, because the reason that Ferrell and his friends came to Florida was to pick up Heather and run away to New Orleans.

King opposed release of the transcripts, pointing out that grand jury witnesses feel free to testify about some matters because they believe their statements will be protected from outsiders. He also observed that he was already ethically bound to disclose any discrepancies in Heather's statements to defense attorneys. Judge Lockett instructed the attorneys to lay out their case in writing, enumerating exactly why he should comply with the motions.

In May, Lockett took the sixty-nine-page transcript to his home for review. He planned to pay special attention to the comparing of Heather's statements to the grand jury with those she made to police following the arrests in Baton Rouge. He also announced before looking over the material that if he decided to release the testimony to the defense lawyers he would also make it available to the public. "If I don't give it to them [the public], then nobody gets to see it," he said.

A month later, Hawthorne was back in the Lake County Clerk of Court's office filing another motion. In the new document, she argued that King's refusal to permit witnesses to answer defense questions about their testimony before the grand jury was a violation of their First Amendment right to free speech. She asked Lockett to schedule a hearing to determine if grand jury witnesses wanted to testify about their statements before the panel.

So it went, back and forth, the jockeying for position and advantages that is part of the sometimes frustrating but often crucial pre-trial proceedings that can take on all the outward appearances of tilting at windmills. Filing and arguing of motions, taking of depositions, and pre-trial conferences seldom outwardly reflect the high drama of a major murder trial, but the outcome of some of the procedures can often make the difference between a conviction or acquittal, and life or death.

9. BLOOD FEUD

Heather's defection, and her decision to point the finger of guilt for the murder of her parents squarely at Rod, was merely the most public example of the breakup of the Vampire Clan. The old cohesiveness and misplaced loyalties that previously helped hold the band together were shattered by infighting, jealousy and self-preservation. They were locked in a struggle for survival.

One at a time, most of the frightened teenagers began turning on their former companions in desperate efforts to escape blame for the killing of the Wendorfs and to salvage whatever they could from their own lives.

Rod and Scott blamed each other for committing the murders.

Rod's story about waiting at the end of the road after Scott sent the girls away, borrowed the combat boots and walked off toward the Wendorf house, was a clear attempt to divert suspicion from himself by pointing the finger at his second-in-command. When he turned on Scott, Rod was continuing a longtime pattern of similar behavior. Fights with Murphy and Goodman, threats to snitch on his mother for reputedly attempting to seduce a juvenile, the dust-up with April Doeden, the bizarre story painting his grandfather as a murderous blood cultist, and the attempt to lay the blame for the murders on a rival vampire lord in Murray all fit in perfectly. Scott was simply the latest of Rod's family members, former acolytes and hangers-on pinpointed as a fall-guy, and the scrawny vampire lord behaved as if he planned to stick to his story until the last dog died.

Scott had no illusions about the seriousness of the trouble he was in, and cooperated with police and other authorities from the time of the arrests in Baton Rouge, through the period of the indictments and waivers of the Kentucky members of the Vampire Clan, into adult court. He also had his own story to tell, and admitted that he was inside the Wendorf house, but claimed that he tried to prevent Rod from committing the murders. As bleak as the prospect of spending the rest of his life in prison was, it beat the possibility of being strapped into "Old Sparky," and he was hopeful that his cooperation would help him avoid the death penalty.

The boys were locked in separate cellblocks, and another juvenile who was a cellmate of Scott's for a while claimed the Mayfield boy put the blame for the murders squarely on Rod. Seventeen-year-old Ahmad Brown told the *Sentinel* that Scott told him Rod walked into the house through the front door and beat both the Wendorfs to death. According to the story, Richard Wendorf confronted Rod and they began arguing. Then Rod started beating the man with a crowbar. Alarmed at the sudden violence, Scott grabbed Rod's arm and shouted, "Are you crazy? Stop! Stop!" Rod responded by turning and giving Scott a look that was so frightening, he was cowed into silence. Scott said Heather's mother heard the racket and as she hurried into the family room, Rod turned his attack on her. After the murders the boys took the Ford Explorer and drove away to meet the girls.

It's doubtful that Scott, Rod or any of their fellow runaways had heard of Akira Kurosawa, but the conflicting stories being told about events leading up to the murders and how they were carried out were giving the case a flavor mindful of the Japanese film director's movie classic, *Rashomon*. Characters in the Oscar-winning 1950 film, including one who is called back from the dead, tell the story of a rape and murder—and each of the narrators gives a version that puts the major blame on others, while casting him- or herself in the best light.

During Scott's first few days at the jail he was treated like a celebrity by some of his fellow inmates. When prisoners were allowed in the dayroom, some of the imprisoned juveniles gathered at the door of his cell to listen to his stories. He basked in the attention and began boasting about being a master of black magic and Voodoo.

It was entertaining for a while, but eventually the fanciful yarns about being able to read people's minds and manipulate supernatural forces started to get old. Curiosity about the reputed blood-sucking cult killer turned to contempt, Brown said. One youth got into a shoving match with Scott after taking offense at his yarns, and others began waiting until he fell asleep on his bunk, then drenching him with cold water tossed through the bars of his cell door. It could have been worse. In most adult prisons the liquid of choice for dousing unpopular inmates is urine, or in worst-case scenarios, gasoline followed by a lighted match.

Scott responded to his ostracism by spending much of his time alone in his cell, crouching on his haunches atop a small table with his hands clasped in front of him, peering silently at the walls like a gargoyle. Sometimes he held the same position for hours, neither talking nor showing other signs of recognizing people around him. At other times he clamped down on the metal bars of his cell door with his teeth. Brown described him as gnawing on the bars like a dog with a bone. Scott told Brown he didn't believe he was a vampire, but Rod thought he was the real thing.

Scott also confided to some of his fellow inmates that he had multiple personalities, although he didn't claim as many as Rod. Scott claimed only three, but they were all distinctly different. The talk about multiple personalities from the two boys wasn't without precedent. Multiple personalities is a staple of jailhouse chatter, especially by inmates who may be trying to lay the groundwork for insanity pleas.

Charity wasn't experiencing the same degree of deeply disturbing problems handling imprisonment as Rod and Scott were, but she was weepy, frightened, and desperately wanted to go home. There was heavy speculation in the local legal community and among courtroom insiders that she and Dana might be helped to achieve that distant goal by working out plea bargain deals for light sentences in return for agreeing to testify against Rod or against both him and Scott.

One of the strongest possible ties between the couple was dissolved when tests disclosed that Charity wasn't pregnant with Rod's child, as the teenage sweethearts had previously believed. Three different pregnancy tests were conducted, and they were all negative.

Another sign that she might be getting ready to move away from the old relationship with her boyfriend occurred when she told police that she never "crossed over" by allowing him to suck her blood. It was a statement that posed serious questions, considering the slash marks on her arms, and had skeptics wondering if she was merely up to a bit of dissembling. Charity claimed that she cut herself sometimes when she became angry. But her mother was one of the skeptics, and blamed Rod for the razor slashes. Charity was too much of "a wimp," Mrs. Remington believed. The girl didn't seem to be the type who would mutilate herself because of some minor tantrum.

The South Dakota woman worried when she helped police trap the runaways that Charity would hold that action against her, but after the arrests the mother and daughter actually strengthened their emotional ties. They frequently talked by telephone, and other family members were also strongly supportive of the teenager.

Charity impressed the jail chaplain with her intelligence, and spent some of the long, solitary hours at the jail on schoolwork. Chaplain Bob Whitworth considered her to be "light years" ahead of other inmates studying for General Equivalency Diplomas. A few months after she was locked up, she was hoping to take the GED test, but it looked like she might have a long wait ahead of her. Adult educational authorities were not expected to send a proctor to the LCDC unless at least twelve inmates were ready to take the test, and Charity's devotion to her studies wasn't typical of her jailhouse peers.

Lighter reading was also available for the Murray girl and her fellow inmates, if they wished to take advantage of a library service staffed at the jail by local volunteers. The volunteers wheel a cartload of books through the cellblocks and loan them to inmates on a one-at-a-time basis. When an inmate finishes one book and returns it, she or he is permitted to borrow another.

Dana was outwardly stolid, but was having trouble dealing with long-term incarceration. She hated the constant regimentation, the inactivity and the uncertainty over her future. From hearing to hearing, Dana's expression never changed. Whether she was shuffling awkwardly into the courtroom or sitting quietly by her attorney, her face was vacant, unemotional and as pallid, round and unreadable as a muskmelon.

Her attorney hadn't ruled out the chances of a plea bargain of some sort, although none had yet been offered, and while the pre-trial proceedings dragged on, Plecas was seriously considering the possibility that her client would become a prosecution witness in proceedings against one or more of her former companions. Brad King continued to state that he wasn't making any offers for plea bargaining, but Plecas said that she had discussed what was vaguely described by the press as "an unspecified comfort zone" for her client.

Maneuvering by the attorneys may not have been responsible for initially turning the defendants against each other, but the legal feints and strategems going on up front and behind the scenes kept the psychic wounds that the teenagers were inflicting on each other open and raw. Each of the lawyers owed total loyalty to his or her own client. When four defendants are accused in the same felony crime, there is seldom any evidence at their trials of D'Artagnan's famous proclamation of "All for one, one for all." The sentiment of the fictional fourth musketeer in Alexandre

Dumas' epic novel, *The Three Musketeers*, is highly laudable, but it is not the stuff of courtrooms. When co-defendants in a serious felony crime are facing the grim possibility of the death penalty or long years behind bars, it's more likely to be a case of every man—and woman—for him- or herself. And devil take the hindmost.

All of the defendants were facing critically serious charges, but Graves, whose client faced the possibility of being executed if King sought the death penalty, was prepared to pull out all the stops. The Tavares attorney figured he needed help from another lawyer and a private investigator to help sort through the courtroom intricacies and demands on time and other resources that were tied to the crushing workload, and he asked the judge to approve beefing up his defense team.

Plecas was undergoing her own problems juggling the responsibilities of representing Dana with the demands of her personal law practice. She was deeply involved as a co-counsel with former O.J. Simpson attorney F. Lee Bailey in a complicated federal securities fraud case in Orlando, and a few weeks earlier had angered Judge Lockett when she failed to show up for a hearing.

Each of the defendants at the hearing, except for Dana, was flanked by his or her defense lawyer. The telltale pallor of longtime incarceration showed plainly on their faces and they looked as pasty-white as real vampires, if there were such things. There was no juvenile posturing or displays of false courage by Rod or any of his followers. They sat quietly at the defense table, dressed in the same blood-orange uniforms they had worn for months. Graves extended apologies to the court on his colleague's behalf, explaining that she was tied up in an important federal proceeding and couldn't fit the hearing into her schedule. The judge was unsympathetic.

"No attorney should fail to attend a hearing without providing substitute counsel in the future," the judge declared as he glared out over the little assembly. "There is no case in any court that is any more important than a capital case.

There is no excuse for failure to be present in this courtroom today." Then he ordered a special hearing for Dana, and announced that Plecas would be responsible for the costs. Because of the absence of Dana's lawyer, all the motions that involved her would have to be repeated at the additional hearing.

Then Lockett turned to the primary reason for the proceeding, a motion by the state seeking court approval to permit the gathering of blood, hair, saliva and handwriting samples from the defendants. After King withdrew a portion of the request asking for specimens of pubic hair, because there was no probable cause to justify gathering those particular samples, the judge granted the motion for the defendants who were represented by counsel at the hearing. The decision about similar samples sought from Dana, again minus the pubic hair, was postponed until she appeared with her attorney for the rescheduled hearing.

Collection of pubic hair can be particularly mortifying. In most jurisdictions donors are required to drop their pants and sit on a specially prepared sheet of paper, then run a fine-tooth comb from a special evidence package through the pubic area in a downward motion to pick up loose hairs and other fine debris. Some collectors insist that they do the combing, and others permit the donor to do it. Additional live hair samples are plucked out of the pubic area in order to obtain the roots, which can be important to laboratory technicians and other experts charged with examining and testing the specimens. Pubic hair samples can be very important in cases involving sexual assault or other sexual activity, but that wasn't a factor in the investigation or trial of the Vampire Clan. Eliminating the request for pubic hair spared the teenagers needless embarrassment.

The state attorney explained that he needed the other samples to compare with physical evidence found at the crime scene and inside the Wendorfs' Ford Explorer, which the runaways drove to Louisiana. "This is a routine request for elimination purposes," he said. Defense attorneys requested that they be allowed to be present when the specimens were taken, and the judge concurred.

In his order, which was later extended to Dana, Judge Lockett directed each of the defendants to provide the county sheriff with no more than thirty cubic centimeters of blood, no more than fifteen head hairs with roots, and no more than three samples of saliva with the collection to be carried out by a licensed medical doctor or a registered nurse. He further ordered each of the defendants to provide a handwriting sample while supervised by a qualified law enforcement officer using standardized forms designed for that purpose.

The blood drawn from the defendants would be compared with samples collected at the murder scene and with the swabs taken from the interior of the Explorer following the arrests in Baton Rouge. The prosecutors also stated that laboratory technicians would be asked to compare saliva residue believed to exist on cigarette butts collected from the Wendorf home with the samples collected from the defendants.

King continued to be coy about the possibility of seeking the death sentence, and another hearing was scheduled to consider the matter. Time was rapidly closing in and putting pressure on the prosecutor for making a death penalty decision. If he failed to make the decision by February 27, which was only a week away, and more than three weeks before the date of the new hearing just scheduled by the judge, he could still go for the death penalty at a later date, but the opportunity to have certain psychological tests conducted on the defendants would be lost.

Judge Lockett also scheduled discussion and arguments during the same hearing to consider putting all or some of the defendants on trial simultaneously, the possibility of moving the trials out of Lake County and potential dates to begin the proceedings. In other matters taken up during the lengthy mid-week proceeding, defense lawyers asked that Heather's court-appointed guardian attend the next scheduled hearing so that he could state his position about the efforts to win disclosure of her grand jury testimony, and about the possibility of entering property seized from the girl and her deceased parents into evidence.

The hearing was filled with minutiae, tying up loose ends and opening new areas of inquiry, but it was a proceeding that was important to the future of the case. All the pre-trial hearings were, and the pique exhibited by the jurist at the absence of one of the defense attorneys was not surprising. Ironically, after Plecas spent six weeks immersed in the federal case in Orlando, the jury failed to reach a decision and the judge declared a mistrial. A new trial was rescheduled and that extended the time crunch for Dana's lawyer. She reported that the conflicting commitments might mean she wouldn't be able to continue working on the Kentucky woman's behalf. If she was unable to get herself excused from the case in Orlando, she said, she might have to turn Dana's defense over to another attorney. Scheduling and co-ordinating the available time of the lawyers involved in the case had been a problem since the beginning of the proceedings; the conflicts and other pressures weren't easing up a bit, and promised to increase the closer the participants came to the trial date.

And so they did when, a few days after the hearing missed by Plecas, King filed a notice in the office of the Clerk of Court affirming that he would seek the death penalty against both of the boys. The notice was filed just in time to preserve the state's right to take advantage of psychiatric examinations. The state attorney indicated that he still hadn't made his mind up about Dana and Charity.

Attorneys for the boys were disappointed by the decision, but they weren't surprised. Graves said he believed prosecutors were asking the death penalty for Scott because they believed he was in the house on Greentree Lane when the Wendorfs were killed. The lawyer indicated, however, that he didn't think the case against his client justified seeking the boy's execution. Graves and Hawthorne, along with the prosecutors, were now faced with preparing for a two-part trial for the boys.

In Florida, death penalty cases are tried first in proceedings to determine guilt or innocence. Then a second minitrial is immediately conducted to determine the jury's penalty recommendation. Judges are not firmly bound by the recommendations, but rarely go against the jury when passing sentence.

Along with homicide investigators, King believed that the boys were alone when they walked into the Wendorf house and Rod bludgeoned the couple to death. When Rod and Scott at last walked into a courtroom for the beginning of their first-degree murder trials, their lives would officially be on the line. Despite constant roadblocks in the higher courts and a long-running controversy over the propriety of carrying out executions in a manner that might cause momentary pain for the condemned, Florida is a leading death penalty state. Since a U. S. Supreme Court ruling in 1976 known in legal circles as *Gregg* v. *Georgia* allowed states to resume carrying out the death penalty, the Sunshine State trails only behind Texas and Virginia in the number of executions. A drifter and killer named John Spenkelink became the first man executed in Florida during ''Old Sparky's'' modern era when he was strapped into the chair on May 25, 1979. Since that time thirty-eight other killers had ended their lives in the old three-legged solid oak chair.

By the time the decision was made to seek the ultimate penalty for Rod and Scott, about 380 people, give or take a few depending on the exact date, were on death row at the Florida State Prison and Union Correctional Institution near the town of Starke—and at the Broward Correctional Institution (BCI), where condemned women are held. The state has the third largest number of condemned killers in the country, after California and Texas. One of the latest death row arrivals at the Florida prison was Glen Edward Rogers, an accused serial killer and low-rent Casanova with strong Kentucky ties. A vicious alcoholic and former carnival roustabout, Rogers was convicted of murdering a woman he met in a bar that was a popular hangout for carnies in the Hillsborough County town of Gibsonton near Tampa. He was also named as a suspect in the slayings of women in three other states before he was captured in a wild police chase and shootout along steep, winding mountain roads near Richmond, Kentucky.

Unless legislators and corrections authorities are successful in efforts to cut down on delays, and grease the wheels of the process, Rogers and his death row neighbors—along with potential newcomers like Rod and Scott—can expect to spend about ten years between sentencing and execution. That's the average time spent on death row in Florida by condemned prisoners who are finally executed. About a half-dozen men have spent more than twenty years waiting for their sentences to be carried out.

Legal roadblocks by attorneys and other death penalty opponents challenging the constitutionality of laws, filing last-minute appeals citing surprising new evidence or attacking the death penalty as arbitrary, racially biased or unfair in some other manner, have made the process agonizingly slow and devastatingly expensive. The state spent about $6 million before notorious serial killer Ted "The Troller" Bundy, who admitted to the sex-murders of more than thirty young women, was finally put to death for slaughtering a twelve-year-old Florida girl he kidnapped from her middle-school campus. But the average cost of executing a killer in Florida is closer to $2 million, according to an analysis by the Associated Press.

Fees for lawyers account for the lion's share of the expense to taxpayers, but other costs of the original trials and appeals, including the paychecks of lower and higher court judges, also contribute to the costs. Add to that the cost of extra prison guards, additional security for death row inmates, meals, clothing and medical care, and the overall expenses mushroom. The only true bargains are the few cents to pay for electricity when the switch is finally thrown, and for the executioner's $150 fee.

The staggering costs of carrying out the will of the people aren't driven up by accident. Despite polls and other national samplings that repeatedly show an overwhelming percentage of Americans support the death penalty, running up the expenses is a deliberate act. Some attorneys, especially those who devote their careers to drawing out appeals of death row inmates, do everything they can to make the process as lengthy and costly as possible in order to saddle the public with a burden that is so frustrating and crushing that taxpayers and legislators will simply give up. Lawyers for one death row inmate in Florida demanded records of all the homicide and sex prosecutions that the state attorney handling the case had been involved in for two years. In another case, a request was made for every document relating to two years of court budgets from the county where the proceeding originated.

No matter how seemingly impractical or frivolous the demands are, each one must be dealt with in meticulous detail in order to avoid errors or omissions that might possibly lead to successful challenges and reversals in higher courts. And as soon as legislators or the courts close one loophole, advocates for the condemned killers open another.

Ironically, the very people who deliberately drive up the costs because they hate the idea of executing serial killers, mad bombers and mutilation murderers are the first to cite the incredible expense as an excuse for doing away with the death penalty. Death penalty proponents who believe that some crimes are so vicious and grotesque that no punishment short of execution is adequate respond that no price tag can or should be put on justice. Harsh crimes deserve harsh punishment, regardless of the cost.

About the time the vampire cult murders began making news in Florida, anti–death penalty activists came up with a new device to slow down the justice process. Two flawed executions that occurred a few years apart provided the opportunity to attack the death penalty with claims that Florida's electric chair was barbaric and violated U. S. Constitutional restrictions against cruel and unusual punishment. Salt-water-soaked sponges attached to the heads of cop-killer Jesse Tafaro and Cuban refugee Pedro Medina, who murdered an elementary school teacher from Orlando by plunging a knife into her chest ten times, were scorched during their executions, leading to the outcry.

During a hearing in Tallahassee examining the constitutionality of the electric chair, a biomedical engineer testified that electrocution was instant and painless, but the expert opinion failed to quell the controversy. Lawyers seeking to retire "Old Sparky" permanently also argued that the declining use of the electric chair across the country was another factor that illustrated it was an unnecessarily cruel means of execution. Only nine other states still use the so-called "hot seat," and some of those offer a choice of electrocution or lethal injection to the condemned. Since lethal injection was introduced for executions in 1977, the method has been adopted by thirty-two states, the military and the United States government. Most observers, especially anti–death penalty forces, adopted the attitude that no one on this side of the veil really knew for sure if electrocution is painless. All the real experts were dead, their brains fried and their respiratory muscles paralyzed by 2,300 volts of deadly alternating current.

Rod and his clutch of vampire colleagues were still cooling their heels at the detention center, awaiting their trials, when the statewide debate was temporarily settled in favor of "Old Sparky." In a razor-thin four-to-three ruling, the Florida Supreme Court upheld the constitutionality of using electrocution as a means of carrying out the death penalty. The ruling effectively ended stays of execution for Leo Jones, a cop-killer from Jacksonville, and Gerald Stano, who scattered the bodies of murdered women around the Daytona Beach area. In Tallahassee, Governor Chiles announced that he planned to move quickly and carry out his constitutional duty to uphold Florida's death penalty.

The reinforced prospect of ending their lives in "Old Sparky," regardless of whether the event might be two years, ten years, or twenty years in the future, had to be terrifying for the two former close friends and vampire enthusiasts from Calloway County. Charity's mother was one person who wasn't losing any sleep over the prospect that

Rod might someday be strapped into the electric chair. If that happened, she would like to pull the switch, Mrs. Remington told the *Daily-Commercial*. In a telephone interview from her home in South Dakota, she said that if Rod was given the death penalty, it was a sentence he deserved. "And the only thing that would make it better is if his mother was sitting right there next to him," she said. Mrs. Remington believed that Sondra shared the responsibility for getting Charity involved in the loony vampire activities.

On another front, King's decision to seek the death penalty made Graves' motion for appointment of another lawyer to help him defend Scott a moot point. There was no question that with the grim specter of execution hanging over the boy's head, he would have two defense attorneys in his corner. The problem lay in deciding who the newcomer was going to be. The murders of the Wendorfs occurred in a rural county with a relatively small pool of criminal defense attorneys to choose from. And with four defendants still awaiting trial and the attorney for another former defendant out of the picture, some of the best and most experienced lawyers were unavailable for duty as assistant or co-counsel for Scott.

Graves believed he knew the right person for the job and suggested appointment of local attorney Kimberly Reed. She was a savvy criminal defense lawyer who knew her way around the local courtrooms, but there was an unexpected problem with her proposed appointment to help out in the murder case. She was a law partner of attorney Jerry Blair—and Blair was a former law partner of Judge Lockett. Blair had even represented the judge as a personal counsel. That's the way it is in small towns and small counties. After a while the local legal communities become so professionally inbred that extreme care has to be taken to avoid conflicts of interest, even the mere appearance of conflicts. Lockett solved the problem by reaching into the neighboring Lake County community of Leesburg, and appointing experienced criminal defense attorney Harry Hackney to Scott's legal defense team.

Rod didn't share a similar problem. Hawthorne already had help from colleagues at the public defender's office. Assistant Public Defenders Bill Lackey and Mike Rogers would share principal duties with Hawthorne at the defense table during hearings and the trial. The defense team was also assisted by a paralegal. Graves and the public defenders were already doing their best for their clients, but with the lives of the boys now at stake they weren't leaving any stone unturned. They busied themselves dredging up every bit of evidence and checked out every hint of extenuating circumstances that might help their clients avoid the electric chair. Hawthorne was already looking closely into Rod's background in Kentucky in efforts that were aimed, at least in part, on showing what she described as "his human side."

On March 28, exactly one month after Rod learned that he would be put on trial for his life, he observed his seventeenth birthday at the jail. There was no cake, and no celebration.

The defense teams were at last in place and ready for the shooting to begin, but no firm dates had yet been set for the trial, or trials. It hadn't even been decided which, if any, of the defendants would be put on trial together. The lawyers for all the teenagers told Judge Briggs that they wanted separate trials for their clients, but the prosecutor wanted the four of them put on trial simultaneously. Before Briggs was able to make a decision about severing the cases, or ordering trials in pairs or groups, he was out of the picture and replaced by a new judge. Now the problem was Judge Lockett's.

Dana was the first of the reputed vampire cultists to be formally charged as an adult, the first to be locked up at the Lake County Jail, and for a while it looked as if she would be the first to be brought to trial. At a pre-trial meeting with defense lawyers, Judge Lockett underscored his determination to begin the trials early the following year. "Our first trial will be in February 1998," he declared. "Whether they're together or separate, there will be a trial in February."

Then Plecas sprung a surprise by announcing that her client had decided not to waive her right to a speedy trial. Despite the scheduling problems, Dana's lawyer was still on board and she informed the court that the young woman planned to exercise her right to go to trial within 120 days of her arrest. Dana was "feisty" and didn't "want to sit around," the lawyer said. Lockett said that he would schedule a trial date for Dana in May. Although there was no time for procrastination, the defense would be ready, Plecas promised.

Any hopes of putting Dana's co-defendants on trial as a group were also severely dampened when Hawthorne and Graves said that they planned to file motions to sever the cases of their clients from those of each other and of the other defendants. In earlier remarks Lockett seemed to have put the icing on the cake before it was baked when he declared that under no circumstance would he put all of the defendants on trial in the same proceeding. "Their cases are significantly different," he said.

Talk of a May 1997 trial date for Dana was a startling development, and a bit confusing for court watchers who added up the time between Dana's arrest in late November 1996 and May 1, 1997. If the trial began on the very first day of the month, more than 150 days would have elapsed between the arrest and the beginning of the proceeding. Even if counting from the date formal charges were refiled after the grand jury indictments were returned on December 17, a May trial would still miss the deadline by weeks.

It was all very perplexing, but where the criminal legal justice system was concerned that was about par for the course. Prosecution and defense of criminal defendants is a game of strategy, tactics—and sometimes the whim of the individual who is being put on trial. There were also other considerations, such as conflicting schedules of the judge and attorneys that were especially complex when multiple defendants were involved and the possibility existed that some or all of them would be put on trial at the same time.

Ever since assuming responsibilities as Dana's defense at-

torney, Plecas' heart had been set on all the defendants going
to trial together as a group. Then jurors would understand
just how minor a role Dana had played in the tragedy, she
believed. But her client was sick and tired of life in a jail
cell, and was anxious to get the show on the road.

There was also a certain tactical advantage to forcing an
early trial while King was busy compiling, examining and
collating the mountain of scientific evidence and other information, lining up witnesses and working out strategy to
prosecute the principal defendants, Rod and Scott. Testimony based on analysis of blood collected during the investigation, almost certain to include learned conclusions
and opinions from expert witnesses with a string of degrees
and authoritative knowledge of DNA, was expected to play
an important role in the trials. But analysis of blood and
DNA were more likely to be factors in the trials of the boys.
The task ahead of the state attorney in preparing to prosecute
Dana and Charity was less exacting. King said that he could
go to trial with Dana by May without the scientific evidence.
He didn't expect that evidence to be critical in her case.

It seemed that Dana's course through the courts had at
last been charted, but the journey for her vampire kindred
still had a ways to go before the labyrinthian twists and turns
of the legal system were fully navigated. For the time being,
from at least some viewpoints, Charity was taking a back
seat. She and Dana were generally perceived by court watchers and some local legal pundits to have been extras in the
dark drama of murder, intrigue and twisted teenage passions.

At that point in the proceedings, with Rod and Scott accusing each other, and Dana insisting on her right to an early
trial, it appeared that about the only chance of any of the
defendants being tried together would be linked to the possibility of teaming up the two girls. Rod and Scott waived
their right to speedy trials a few weeks after being returned
to Florida. But Charity and her attorney hadn't yet decided
if she would waive, or follow the lead of the older girl and
force court authorities to proceed. Time was rapidly running
out, however, and the decision had to be made soon.

The prospect of an early trial wasn't the only development that lifted Dana's flagging spirits during the lengthy meeting with Judge Lockett. King finally disclosed that the state would not seek the death penalty against her or Charity. Dana greeted the revelation by expelling a huge sigh of relief. She still faced the dreary possibility that she might be saddled with a sentence of life in prison without parole. But for the first time in months, she and Charity could close their eyes at night without being tormented by the specter of ending their lives in the old electric chair constructed by convict labor long before their parents were born. Although more than 230 killers and rapists have been put to death in the chair since it was first used in 1924, no woman had been executed there.

But six women were under sentence of death in Florida, and were locked up in a special section of the BCI in Pembroke Pines near Fort Lauderdale waiting out interminable appeals. Among the most notorious were serial killer and hitch-hiking prostitute Aileen Wuornos; Judias "Judy" Buenoano, a serial poisoner who specialized in family members and boyfriends, (and was executed in Florida's electric chair in 1998;) and Deidre Michelle Hunt who gunned down a bound teenager while her married lover captured the unforgettable moment on video. King's decision had put to rest any chance that Dana or Charity would one day join their dismal sisterhood.

In April, less than one month before the May 5 date for Dana's scheduled trial, and after jury notices were already mailed, Plecas reported that her client had experienced a change of heart. After a long talk with her lawyer, she waived her right to a speedy trial. The decision was a relief to her lawyer, and a paralegal helping out with Dana's defense told lawyers that she believed the Kentucky woman had finally realized the dangers of being the first one of the group to be put on trial. Plecas was sincerely worried that if her client went to trial before her companions, all the horror and outrage over the murders would be heaped upon her. It "would be like a sheep led to slaughter," she told reporters.

Judge Lockett was considering putting the two boys on trial together in February of 1998 and setting a trial date sometime later for the two girls. After Dana's last-minute reversal of her decision to insist on an early trial, it appeared even more likely than before that she and Charity might also be tried in tandem. But February was still months in the future, and consideration of bringing the reputed Vampire Clan to trial in pairs, possibly in back-to-back proceedings, was far from a done deal. Attorneys on both sides of the case still had an enormous amount of work to do: interviews to be conducted, laboratory and other forensics tests to be carried out and results to be examined, motions to file and documents to be collected.

Hawthorne asked Lockett to order Heather's guardian, and family members and friends of the girl, to turn over various items to the defense. Among material the assistant public defender asked to see were letters that Heather had written after her arrest to her sister Jennifer, Jeanine LeClaire, Jeremy Hueber and members of the Queen family in Dallas. The lawyer stated that she had requested the material numerous times as part of the discovery process, but complained that Tally and others were dragging their heels and hadn't complied with the requests. She asked Lockett to issue a court order for the material and to set a time limit on compliance.

The assistant public defender was waiting to see the letters when she canceled plans to take a deposition from the girl on June 3. Hawthorne wanted the correspondence before she talked to Heather, and one of her main motivations for sticking so stubbornly to her guns was a desire to straighten out the discrepancies in accounts tracing her actions on the night of the murders. The hard-driving lawyer claimed that the letters were self-serving, and she wanted to compare them with other information.

King had already released most of the state's evidence in the case through the discovery process, including copies of the crime scene video taken by LCSD detectives inside the Wendorfs' home before the bodies were removed. He also released an audiocassette tape made by Baton Rouge police while they were closing in on the runaways and comparing the Ford Explorer parked at the Howard Johnson's Motor Lodge with a radio description of the vehicle. The state attorney claimed, however, that he couldn't turn over the letters because they were private correspondence from Heather to other people, and said it was his understanding that the defense attorneys "want what I don't have."

Hawthorne also asked for a court-appointed guardian for her client because she had run into a roadblock in efforts to obtain his medical records. Rod's mother was so deeply mired in her own troubles with the criminal courts in Kentucky that she couldn't function as the legal parent to waive his privacy rights to the records, as she would in a normal situation. A court-appointed guardian was about the only solution. In the absence of a firm helping hand from his mother, a guardian could help the seventeen-year-old negotiate his way through the court system. Other decisions involving legal strategies that called for input from a parent or other concerned adult capable of advising the boy also had to be made.

Lockett settled the guardian problem by appointing Tavares lawyer Jodi Anderson to advise the boy and generally handle matters for him that would normally be the responsibility of a parent. Sondra later indicated that she wasn't notified about the hearing or plans to name a guardian, and said she would have preferred that her parents take on the responsibility. Harrell and Rosetta Gibson had moved back to Florida.

The judge also rescheduled Heather's deposition for October 14, and agreed to order Tally, Jennifer, Jeanine LeClaire, and Queen family members in Dallas to turn over material the defense was seeking as part of the discovery process. The materials included the letters, along with sculptures and drawings created by Heather. The Lake County

Sheriff's Department was designated to take custody of the articles until the trials were concluded.

Tally was scheduled to participate in a Florida state cultural affairs panel in Tallahassee on October 14, so Hope was designated to represent Heather during the depositions. The lawyers for Rod and Scott planned to ask Lockett to compare Heather's statements at the deposition with her testimony to the grand jury and look for discrepancies.

Heather showed up at the judicial center to give her deposition wearing a short, multicolored outfit that buttoned down the front, three or four necklaces, Roman-style sandals and dark glasses. Her hair was its natural honey-blonde. The old Morticia Addams look had been permanently relegated to the trash can. Graves and Hackney, Hawthorne and Lackey, Carle and Plecas represented the defendants at the proceeding, and Hope was there to advise Heather.

The three hours set aside for the deposition were marked by frequent breaks and invocation of Heather's Fifth Amendment rights not to reply to certain questions in order to avoid self-incrimination. When she was asked if she had taken a turn driving her father's car during the trip to Baton Rouge, Hope asserted her Fifth Amendment rights but she answered ''no'' before he was able to complete the objection. The lawyers ran out of time before anyone except Hawthorne and Lackey were able to ask questions. They indicated that they might seek to continue more questioning later, and Hawthorne was considering asking Judge Lockett to compel Heather to be more forthcoming.

The defense attorneys were spending considerable time taking depositions. Early in November, almost a full year after the murders, Graves, Hawthorne, Carle and Plecas coordinated trips to Kentucky and Louisiana to take statements from witnesses in those states.

10. THE SCENT OF BLOOD

While Rod and his vampire kindred were encamped at the Lake County Detention Center in Tavares waiting out the painfully slow pre-trial process, back in Murray, authorities were still working to clear away the wreckage and human detritus he left behind him.

Rod was as erratic and destructive as one of the deadly whirlwinds that skims across Kansas and other Great Plains states in Tornado Alley, sometimes moving north and east to spread misery in Kentucky and the Midwest. There was no telling exactly which direction the whirlwind would take, where it would touch down and how much damage it would leave in its wake.

A few months after the dust-up at Grogan's Trailer Park, April Doeden had a change of heart and walked into the office of Calloway County Attorney David Harrington in Murray to announce that she wanted to drop the charges against Jason Jones. Then she melted back into the shadows of Calloway County. When employees at Harrington's office tried to get in touch with her, they learned that she had moved out of the trailer park without leaving a forwarding address or other means of contacting her. Some of Harrington's employees checked with the Department of Social Services and learned that she was staying with friends.

Since April had basically stepped out of the picture, Harrington got together with Jason's court-appointed attorney and worked out a deal utilizing an element of Kentucky criminal law that is similar to probation and is known as a diversionary agreement. According to the pact, which was given the official stamp of approval by Judge Furches, Jason was advised that if he stayed out of trouble for twelve months from the date of the agreement the case would be dismissed. Harrington had previously trimmed the charge from a felony to wanton endangerment, second degree, a class-A misdemeanor. Jason agreed to the terms, which included the stipulation that he avoid any contact with April.

Otha Cooper consented to a similar deal on the charges filed after he leveled the nervous barrage of gunfire at the carful of teenagers in November. Cooper had never been in trouble with the law before and the county attorney consented to drop charges if he kept his nose clean for one year from the date the agreement was signed. As part of the pact, Dana's father also agreed to pay some restitution of the costs of the proceeding, not to exceed $100, and to stay away from the teenagers who were in the car and had filed the complaint.

Sondra Gibson's legal problems weren't as easy to solve, and they were growing more complicated and serious as time passed. She admitted writing to the fourteen-year-old boy, but claimed that the content of her letters was misinterpreted and that charges were being trumped up for revenge. Dennis Lortie, a public defender, contended that the letters were protected speech and disclosed that he planned to file a motion asking that the charges of criminal solicitation to commit third-degree rape and third-degree sodomy be dismissed.

The charges were eventually dropped, but only as part of a court process that landed the woman in even more serious trouble than before. The local prosecutor believed that the accusations of attempting to entice a minor into an act of sexual intercourse constituted a crime that was more serious than a mere misdemeanor, and presented the information about Sondra's alleged misbehavior to a Calloway County grand jury. Two months after the misdemeanor charges were wiped off the books, the panel met in the Miller Annex to consider the evidence against Sondra and returned an indictment charging her with criminal attempt to commit first-degree unlawful transactions with a minor. The new felony charges carried a possible penalty of one-to-five years in prison.

Sondra scrapped her previous plans to move to Paducah. Instead, she returned to Florida, and apparently moved around for awhile between Lake County, to be near her son, and Daytona Beach, where her older sister and grandmother lived.

While Sondra was trying to figure out how to deal with the mess she was in, the story about a rival vampire clan that was the blood enemy of the jailed Kentucky teenagers was resurrected in a letter from one of Charity's relatives. Donna Ronning, a sister of Charity's father, wrote to a reporter for the *Daily Commercial* from her home in Montana and said she had heard that some would-be vampires from Murray who were rivals of Rod's band had traveled to Daytona Beach. Mrs. Ronning said one of the rival cultists wrote to her niece, and she complained that the vampire gang was able to get mail to Charity more easily than the girl's family was.

The hard realities of the predicament Charity had gotten herself into were coming down with crushing force on the girl and on members of her family who loved her. The willow-thin teenager's prospects for the future appeared to have been badly squandered, and she was having a hard time dealing with living the life of a jailbird. She was frightened, lonely, bored and cold. Charity spent much of her time sleeping, and if some reports are to be believed, she and Rod managed to exchange a letter or two. She also corresponded for awhile with Sondra, who said that she expected to become Charity's mother-in-law some day.

Carle asked jail authorities to permit his client to wear thermal underwear beneath her jail uniform, but was turned down, her aunt complained. Mrs. Ronning wrote to the reporter that her niece was allowed only a man's T-shirt to wear under the jail uniform, and said it didn't help much because it left Charity's arms uncovered. "I have to say humanity isn't an 'in thing' in your county," she groused. "Poor girl has no fat or muscle to keep her warm . . ."

Temperatures outside the jail were running in the mid-nineties, but Charity's bunk was right in front of the business end of an air conditioner. Corrections officials kept temperatures inside the institution at a steady seventy-four degrees throughout the summer months, and an LCDC spokesman told the press that although Charity might consider that too cold for her personal tastes it was simply too bad. That was the kind of thing people sometimes had to put up with when they were behind bars.

Mrs. Ronning also indicated in her letter that she was upset because jail authorities confiscated a crossword puzzle clipped from a newspaper that Charity's grandmother had slipped inside. Corrections authorities at the LCDC forward letter mail to inmates, but remove checks, money orders and newspaper and magazine clippings. Crossword puzzles were treated just like any other clippings. They weren't allowed to be mailed to Charity or to any other prisoner.

The fuss over the letter reportedly mailed to Charity from the rival vampire band and censorship of her mail was a minor flap, but it helped underscore one of the problems police investigators, defense lawyers and other court officers were experiencing in their efforts to play down the more outlandish aspects of the sensational murder case. Carle responded to the report of cultists in Daytona Beach by telling the press that vampires had nothing to do with the facts of the case. Similar remarks were made by others. But every time defense lawyers, prosecutors or law enforcement officers tried to bury vampires by tossing another shovelful of dirt over their coffins, the creatures of the night stubbornly clawed their way out of their graves, and the whispers and speculation about a chilling cult of blood-sucking teenagers began all over again. Unlike the legendary blood-suckers of

Bram Stoker's classic *Dracula* and other horrid revenants described in literature and film, the Vampire Clan(s) seemed to be casting their reflections just about everywhere.

While Charity was complaining about her goosebumps, Kentucky authorities at last caught up with her boyfriend's mother in Tavares and took her into custody. She left Daytona Beach after breaking up with her boyfriend, Smoke, and moved back to central Florida to be closer to Rod. A couple of days after her arrest, Sondra was transported to Murray and booked into the Calloway County Detention Center. Early in August she appeared before Circuit Judge Dennis Foust for arraignment and entered a plea of not guilty to the single felony charge against her.

Steve West, her new court-appointed attorney, told the judge that after talking with Sondra's parents he decided that his client should undergo a psychiatric evaluation to determine her competency to stand trial and her ability to understand the nature of the offense at the time it allegedly occurred. Commonwealth Attorney Mike Ward, who represented the prosecution at the hearing, had no objections to the request and it was approved by the judge.

Psychiatric evaluations were becoming a family tradition. Shortly after return of the fugitives to Lake County from Baton Rouge, Dr. Harry Crop, Ph.D., of Gainesville, was appointed by Judge Briggs as a confidential expert to examine Rod to determine if he was competent to stand trial and cooperate in his own defense. Dr. Crop conducted the examination in a private room at the jail, and according to the order his conclusions were reported to Rod's defense attorneys and were not to be shared with the state.

Sondra was transported to Kentucky's Psychiatric Evaluation Center in Madisonville to undergo a battery of tests and interviews by mental health professionals. Madisonville is a couple of hours' drive northeast of Murray in Hopkins County, and is home to the Western District Headquarters of the Kentucky State Police Department, as well as the psychiatric evaluation center.

After several days of observation and tests at the center,

Sondra was returned to Murray, issued a white-and-black-striped uniform of pants and blouse and locked up once more in a cell. The psychiatric report was sealed by court order, but during an interview with Mahanes in the jail's legal library she claimed that doctors at the center concluded that she was "perfectly sane."

The interview ranged over a broad area and the prisoner and reporter talked about her predicament, about Rod, about his father Rick Ferrell, Charity and others who had played roles in the complicated stew their lives had become. She was cooperative and appeared eager to share her story, but refused to discuss her son's case except to say that he'd told her he didn't remember having anything to do with the murders. He had blackouts, she said. Rod's lawyers had cautioned her to wait until after the trial to talk about the proceedings against him, Sondra explained.

Rod was merely following in the footsteps of his father when he became attracted to role-playing games, Sondra indicated. She said that when she first met Rick Ferrell he was already playing "Dungeons & Dragons," and she later learned that he had turned more recently to "Vampire: The Masquerade." She wrote to him, hoping to learn more about the game, but he never responded to her letter. Except for her parents and a grandmother, most of her family had turned against her and Rod, she added.

Sondra said that for a while before her arrest in Florida, she was living in the same small town where Heather was resettled by her relatives. She was upset about the grand jury decision clearing Heather, " 'cause here's my son looking at the electric chair, and she just walks," Sondra said. She declined to identify the town she was referring to. She said that she was sorry she had brought Rod back to Murray, but wanted to get him away from Heather, Jeanine and other people he had been hanging around with in Florida.

All the fuss about a bloodthirsty vampire cult was misdirected, according to the woman's account. The focus on vampires was merely a clever smokescreen for the evil that was really going on. Kids in Murray and Eustis were up to their ears in an "old-fashioned . . . devil worshipping . . . Satanic cult," she confided, once lowering her voice to a conspiratorial whisper. The vampire nonsense was part of a coverup for the activities of the Satanists, and her son was pulled into it "for a while."

Sondra alluded to threats from a boy and a girl, teenagers who were part of the mysterious underground of sinister diabolists in Murray, while explaining why she had written the letters to the fourteen-year-old. She wrote them because she was afraid for her life. It was a strange story, told in bits and pieces, with huge holes that left many questions unexplained, but she seemed to be saying that if she wrote the incriminating letters, the people she feared would leave her alone. It was part of a darkling ritual she had to undergo, and she could select whomever she wished to assist her in consummating the act.

The story was like so many others that the mother and son were known for telling. It was filled with dead-ends, confounding twists and turns, hidden meanings and hints of profound secrets lurking just behind the bare-bones construct that was being laid out. It hinted at terrible images of a little Kentucky town that was festering with counterfeit vampires, real-life Satanists and all manner of demonic goings-on. And it was all happening in a God-fearing community that supported more than one hundred churches. While preachers were delivering sermons at Sunday morning services and leading their flocks at Wednesday night prayer meetings, and innocent children were in Sunday school classes learning about Jesus casting out demons, Old Scratch himself was stalking the streets and working his evil in their very midst. It was a sobering thought.

Mahanes dutifully recorded all the woman's remarks, but reserved personal judgment on her story. Sondra's reputation for veracity was about as moth-eaten and shopworn as the word of a White House fund-raiser—or her own son.

All the efforts to clean up the wreckage left in the wake of the Vampire Clan weren't confined to the criminal courts. The sudden, savage murders of Richard Wendorf and Naoma Queen Wendorf left family members and civil authorities with two estates to settle. Between the two of them, Richard and Naoma left four daughters and other possible beneficiaries. Two estates and different beneficiaries also meant more lawyers moving into the lives of the couple's survivors to deal with business matters. Bill Barfield, a lawyer from the town of Maitland, assumed the legal responsibilities for handling Richard Wendorf's estate. Michael Magruder, a lawyer from the Osceola County town of Kissimmee, a few minutes' drive south of Orlando, opened the estate for Naoma Ruth Queen. And Heather's guardian, civil attorney Lou Tally, and her criminal defense lawyer James Hope, were still waiting in the wings.

The problems handling Richard's estate were relatively simple and straightforward, especially after Heather was cleared of any criminal participation in the murders. She and her sister were the principal beneficiaries. It was a different story for their mother, even though she had lived with their father in a common-law marriage arrangement for twenty years. The state of Florida doesn't recognize common-law marriages, and Naoma was never divorced from her legal husband, Joseph Queen. He was still living, and he and their daughters, Paula and Sandy Queen, made their homes in Dallas.

According to Magruder, Joe and Naoma Queen worked out an amicable separation, but he didn't know why they had never bothered to get a divorce, or why she had lived with Richard Wendorf for approximately two decades in the common-law relationship. People who knew more about Naoma and Richard's motives for the unorthodox living arrangements weren't volunteering the information.

Attorneys were more willing to talk about plans for the house where the murders occurred. After sheriff's investigators finished with the property as a crime scene, the house and contents were released to Jennifer, but that didn't mean she was the new owner outright. The lawyers took an inventory of property inside the house, and family members began making arrangements to have the blood-splattered walls and floors cleaned, and other signs of the butchery that occurred there removed. While the interior of the house was being put back into shape, relatives of the dead couple were also looking around for a buyer. Tally told reporters that he didn't expect either Jennifer or Heather to buy the house and move in. The three-bedroom brick home was too big for either of them to keep up, even if they were adults.

If the couple's survivors were unable to find an acceptable buyer on their own, the house would be listed with a real-estate agent, the attorneys said. According to Florida law, realtors were required to inform prospective buyers that a violent crime had taken place in the home. It was a requirement that had advantages or disadvantages, depending on the prospective new homeowner. Some people would find the idea of moving into the murder house too grisly or depressing to contemplate. Certain other buyers might experience a vicarious thrill living in a house where two people were so savagely bludgeoned to death.

In California, after pregnant actress Sharon Tate and four other people were chopped and slashed to death by a band of Charlie Manson's hopped-up hippies, the real-estate agent listing the Benedict Canyon home was flooded with calls from people wanting to buy it. But new tenants who signed a lease for a handsome Beverly Hills mansion loved the home until they learned that Lana Turner's mobster boyfriend was stabbed to death in one of the bedrooms. Then one of the tenants called the real estate agent in tears, and said that she was scared to death to live in the house. He helped her break the lease.

The ghost element can also be a factor. Houses and other locations where especially sensational or ghastly murders have occurred often wind up being linked to hauntings by ghosts or demons, or other fearsome supernatural beings. Most states have laws requiring sellers and agents to advise potential buyers about deaths occurring in homes going back a certain number of years, especially if they involved violence. Some states have similar restrictions about homes that are said to be haunted, and permit lawsuits for non-disclosure if prospective buyers aren't warned. But the laws vary from state to state.

Florida statutes require sellers and their agents to disclose material facts that are not readily discernible, but could affect the value of a home. It was unlikely that anyone who might contemplate buying and moving into the Wendorf house would be unaware of the tragedy that occurred there. That would be especially true of anyone who lived in central Florida.

Regardless of who might buy the Wendorf house, the slayings left behind a community that was traumatized and scarred by the scent of blood. Eustis High School and, to a somewhat lesser extent, Calloway County High School were each imprinted with the horror of the murders and the transgressions and atrocities committed by the vampires-in-training who once roamed the hallways and campuses. It was common knowledge among their classmates that Heather and Rod were not the only students at Eustis High who, at one time or another, and to varying degrees, were caught up in the vampire mania.

A similar sense of unease was felt among high school students in Calloway County, where Sheriff Scott estimated that as many as thirty young people from the community may have been involved in the local vampire underground. Several of them, in addition to Rod, Charity and Dana, attended or previously attended CCHS. If what police in three states were saying was true, a monster had walked in their midst and infected others with his evil.

Of more immediate concern, if the sheriff was correct, the virus was still alive and virulently present. Youngsters and adults were bothered by unsettling questions that cast a pall of fear over the community and left many people wondering if the vampires had only been forced deeper underground and were merely in hibernation. Who were the remaining members of the vampire cult? What were they up to? And who may have purposely, or inadvertently, done something to earn a place on their enemies list?

11. SUNLIGHT AND ASHES

Most people in Eustis and neighboring communities were looking forward to burying the notorious Vampire Clan in the ashes of the trial—one way or another. Students and faculty members at Eustis High School made it plain when they were asked about the sensational murder case that they were sick and tired of being associated with gruesome murder and stories about members of a bloodthirsty vampire clan roaming their hallways and sharing their campus. Radio talk show hosts and other people were circulating jokes about EHS that made it sound like vampires were hanging from the stairwells, lurking in closets and hiding coffins away in secluded storerooms for midday naps.

Everyone at the school was anxious to turn the focus at EHS back to accomplishments in such pursuits as academics, athletics and character-building. While the Wendorf sisters were living with relatives and working to get their lives back together, a couple of Jennifer's classmates were graduating as valedictorian and salutatorian. The top graduate talked of plans to register at the University of Florida in Gainesville, identified her dream job as "aerospace engineer," and said her hero and the person with the most influence in her life was her "Dad." Like Jennifer, the salutatorian planned to register at FSU. She said that she would like to be the CEO of a major corporation, and identified her heroes as Jesus Christ, her parents and her sister.

Attitudes were much the same in Calloway County, where law enforcement authorities, former classmates and family members and neighbors of the western Kentucky teenagers were anxious to put the atrocities attributed to Rod and his Vampire Clan behind them. A new class of students had registered at CCHS and Murray State College, another tobacco crop was in the fields, and a fresh breeze was sweeping through the county, blowing away all the rot, corruption and evil left in the wake of the Vampire Clan. People were ready to move on with their lives.

Before all the deceit, evil and misguided teenage freakiness could be exposed to the light of the sun and begin to bring a degree of closure to the troubling spectacle, however, a judge, prosecutors, defense attorneys, a jury and support staff had to bring the defendants to trial. No matter how anxious Dana or anyone else might be to get the show on the road, it was a process that couldn't be rushed.

One of the roadblocks still to be negotiated was directly linked to the unrelenting blizzard of publicity identifying the defendants as members of a murderous Vampire Clan, involved in gross blood-drinking rituals and general teenage lunacy. Rod's lawyers with the public defender's office wanted a court order to hold the trial outside Lake County.

Hawthorne cited the publicity in a formal change of venue motion, and presented the court with a stack of newspaper articles about the case that referred to activities of a vampire cult. An affidavit from Rod was attached to the motion, handwritten in fine script that slanted slightly to the right. "The publicity has continued non-stop since the date of the arrest and your affiant has a well-founded fear that a fair and impartial trial cannot be had in Lake County, Florida or any of the surrounding counties where the publicity has extended," he wrote.

In the motion, Hawthorne and her boss, "Skip" Babb, called the publicity "extensive" and "pervasive," and said that, of all the prospective grand jurors in the original pool, only one individual hadn't heard of, or had at least some knowledge of, the case. Publicity surrounding the manhunt, arrest and prosecution of the "five young people allegedly involved in this case has been extensive and pervasive," they stated in the four-page document. Television, radio and both daily newspapers in the county had broadcast or printed stories about the case on a near-daily basis.

Using words and terminology like "vociferously reported in the media," and "publicity surrounding the case continues like a winter blizzard," the lawyers contended that the problem was exacerbated by the fact that juvenile crime had "become the story of the '90s . . . Additionally, the twist of alleged 'vampire cult' activities, with rumors of bloodletting, and ritualistic voodoo, enhancing [sic] the macabre interest in sensationalizing the case."

Rod's lawyers claimed a fair and impartial trial could not be obtained in Lake County, or any county which received much of its daily news from Leesburg's *Daily Commercial* and/or the *Orlando Sentinel*. Any effort to obtain impartial jurors in the county would be futile, and failure to change the venue would violate their clients' rights under the U.S. Constitution and the Constitution of the State of Florida, they contended.

The defense move presented a knotty problem for a judge to deal with, but it was not a development that was either unique or unexpected. Almost every high-profile felony case that attracts publicity can be expected to spark requests by defense attorneys for changes of venue. And the vampire-cult murders were definitely high-profile, especially in central Florida. Moving the trial to Ocala in Marion County, Orlando in Orange County, Sanford in Seminole County or all the way to Daytona Beach in Volusia County wasn't likely to make that much difference when time came to begin selecting a jury pool. The publicity was pervasive and prospective jurors in surrounding or nearby counties were almost as likely to have read, heard or watched reports about the sensational case as were the men and women of Lake County. The defense request to rule out surrounding counties if the change of venue was granted appeared reasonable.

Marion County, Orange County and Seminole County were each touched by the case in some manner. Four of the five teenagers arrested in Louisiana were lodged for awhile in the juvenile detention center in Ocala, Marion County, and State Attorney King had his main offices there. Ocala was the center of Florida's Fifth Judicial District, an area encompassing Marion, Lake, Citrus, Sumter and Hernando Counties. The old Buick that four of the suspects drove from Kentucky was abandoned near Sanford in Seminole County. And Wendorf family members were settled around Orlando in Orange County. The teenage girl who had made up the story about a conversation with Heather that never occurred, then repeated the fiction before the grand jury, also lived in Orange County.

From the beginning of the case, the public defender's office took a lead role in efforts to squelch sensationalistic references to vampires or cultish activities. Barely two weeks after the fugitives were rounded up in Baton Rouge, Babb issued a formal statement aimed at accomplishing that purpose.

"Our initial inquiry supports what law enforcement has repeatedly found that this case has nothing to do with vampires," he declared. "When you need information about the progress of this case, please refer to it as the Wendorf case."

Babb's attempt to divert attention away from the more far-out aspects of the lurid case was a doomed effort, simply because the teenagers were so clearly obsessed with vampires, blood and the supernatural. The gruesomeness of the murders, with all the gore and feral savagery they were surrounded by, such as the Vampire Clan symbol reputedly burned into the flesh of the victims, was impossible to ignore.

Despite the care taken by Babb, by Lake County Sheriff's Department spokesmen and by defense attorneys and other authorities closely involved with the case to avoid publicly linking the murders to the work of a crazed blood cult, a few comments about vampires were even made by officials who were part of the local criminal justice system. In statements made by Judge Miller after refusing to set bail for Dana during the video-phone hearing at the jail, the jurist was quoted in the *Commercial* as saying, ''. . . since this seems to be a national vampire group, posting bond wouldn't be a problem.''

Assistant Public Defender Bill Stone told reporters following the hearing that despite rumors going around, he didn't see any cuts on her, or sharpened canine teeth. Then he complained about the adverse effects of national news coverage, but—for the time being at least—nixed the idea of moving for a change of venue. Asked if the trial could be moved in order to find jurors who hadn't heard about the case, he responded, ''Where? To China?''

The reputed Vampire Clan attracted international attention, and sparked stories in Canada, England and Australia. *Who Weekly*, a popular journal published Down Under, devoted the entire front page of a December issue to the headline: ''VAMPIRE KILLERS—A cult of blood-sucking teenagers face charges they murdered two of their parents.'' Headshots of Rod and Charity taken after their arrests in Baton Rouge were shown along the bottom of the cover page against a backdrop of graffiti prominently featuring the word ''Vampire.'' Six full pages, with a large picture of Rod jumping on a grave in the old Salem Cemetery, were devoted to the copiously illustrated story inside.

Closer to home, the *Sentinel*'s scoop based on the exclusive telephone interview with Rod was carried at the top of the page under the banner headline: ''INTERVIEW WITH THE VAMPIRE.'' The headline, which was a play on the title of Anne Rice's book and the subsequent movie, was creative, timely and a sure attention-grabber. It was also exactly the type of thing that lawyers and many other court and police officials were still desperately trying to keep from being associated with the case in the public mind. No matter how hard they tried to play down the vampire angle, however, the press and the public weren't listening. Other major stories appeared in *People* magazine, *USA Today*, and in the weekly supermarket tabloid, the *National Examiner*. Shock jock Howard Stern mentioned the case on his New York–based, nationally broadcast radio show.

Rod, Heather and their friends hadn't yet been brought back from Baton Rouge when a segment of NBC-TV's *Today Show* was broadcast to millions of people across the country reporting that police believed some of the teenage suspects drank the blood of the murder victims. A Miami-based correspondent cited his source as a Louisiana law enforcement officer who insisted on anonymity. Ultimately, the allegation was shown to be false. *Dateline NBC* also did a segment on the story, and Oprah Winfrey discussed it on her talk show. Television's *Inside Edition* staffed the hearings in Baton Rouge, its electronic tabloid competitor, *Hard Copy*, sent reporters to the Eustis High campus on Washington Avenue to ask students if they knew other vampires at EHS, and the story was reported on *CNN*.

America's Most Wanted, the long-running crime-fighting show on the Fox TV network, broadcast a segment on the first Saturday night of 1997 that included an interview with a Kentucky State Police official and an expert on cults who offered advice to parents about warning signs to be on the lookout for. The show was a departure from the usual construct for the popular program, which was known since its inception for focusing on suspected criminals still on the loose. After surviving a cancellation scare the previous May, show producers decided to broaden the scope of their coverage to include feature stories, crime prevention and safety tips and other related subjects. The Vampire Clan story was one of the first.

The *Daily Commercial* broadcast its own report during the newspaper's *News Makers* program on Lake County Cablevision's channel TV-13 showing portions of the videotapes taken of the teenagers being questioned by police in Baton Rouge. The show was repeated on five different days and nights, each time showing the same excerpts from tapes which were heavily edited before they were turned over to defense attorneys and ultimately made available to the press.

Steven Murphy, who insisted on anonymity for his interview with the hometown reporter in Murray, appeared with his mother on the *Jenny Jones* show. Lots of people either hadn't seen Babb's cautionary news release—or they weren't paying any attention.

During arguments in one motion, Graves declared that ''ninety-nine percent if not one hundred percent of the spin on the case is on vampires. The criminal charges ain't got nothing to do with vampires. Now what we have in the process is the spin and marketing tool of media weighed against the defendants' rights to a fair trial and in that respect the media fall woefully short.''

After King released the videotaped meeting between Rod and Charity inside the Baton Rouge Police Department interrogation room, Hawthorne and Lackey criticized him for letting the press see and listen to it before it was turned over to the defense. Hawthorne accused King of acting in ''bad faith,'' and said that the incident strengthened the argument for a change of venue. Lackey told reporters that even though lovers didn't enjoy the same privacy privileges afforded to clients and their lawyers, he believed the young couple ''had a reasonable expectation of privacy.'' The attorney pointed out that the tape was inaudible until King arranged for sound-enhancement technicians to work on it at the FBI Academy in Quantico, Virginia.

Near the end of August, almost exactly nine months after the fugitives were arrested, Judge Lockett ordered separate trials for the defendants. He also kept to his previously stated plan to begin the trials in early 1998. Rod was scheduled for trial in February, Scott in April, Dana in May and Charity in June. And there was no order for change of venue; each proceeding was entered onto the local court calendar.

King had opposed separate trials, which were sought by Hawthorne and Graves, whose clients were facing the possibility of the death penalty. The prosecutor argued that dealing with the defendants one at a time would greatly increase the expenses. Some witnesses, including several from out of state, would have to be brought to Lake County four times instead of just once for a single trial. Lake County taxpayers would pick up the bills for transportation, lodging and meals. The judge's decision also seemed to assure that considerably more court time would be spent in the proceedings than would be necessary if the defendants were put on trial in groups or all at once.

The Kentucky youths showed little emotion while they sat at the defense tables, watching, listening and occasionally turning to whisper to an attorney as the critical discourse and maneuverings continued around them. Despite the judge's action finally setting trial dates, their immediate future was unchanged. They would stay right where they were, buried alive in the concrete-and-steel bowels of a maximum-security county jail that was as claustrophobically confining as a mausoleum. They were jailhouse pallid, and Rod and Charity were showing even more startling changes in appearance. During the long weeks they had been locked up, their hair had become two-tone. Near the roots and the tops of their heads, their hair was a natural butternut brown. Farther down, it was black from the dye they had applied when they were free and playing at being vampires.

Charity's hair was neatly cut to shoulder-length, with bangs that curled over her forehead. Except for the color, Rod's hairstyle hadn't changed, although once more he was nurturing a scraggly, dark brown goatee. He continued to wear his hair straight, and it was so long that his lawyer had tucked the ends into his shirt. Hawthorne told reporters that Rod was in solitary to isolate him from Scott, and jailers wouldn't give him a haircut.

The surprise alterations in the hairstyles of two of the young defendants didn't stir up the kind of commotion in the national press that O.J. Simpson prosecutor Marcia Clark's famous makeover created when she showed up in the courtroom with a short new shag replacing her old tightly curled hairdo. But the development was dramatic enough to spark some light courtroom chatter, and an aside from Plecas to Charity's attorney, whom she called by his nickname, "Tommy," that his client should get a haircut or a dye job.

Appearing in court with a two-tone hairdo was no way for the girl to look.

At their next court appearance, both teenagers showed up with hair that appeared to be natural brown from the roots to the tips. For the first time in years, Rod's hair was also neatly trimmed above his ears and it accentuated the thinness of his saturnine features. His nose looked longer than ever, and redder than ever.

There was still plenty of time for even further experimentation with physical appearances if the defendants wished. By the time Rod's trial began, they would have already spent about fifteen months in jails and juvenile detention centers. The June trial date set for Charity meant that she would spend a total of about nineteen months waiting to learn her fate. Scott would spend his eighteenth birthday in jail before his trial, and Rod's eighteenth birthday was March 28, the month after his trial was scheduled to begin. Both boys were sixteen when the Wendorfs were murdered, and if they were convicted and sentenced to die in the electric chair, they would be among the youngest killers sent to death row in modern Florida history.

As a prisoner in solitary, Rod was faced with a situation long-term convicts call "twenty-three and one lockdown." That meant that except for court appearances, conferences with his attorneys and occasional visits from his mother or other family members, he was locked in his cell twenty-three hours a day. The one hour a day he was allowed outside was set aside for minimal exercise and showers. It was a situation designed for ennui, melancholy and claustrophobia. Rod's twice-a-week visits with Sondra stopped when she was arrested and locked in jail herself, but the mother and son continued to stay in touch through the mails. Rod wrote from his jail cell; Sondra from hers.

Scott was still celled in a general population area of the jail's juvenile section, and his hair was fashionably cut well above his shoulders. Dana's hairstyle also hadn't changed. It was naturally curly and naturally black, but she grumbled to her lawyer that it was falling out. The long months in jail were wearing on her, and she complained of other symptoms of stress, including weight loss and heart palpitations. She indicated that she was having trouble dealing with some of her fellow inmates, and became so dispirited that Plecas directed her receptionist to begin regular visits with her. Three times a week, Felipa "Josie" Gonzalez made the trip down the street to the detention center to listen to Dana's troubles and try to cheer her up.

Josie seemed to be an excellent choice for the job. She was a self-starter: an attractive, energetic individual who dressed neatly, kept her hair perfectly coifed and her nails long, worked hard and was a pleasure to be around. She functioned as a "Jill-of-all-trades" for her boss, answering telephones, running errands, making bank deposits for the law office and doing her best at whatever assignment she was asked to carry out.

During the second weekend in July, Plecas was out of town when one more quirky wrinkle was added to the already outlandishly strange case. The lawyer lost her receptionist and Dana lost her visitor when "Josie" was arrested and locked up in the same jail in Tavares that held the miserable remnants of the Vampire Clan. The receptionist was assigned to the jail's medical wing after corrections officers discovered during the booking process that Josie Gonzalez was living a lie. The thirty-three-year-old Mount Dora resident wasn't ill—and wasn't a woman—but was a man on the lam from Bowie County, Texas. He was placed in the dispensary to protect him from harassment by other inmates. Gonzalez was on ten years' probation in Texas for a house burglary conviction when he left the state in 1993. After he failed to report to his probation officer, authorities issued a warrant for his arrest.

Gonzalez worked for Plecas for about seven months, and no one suspected the charming employee was anything other than what he presented himself to be. The masquerade was uncovered after agents with the Lake County Sheriff's Department's narcotics unit stopped at Gonzalez' home looking for another man they wanted on a witness-tampering charge.

He wasn't there, so the agents ran information from Gonzalez' driver's license through the police computer and discovered the outstanding warrant.

Plecas was stunned when other employees telephoned and told her about the arrest and the equally startling discovery at the jail. The lawyer visited her former employee, offered what support she could and advised him to waive extradition. Plecas later told reporters that she didn't believe Gonzalez would return to work at the law office. During the visit, her former receptionist had no makeup, his hair was mussed and he appeared sad and withdrawn.

For Dana, the perplexing development was just one more disappointment to deal with. For a while she flirted again with the idea of demanding an early trial, but was talked out of it.

The dreary routine of the defendants, meanwhile, was broken by occasional visits from family members who made the long trips to Tavares from Kentucky or other states when they could scrape together the money, get the time off from work and make all the other necessary arrangements. Jail regulations permit each prisoner one day during the week and one day during the weekend for visits. The days of the week are selected according to the first letter of the last name of inmates and the cellblocks they are assigned to, in order to spread out the workload and avoid accusations of favoritism. The visits, as eagerly as they may have been anticipated, must have been bittersweet. Jails and prisons are uniformly unpleasant places to be, not only for inmates, but for relatives and friends who visit there.

When the Lake County Detention Center was designed, a visiting room was built into the plans that permitted inmates and their friends or relatives to sit at tables together, touch, hold hands or kiss. That wasn't satisfactory to the sheriff and his senior corrections officers because contact visits of that kind virtually invite the passing of contraband. In jails and prisons that allow contact visits, drugs, alcohol, written messages and other illicit materials are passed to prisoners by mouth, feet and hands. Prohibited material is smuggled into visiting rooms inside baby diapers, packed into body orifices, and secreted in the folds of clothing.

The LCDC visiting room was reworked to provide maximum security, and contact visits were firmly ruled out. When Rod, Scott, Charity or Dana were led from their cellblocks to the visiting room, he or she would sit down on a stool in front of a heavy glass partition with a telephone at the side. Their visitors entered the room from an elevator, and sat down on stools next to telephones on the other side of the glass. Visitors and inmates were permitted to look at each other and talk to each other, but no touching was allowed. Inmates constantly ask for contact visits, but Captain Drinan rejects every request. "As far as I'm concerned, if they want a contact visit with their family, then they need to behave themselves and stay out of jail," he says. "We're tough here. We don't cut any slack."

12. RETRIBUTION

"I was not a Betty Crocker type. Not by a long shot."

—Sondra Gibson

On a Monday morning, February 2, more than fourteen months after the brutal murders of Richard and Naoma Wendorf, Rod Ferrell went on trial for his life.

When the skinny seventeen-year-old Kentucky youth was led into the courtroom of Judge Jerry T. Lockett for the beginning of jury selection, his hair was trimmed neatly over his ears, a pair of glasses was perched on his long nose, and he was dressed in a pair of crisply pressed slacks, white shirt, necktie and sweater. He had the look of an "all-American boy" from the placid 1950s. But real all-American boys were free and chasing all-American girls. Rod hadn't tasted freedom, or been within shouting distance of an all-American girl for more than a year. And he was up to his big ears in a desperate fight for his life.

After the long months behind bars he was vampire-pale, and sat quietly beside his attorneys, calmly watching and listening during the opening stages of the deadly serious courtroom contest that was expected to determine if he would spend the rest of his life behind bars, or die in Florida's electric chair. There was no repeat of the juvenile posturing and playing up to cameras that had marked his transfer from Baton Rouge to the Lake County Jail.

The final weeks leading up to the trial were dramatic and filled with new revelations about the double slaying, its immediate aftermath, and Rod's erratic behavior during his uneasy reign as the most notorious inmate in the Lake County Correctional Center. In December he had scuffled with a fifteen-year-old fellow inmate, and created a mini-stir with fanciful speculation about launching a bloody escape attempt.

During hard-fought battles in the courtroom over the admissibility of evidence and other matters, grisly details continued to emerge, indicating that Naoma put up a fierce battle for life, dousing her attacker with hot coffee and raking him with her fingernails before she was bludgeoned so viciously with a crowbar taken from her husband's garage workshop that her skull was crushed and her brain matter oozed out.

The young defendant also lost a last-minute effort to have the videotaped confession he made to police in Baton Rouge ruled inadmissible as evidence. He claimed he drank almost a full bottle of red wine in twelve minutes shortly before his arrest, and didn't understand his rights.

"I wanted to go ahead and see Miss Keesee and I figured if I didn't go along with what they wanted I wouldn't be able to see her," he declared. "I didn't understand the rights back then. If I'd known the impact and known about appointing an attorney [to represent him], I wouldn't have spoke," he said. Ferrell's lawyers contended his juvenile rights were violated, and that he was shackled, coerced and threatened by police in Baton Rouge. Lockett ruled against the motion, and said there was "no proof of unconstitutional threats or coercion." Scott, Dana and Charity were present in the courtroom for similar proceedings, and the judge announced matching decisions in their cases. The confessions would be admissible during their trials.

Rod demonstrated long before the hearing that he didn't need to guzzle a bottle of wine or make a deal for a visit with his girlfriend as an excuse for digging himself into holes by running off his mouth. On December 2, 1997, and again on December 3, the same day as the dust-up with the younger inmate, he approached a pretty corrections officer with honey-blonde hair named Desiree Nutt and began chatting about his case, and about the nuts-and-bolts of a scenario for an escape. The young guard recorded the highlights of the accused killer's remarks on scratch paper, then filed a full report with her superiors.

The incident was publicly disclosed during a pre-trial hearing before Lockett on a defense motion to suppress the report. According to the guard, even though she had advised Rod she didn't want to know anything about his case, he began talking to her about it while she was assigned to the juvenile pod at the jail. He said he knew there were manned gunports on the roof of the jail, and asked if there were cameras in the air-conditioning vents. "But if someone wanted to get out, they could just crawl out through the vents, right?" she quoted him as asking.

Nutt wrote that Rod suggested he could "take out the officer in the shower room," squeeze through a small window, "take out the property person" and make his escape through the vents. "I could take out so many of the dumb deputies. They're not careful at all. Anyway, I'm an amateur assassin," he reportedly boasted. A few days after the one-sided conversation, the guard quit her job at the jail and went to work for a private security service in Jacksonville. Rod stayed right where he was, and there was no dramatic escape bid. The big talk about breaking out of jail and leaving a trail of bodies behind him was apparently merely one more example of his penchant for boasting and talking himself into trouble. Even facing the possibility of death in the electric chair, he couldn't stop running off his mouth.

But he let his lawyers do his talking for him at the trial, and seemed content to occupy himself using crayons to scribble pictures of gargoyles on a yellow note pad while the defense and prosecution teams questioned members of the jury pool about such matters as their attitude toward the death penalty, mental illness, drug abuse and self-mutilation.

Rod's mother, Sondra, sat with a paralegal and an investigator from the Public Defender's Office, intently listening and watching the proceedings from the spectators' seats. As part of a plea agreement the previous November, she was released from custody after pleading guilty to attempting to arrange a sexual encounter with Steven Murphy's fourteen-year-old brother Josh. According to the pact, she was sentenced to a three-year prison term with credit for time served, and the remainder probated for five years. Calloway Circuit Court Judge Dennis Foust consented to the agreement after considering a report by the psychologist in Madisonville who evaluated Sondra and indicated he believed she was delusional. She claimed she was raped by her son's friend, Steven, and believed her life was in danger if she didn't participate in a crossing-over ritual that included having sex with another member of the vampire cult, according to the report. As soon as Sondra was free, she moved back to central Florida to live with her parents in Umatilla, where she would be near her son.

Members of the Wendorf and Queen families watched and listened to the proceedings from seats on the other side of the aisle. On Tuesday, Jennifer attended the second day of voir dire. Seated between her uncle and aunt, William and Gloria Wendorf, the eighteen-year-old peered intently at the jury prospects as they were questioned, occasionally dabbing at tears or brushing at her nose. The family tragedy was predictably difficult for her, and she had withdrawn from FSU to attend the smaller Tallahassee Community College.

After nearly three days of voir dire, a jury of nine men and three women, with two female alternates, was selected from thirty-five potential jurors. Lockett previously trimmed the original pool from sixty-two, after examining questionnaires filled out by the candidates. Several would-be jurors were dismissed by the judge and attorneys after observing that the crime was simply too grisly for them to deal with emotionally, and others were dropped from consideration after they said they could not vote for the death penalty. One candidate was excused after she reported she couldn't vote for a life sentence, because of the expense to taxpayers and privileges that are available to convicts.

Another woman was excused after she said she knew the crime was extremely brutal, and added: "I remember him [Ferrell] having long black hair and sticking his tongue out and laughing. Even being in the same room with him is rather unnerving."

By Thursday morning, the fourth day of the proceeding, spectators and jurors were prepared for a trial that some observers expected to last four weeks, while focusing on defense claims that Ferrell suffered from a personality disorder and was intoxicated when the twin slayings were committed. They were in for an early surprise.

King was only a couple of minutes into his opening statements before the nervous defendant decided, at almost exactly 9:30 AM, to change his not-guilty plea to pleas of guilty to both counts of first-degree murder, guilty to a single count of armed burglary and guilty to one count of armed robbery. After the shock announcement by Lackey and Hawthorne, the jury was ushered into their chambers, and the courtroom was cleared so the defense team could confer with Rod's mother. Sondra had broken down in tears at the surprise announcement. When, during a break, reporters asked her about the surprise development, the distraught woman replied with the cryptic observation, "We live forever." Later, she explained that the remark could refer to either Christian or vampire immortality.

Rod's heartbroken grandfather also talked briefly with reporters, and repeated a comment that was hard to believe the first time he made the observation during the manhunt for the runaway teenagers, and was even more difficult to accept after Rod's courtroom admission that he had brutally bludgeoned two people to death. "Rod's a good boy," Gibson said.

Shortly before noon, Rod stood before the judge to formalize the plea change. Wiping at his nose and speaking in a voice that was reed-thin, shaky and barely audible, he assured Lockett that he understood the terms of the plea and was aware of his legal rights. Rod knew that he still faced the very real possibility of receiving the death penalty, and the best he could hope for would be life in prison without the chance of parole.

The chips were down and Rod was making a desperate, last-minute gamble for life. King was solidly for the death penalty from the beginning of the case, and had refused to offer plea bargains to any of the defendants. He stated clearly that the plea did not change his position: he was still intent on sending the vampire clan leader to the electric chair. It was up to the defense team to convince the jury and the judge during the punishment phase of the suddenly abbreviated trial that their client deserved to live, by presenting mitigating factors to the jury. King was expected to counter any evidence about the dreary circumstances of Rod's childhood that blighted and twisted his life, with aggravating factors—such as the heinous nature of the crime, and the calculated and premeditated manner in which he believed it was carried out.

According to the Florida State Criminal Code, after listening to the arguments of both sides, the jury was required to make a recommendation to the judge for life or death. Unlike the guilt phase of a trial, in the penalty phase, juries are required to reach only a simple majority for their recommendation. Regardless of the jury's opinion, however, the ultimate decision is up to the judge. It was Lockett's call.

The surprise plea set off a new round of motions, and it was a week before the jury was reconvened for the beginning of the penalty phase. Rod's lawyers were especially determined to prevent the prosecution from showing crime-scene and autopsy photographs to the jury, or allowing Jennifer to testify about discovering the bodies of her murdered parents. They also sought to prevent introduction in the trial of DNA evidence. This evidence had been acquired from laboratory analysis of tissue lifted from under Naoma Queen's fingernails. They also hoped to block King from telling the jury about Jennifer arriving home and discovering the mutilated bodies of her parents. Lockett ruled for the prosecution, permitting use of the DNA evidence and the photos. The judge said earlier, after Rod's guilty plea, that he wanted the jury to get an overview of the case, which wasn't made available to them during the guilt phase. But he sided with the defense on the question of allowing the prosecutor to tell the jury about Jennifer's grisly discovery of her parents' bodies.

A few days later, during a special hearing, Lockett also agreed to keep from the jury any references to the maiming of the puppies in Murray, the burglary in Louisiana, or Rod's reputed willingness to shoot police if he considered it necessary. Lockett ruled, however, that King could present information to the jury from statements that Rod made to Gussler and to Baton Rouge detectives. In one of the statements, Rod talked to Gussler about the excitement and sensation of power he felt during the slayings.

"There was a rush to actually . . . feel that . . . I was taking a life, because that's just like the old philosophy about if you can take a life you become a god for a split-second, and it actually kind of felt that way for a minute." Then, in a surprisingly clear-eyed moment of percipience he asked, "But if I was a god, I wouldn't exactly be here, would I?" Scott shared the "rush" during the killings, Rod claimed.

In the meantime, Rod's mother talked with reporters from her parents' home in Umatilla and denied her statements in the Kentucky psychologist's report that she had been raped by Steven. He had a crush on her, she said, and the letters to Josh were designed to fend off the older boy. Since that time she had decided that was a big mistake.

The proceedings Thursday morning were gruesome and heart-wrenching. William and Gloria Wendorf bowed their heads and cried when the grisly photographs of the murder victims were attached to a courtroom easel and pathologist Dr. Laura Hair graphically described the injuries. Hair told the jurors that Richard Wendorf had twenty-two wounds on his head, his skull was fractured and the crowbar bit into his brain. Naoma was beaten so viciously that her brain stem was severed—a condition that would have immediately stopped her breathing.

Testimony by Lake County Sheriff's Deputy Jeff Taylor, who was the first law enforcement officer to enter the home, was equally graphic. Describing Wendorf's body, Taylor testified, "The glasses were bashed up, and the thing that stands out is that his face looked like hamburger." Turning to a description of the body of Naoma, Taylor said: "She had what appeared to be a large hole in the back of her head, and a pool of blood under her head."

Another former Eustis High School student, who wasn't previously publicly identified in press accounts, also testified about exploring aspects of the occult with Rod, then meeting members of his vampire clan members. Seventeen-year-old Audrey Presson said Rod introduced her to his Kentucky friends on the night before the murders. She said Scott told her at that time, "We're going to have some fun tomorrow night." King advised jurors that the remark referred to the killings.

Ms. Presson, who moved to New York several months before the trial, said that when Rod was a student with her in Eustis, they tried together to read and figure out some of the spells in the *Necronomicon*. But it was very confusing. "He was a regular kid with long red hair; dorky, I guess," she said of Rod, prior to his move to Kentucky. The witness said she abandoned her interests in the occult after the murders.

Rod's defense team focused much of their effort to keep him off death row on the testimony of mental health professionals and family members, who were called on to support the thesis that he suffered from mental illness and was a victim of disgustingly gross forms of child abuse.

Dr. Wade Myers, an adolescent psychiatrist, told the jury that Rod had taken speed (amphetamines), smoked marijuana and was mentally disturbed on the night of the murders. He had a learning disability, a history of depression and drug abuse, and had trouble distinguishing fantasy from reality, the expert witness declared.

"Rod was basically an outcast for a good part of his life. He didn't fit in. He was teased. He used drugs in his early teens. He didn't get involved with any positive social activities." The University of Florida psychiatrist added that Rod began hearing voices of angels and devils as a young boy, and smelled sulfur as if a devil was nearby.

Dr. Myers testified that during his interview with Rod, the youth "said delusional things, like he could lift a two-hundred-pound man with one hand, that he could smell blood through walls." Rod's diagnosis pointed to a "schizotypal disorder" that was marked by trouble with relationships and other problems, the witness said.

Myers and Dr. Harry Krop, a forensic psychologist from Gainesville, both repeated horrid stories about a childhood gang-rape that Rod reputedly endured at the hands of friends of his grandfather. "There was a large group of adults and children. They were practicing dark magic to release evil into the world," Krop testified. He said Rod was six years old when he "was sodomized by several of his grandfather's friends."

Myers said the rape reportedly occurred while the boy was on a fishing trip with his maternal grandfather. "Rod came home shaking and upset," the psychiatrist said. "He told her [Sondra] he'd been abused by several men out on the fishing trip. She never felt comfortable letting him be with his grandfather again." Rod claimed the cult was called the "Black Mask," and sodomy, sadism, masochism and mutilation were practiced as part of the rituals.

Harrell Gibson later repeated his denials outside the courtroom that he or his friends had anything to do with cults or had molested his grandson. Rod spun fantastic stories, and lived in a "teenage dream world," Gibson told reporters. It must have been the boy's maternal grandfather, Bobby Ferrell, he suggested. But when King was asked about that version of the story, he said Rod was talking about his grandfather Gibson, not his grandfather Ferrell.

Bobby Ferrell was deceased and couldn't be called on to testify, but his son was available. Rod's long-absent father,

Rick Ferrell, an aviation insurance underwriter, travelled from Frederick, Maryland to testify for the defense. The witness said he believed he could have made a difference in his son's life if he had been allowed more visitation with the boy. Rick Ferrell said he married Sondra, who was a Murray High School classmate, on April 9, 1980. Three weeks later, they separated, he joined the U. S. Air Force in July, and about a year after that he got a divorce.

Ferrell said he hadn't seen his son since 1987, when he took him for a ride on a Cessna. But he denied that he abandoned the boy. "It was difficult to arrange visitations," he said. "Dealing with Sondra was exceptionally difficult. One minute she was extremely friendly, and the next minute she was . . . difficult to work with. She was accusative and fabricated awful lies."

Sondra also testified for her son. Tearful at times, the thirty-five-year-old woman, who another witness had described as walking around Murray holding hands with her son and looking more like his girlfriend than his mother, told the jury about their nomadic wanderings between Kentucky and Florida while the boy was growing up. She said she abused drugs and turned tricks as a prostitute. She also disclosed a brief second marriage with a husband who moved with her to Michigan, leaving Rod behind with her parents. Sondra sobbed while testifying that, after learning her new husband had told her son she was permanently abandoning him, she boarded a Greyhound and returned to Kentucky. Rod was waiting for her when she climbed off the bus in Murray.

Sondra conceded she wasn't a conventional mother, and during questioning by Hawthorne said she was agreeable to permitting Rod to keep a Satanic altar in his bedroom with skulls, pentagrams and an inverted cross.

"Uh-huh, still do," she replied to a later question. "I was not a Betty Crocker type. Not by a long shot."

Some of the most bizarre testimony was presented by Rod's former friend, now turned adversary, Steven Murphy. Rod blew a kiss to "Jaden" as the assistant manager of a

Murray fabric store walked confidently to the witness stand, then proceeded to lift the shroud from the darkly hidden netherworld of real-life vampires. The jury of homemakers, salesmen and retirees listened with rapt attention as Rod's former vampire sire described a bizarre lifestyle that seemed part gothic horror, part teenage silliness.

Murphy explained that vampires don't kill, and are expected to show "the highest admiration for life. We have to live by the laws that surround us. We're not superbeings who can twist things the way we want them," he explained. He scoffed at some of the reported weaknesses and powers that are ascribed to vampires in popular legend, such as fear of garlic, crosses and sunlight—and the gift of immortality. "I am nineteen years old. I can die," he said.

When Murphy was asked if he had fangs, he opened his mouth and stuck out his tongue. His tongue, like his ears, was pierced and a jeweled stud was plainly visible. But his incisors appeared normal; there was no sign of blood fangs. Nevertheless, Murphy said, vampires do crave blood, human or animal.

The witness said he initiated Rod into vampirism during a crossing-over ceremony in a Murray cemetery that involved slashing their arms and sharing each other's blood, following by a lengthy period of meditation. As the senior vampire who initiated Rod, Murphy said he became the younger boy's sire and was responsible for his behavior. And although he explained the rules of vampire conduct to Rod, the witness said, his protegé violated those principles when he organized his own band of followers that included Scott, Dana, Charity, Heather and Jeanine LeClaire.

The Wendorf murders were not vampiric, Murphy explained, because Rod didn't bleed the bodies. "There was no bloodletting. He did not take from them."

Murphy claimed that he was still fond of Rod, but knew soon after learning the Florida couple had been bludgeoned to death that his former protegé was responsible. However, he said he didn't believe that Rod should be put to death for the slayings. "We're all allowed one major faux pas. I don't think he deserves the electric chair. That's the easy way out.''

The jury didn't agree with Rod's vampire sire. After listening to closing arguments at the conclusion of the eight-day proceeding, they deliberated four-and-a-half hours before reporting a unanimous recommendation for the death penalty. Rod lifted his eyebrows and shrugged his shoulders, and his eyes reddened as if he was fighting back tears. But when the dreadful finding of the jury was announced, he stood quietly between his attorneys with his hands folded in front of him, without any other show of emotion.

The timing of Rod's trial and the jury decision was especially ominous because Old Sparky was ready to sizzle back into business. Florida Governor Lawton Chiles, state legislators, corrections and other officials had ironed out the difficulties over the embarrassing flameouts during the two earlier botched executions, and three men and a woman were scheduled to die in the electric chair during a nine-day period through the end of March.

But Rod still wasn't ready to be loaded into a Sheriff's Department cage car to begin the roughly hour-long drive to death row at the Florida State Prison. The day before his scheduled sentencing, the admitted double-murderer, Charity and members of the Wendorf family testified before Judge Lockett outside the presence of a jury in what is known as a ''Spencer hearing.'' The hearing was a new requirement written into the criminal code by state legislators, and apparently represented Rod's last chance to avoid the electric chair.

Charity's attorney was openly angered at the subpoena requiring his client to testify, and she invoked her Fifth Amendment rights against self-incrimination by refusing to answer ten questions from Hawthorne, including queries about her possible drug use and whether or not she told Rod she was pregnant. While Carle hovered protectively a few feet away however, his client—dressed in a neatly pressed gray pant suit and a pair of handcuffs as her most visible accessories—told about meeting Rod at school. Although he acted normal at first, he later developed mood swings and she saw him using marijuana and LSD, Charity testified. When Hawthorne asked if she used drugs, the seventeen-year-old witness invoked the Fifth Amendment.

Charity was still anticipating her own trial, and anything she said at the hearing could be used against her by the prosecution. It was a different story for Rod, who had already been convicted, and his testimony was more revealing. After seating himself at the witness stand, he said that when he observed William Wendorf and other members of the family crying or struggling to hold back tears during the trial, he began for the first time to see the victims as real three-dimensional people. And he blamed Heather for the murder scheme, claiming she repeatedly said during telephone conversations that she wanted her parents dead. When he asked her again after coming to Florida if she still wanted him to kill her parents, she said she did, he claimed.

Rod said he also asked Scott three times while they were driving to the Wendorf house if he still wanted to go through with it, and his friend agreed that he did. "I asked Scott how he felt taking out the parents," Rod stated, "because at that time I was under the impression that Heather's parents had hurt her."

The next morning, Friday, February 27, Rod stood beside his attorney, Candace Hawthorne, wearing handcuffs and his blood-orange jail uniform for what was expected to be his last appearance before Lockett. The fifty-five-year-old judge confirmed the jury's recommendation and sentenced Rod to death.

In passing the sentence, Lockett acknowledged Rod's miserable home life and observed that he came from "one of the most dysfunctional families anyone could be cursed to come from." That, however, was no excuse for the murders, he said. "I think you are a disturbed young man. I think your family failed you. I think society failed you."

Lockett said that in some respects he believed that Rod's mother "should be on trial for some of this," because she had failed to get the help he needed, even after she became aware he was involved in self-mutilation and vampirism.

The distressed jurist, however, also struck out at another much younger person who was closely involved with the condemned youth, and called for prosecutors to reopen the case against Heather. "There are significant questions remaining regarding the involvement of Heather Wendorf in the murders of her parents," the jurist declared. The strong suggestion of the court to Mr. King, our elected state attorney, is that the grand jury be reconvened and these witnesses be presented to the grand jury in an effort for Lake Countians to understand once and for all whether Heather Wendorf was involved in these brutal killings."

While Rod was packing up his meager collection of personal effects and beginning the drive away from the jail for processing into the state correctional system, Sheriff Knupp added his support to the judge's call for another look at Heather's role in the slayings. Captain Daniels talked with reporters and said his boss "believed at the time, and still believes, that there was sufficient probable cause for her arrest." Daniels said Knupp was hopeful that a new grand jury could find evidence of her role in the tragedy.

King responded, however, that he doubted he would follow up on the judge's request. He indicated there was no point in bringing indictments against someone you couldn't prove was guilty. The prosecutor said he was more concerned at the time with directing his energy toward the cases of the remaining defendants.

Almost exactly one month after Rod was locked up on death row, one of those defendants, Scott Anderson, pleaded guilty to participating in the double murder at the Wendorf home as the condemned youngster's principal accessory. The plea was part of a bargain with the prosecutor that included King's agreement to waive the death penalty and settle for a sentence of life in prison without the possibility of parole. Scott was subdued and seemingly contrite as he stood before Lockett early in April, while the judge pronounced the agreed-upon sentences of life in prison without parole on the charges of armed robbery and armed burglary, and to a second life term for being principal to the first-degree murder of the Wendorf couple. The sentences were ordered served consecutively. Scott was transferred from the jail and processed into the state corrections system.

On Wednesday, March 31, the day before Scott entered into his plea bargain agreement and formally changed his plea, spree killer Daniel Remeta died in Florida's electric chair. The last of the four killers put to death in the nine-day span, he was executed for the slaying of a convenience store clerk in Ocala and was also convicted of three murders in Kansas and one in Arkansas during a five-state crime spree. The day before Remeta died, Judy Buenoano became the first woman executed in Florida since 1848, when a freed slave named Celia was hanged in Jacksonville for killing her former master, a Florida planter. Leo Jones was executed on Tuesday, March 24 for the fatal shooting of a Jacksonville policeman in 1981. Jones' execution was carried out a day after the first of the quartet, serial killer Gerald Stano, was put to death for the 1973 strangulation slaying of a seventeen-year-old hitchhiker. Stano confessed to the murder of forty-one women in Florida, Pennsylvania and New Jersey.

With the two principal defendants in the vampire murder case both locked securely away in maximum-security prisons, only the girls remained behind at the Lake County Correctional Center to be put on trial. But by the time Scott was sentenced, Rod's public defenders had already filed for a new trial and were seeking permission to interview the jurors whose recommendation helped make him the youngest resident of Florida's death row. Hawthorne claimed in the action that the jurors didn't give sufficient weight to aggravating factors against mitigating factors in reaching their decision, and didn't give sufficient attention to Heather's role in the tragedy.

While his lawyers stepped up their efforts to spare the vampire prince from the electric chair, Rod was busy on death row reading correspondence from prison groupies and forging a friendship with another of Florida's most notorious killers: Danny Harold Rolling. The son of a Louisiana policeman, Rolling is the infamous mutilation murderer known as the "Gainesville Ripper," who slaughtered four coeds and a young male roommate of one of the girls in a ghastly blood feast at the University of Florida and another smaller college in Gainesville. One of the girls was decapitated, and her head was left on a dresser where it would be the first thing anyone entering the room would see. Rod Ferrell and Danny Rolling were true brothers in blood.

AFTERWORD

The horror that descended on the families of Richard and Naoma Queen Wendorf left entire communities stunned, anguished and undergoing painful self-examination. How could such a calamity have taken place? Why did it happen? And what could be done to prevent something like it from occurring again?

Reverberations of the tragedy extended far beyond Lake and Calloway Counties, where the same questions were being asked, and saddened law enforcement and social agencies, churches, and public servants and community leaders were left to clean up after the devastating emotional trauma and legal clutter scattered by the Vampire Clan.

The grisly double murder of two loving parents and the suspicions that they were victims of teenagers banded together in a deadly blood cult was a national story, and the questions raised by the atrocity were part of a national concern. Writing off the rapidly escalating violence initiated by Rod, which eventually reached out to ensnare his companions and end the lives of the Wendorfs, as a simple case of teenage growing pains, or misdirected rebellion by adolescents intent on asserting themselves and moving into adulthood, simply won't do.

Every adult has been a teenager, and only a minuscule

few have shown themselves to be capable of the kind of monstrous acts committed at 24135 Greentree Lane, or of the almost casual cruelty to animals attributed to Rod and one of his former cronies. That requires a special personality, a unique mindset, and a deadening of the societally cultivated sense of values, fair play and compassion called conscience.

Perhaps the most frightening lesson arising from the round of pained introspection sparked by the outrages blamed on the Vampire Clan is the unsettling realization that the perplexing flash of violence isn't merely an isolated incident, but a symptom of a deeper, more pervasive malady affecting young Americans.

Similar convictions have been voiced before, but the rapidly burgeoning cruelties of the sort linked to the Vampire Clan, and other groups of young people, that are suddenly rolling across the country are taking on a frightening new significance. Adolescents who should be concerning themselves with studies, proms, teenage crushes and zits are making headlines by banding together in groups, loose-knit fraternities and sororities, or cults, and committing unspeakable crimes.

The new barbarians are not members of traditional street gangs from tough urban neighborhoods, with names like "Bloods," "Crips," "Latin Kings" or "Gangster Disciples." They are composed of the sons and daughters of weekend golfers and soccer moms; solid white-bread Americans who for some inexplicable reasons are banding together in criminal conspiracies. They are from the suburbs and from small towns like Eustis and Murray, warm, secure personal havens carefully selected by loving parents to shield and protect their young from the violence, temptations and evil of the big cities. No one, it seems, has given much thought to protecting the parents and other adult authority figures from the kids.

A few months before the Wendorfs were slaughtered in their home, a couple of hundred miles west and downstate along Florida's Gulf Coast, a group of boys calling themselves "the Lords of Chaos" (LOC) launched a short, savage crime spree that began with armed robbery, carjacking and arson, and culminated in the execution-style murder of the band director of their high school. Headed by a nineteen-year-old who called himself "God," the Fort Myers gang was planning to torch the Riverdale High auditorium when the teacher surprised them and chased them off. He warned them to expect a visit from authorities the next day, and a few hours later the club leader, Kevin D. Foster, reputedly blasted him in the face with a .12-gauge shotgun.

All the boys except Foster were superior students at the school, and when they were rounded up they were already planning to steal costumes from employees during their upcoming Grad Night party at Disney World, then shoot down as many black people as they could. The gunman's accomplice in the shooting of the teacher was a member of the school band and had a $20,000 scholarship to the University of Florida. He later pleaded guilty to his role in the slaying and was sentenced to life in prison without parole. Several other members of the group either entered into plea bargains or were convicted of felonies, and sentenced to long prison terms.

A few weeks before "the Lords of Chaos" were rounded up, students at a Waynesville, Missouri, boarding academy for troubled boys hatched a plan to take over the school and form a cult like the Branch Davidians, who attracted notoriety during the fiery standoff with federal agents in Texas. Two of the would-be cultists, a fifteen-year-old and a nineteen-year-old, lured a classmate from Boca Raton, Florida, into a woods where the younger boy slashed his throat with a pocketknife. They killed him because they believed that he opposed the plan to take over the school.

In October 1997, almost eleven months after Rod and his fellow fugitives were apprehended, seven high school chums were arrested following a bloody murder spree in Pearl, Mississippi, a near suburb of Jackson, that claimed the lives of three people. The gang was broken up after sixteen-year-old Luke Woodham stabbed his fifty-year-old mother to death, then stalked onto the Pearl High School campus and began blasting away at classmates with a hunting rifle. Two girls, including the boy's former girlfriend, were killed and seven other students were wounded. A few days after Woodham was taken into custody, police arrested six other boys and, along with their gunman pal, charged them with conspiracy to kill fellow classmates. The boys, who were described by authorities as being of higher than average intelligence, hung around together and favored black clothes. They called themselves "The Group," and shortly after the shootings police began investigating reports of possible Satanic connections.

The savagery of the acts committed by bands of teenagers like the Vampire Clan, the Lords of Chaos, The Group, the boarding academy boys, and later school shootings in Kentucky and Arkansas occurring in such rapid succession, has law enforcement professionals, social scientists and concerned parents asking themselves, What in the world is going on in smalltown America? Are the Vampire Clan and The Group merely an aberration, a temporary quirk, or are their violent acts a warning of worse to come; a peek into the future at a permanent slide into chaos and anarchy?

The usual scapegoats have already been cited by soberminded psychologists, editorial writers and politicians about broken homes, the television wasteland, and guns. Rod's homelife was less than ideal, but he had grandparents nearby who were loving and supportive. Scott lived through some wretched years with his family, but Howard and Martha Anderson were at last working hard to pull their lives together and making sincere efforts to be more effective and supportive parents to their boys. Charity's parents were divorced but they were loving to her and she had other close relatives who were attentive and concerned. A majority of the LOC teenagers and the boys from Mississippi came from two-parent homes with solid middle-class underpinnings.

Trash television, as bad as it is, doesn't appear to have figured prominently in the grave that members of the Vampire Clan dug for themselves. They were too busy with other things to spend hours staring blankly at the tube. Television didn't make Rod, Dana, Charity or Scott begin sharing blood any more than role-playing characters from "Vampire: The Masquerade" did. "Vampire," "Werewolf," "Dungeons & Dragons" and other games like them are exciting, intellectually challenging pastimes that encourage players to use their minds and their imaginations. The dreadful psychic and emotional damage that shaped Rod's character and led to his murderous behavior was present in his life long before he developed his interest in vampirism.

Finally, handguns had nothing to do with the horrendous cruelties blamed on Rod and the Vampire Clan. The Wendorfs were chopped to death with blows from a crowbar, a household tool that is only a little less common than a hammer. The puppies at the shelter were stomped and ripped to pieces, not shot. When Rod fought with his friends, the boys used their fists and feet. There is no indication that any member of the Vampire Clan ever shot at or threatened anyone with a handgun or a rifle. It seems that the only firearm Rod and his friends had anything to do with was the stolen sawed-off shotgun, and they dumped that in the Mississippi River almost as soon as they got their hands on it.

It's true that the teacher who crossed the LOC was killed with a gun, and Woodham also used a firearm at the school. But he stabbed his mother to death. The crowbar wielded against the Wendorfs and the knives used to fatally stab Woodham's mother and the boy at the academy in Missouri were as deadly effective as any .45 automatic or shotgun would have been.

Other answers will have to be found to explain the troubling outbreak of violence and misbehavior that is raging across America with all the unpredictable craziness of a tornado. Teenagers like Charity, Dana, Scott, Heather and others don't carry guns and aren't typical of the usual candidates for serious trouble with the law. They don't fit into the mold—yet each one of them wound up in handcuffs and shackles, accused of horrid crimes. If there is a common denominator, it's that each of them so intently hungered to belong that they allowed themselves to come under the sway of a manipulative peer with an air of authority who promised an opportunity to become part of an exclusive group sharing shadowy secrets. Members of cults are taught to believe that they are specially chosen and must be slavishly devoted to the leader or the group.

Rod attracted his recruits the same way Marshall Applewhite collected the poor deluded people who followed him in suicide, and had much the same appeal as David Koresh. Each of the doomed devotees of Applewhite and Koresh was brainwashed and inexorably weaned away from the influence and protection of any family member who was not part of the group. If a member deviated from the wishes of the leader, or indicated that he or she might pose a threat to his authority, the troublemaker was cast out. When Rod was unable to control Murphy and Goodman, he fought and severed his relationships with them.

Failure to understand destructive cults—and that's exactly what Rod's followers were: the nucleus of a cult—strengthens their power and provides them with the lifeblood they need in order to feed. Murray's Vampire Clan was bizarre and wildly offbeat; exactly the type of organization that can attract certain vulnerable teenagers if the timing and chemistry is right and they have a bit of the rebel in them.

With their leader defanged and the remainder of the band equally powerless, the vampire cult that was cultivated in Murray, and bloomed into a horrible maturity in central Florida, is unlikely to be resurrected—regardless of some local fears. But other cults, gangs or groups that are equally destructive may emerge at any time, and almost certainly will. Then there will be more bloodshed, and more young lives forever blighted.

Even if one or more of the defendants is cleared of all responsibility for contributing to the murder of the Wendorfs, their lives will never be the same. While Scott was crouching in his cell, he might have been in Mayfield, graduating from high school and following his dream to enlist in the Navy and see the world. It is highly unlikely now that he will ever serve aboard a sleek little hunter–killer destroyer like the USS Kidd, an aircraft carrier like the USS Nimitz or one of the hundreds of other ships in the Pacific and Atlantic fleets. He will never walk down the gangplank with a favorite shipmate to pull liberty in Yokosuka, Bangkok, Naples, Marseille or San Diego. The outlook for Rod is also grim, even more so.

Dana and Charity have already wasted some of the best days of their lives in jail. Dana might have been creating a real family of her own with a husband and children to provide the love and companionship she seemed to have been so desperately seeking. Charity has the intellect to excel in her studies and could have been putting her mind to good use building an academic record and qualifying for a college scholarship, while enjoying high school dances and all the other wholesome social experiences available to a pretty teenager. Even if Charity or Dana walk out of the courtroom as free as Heather after their trials, the experience will have left indelible marks on their psyches. Like Heather, they will need to ''decompress,'' and the healing will take time.

Heather, Jeni and other survivors of Richard and Naoma Wendorf have all suffered terrible trauma as a result of the savage act that occurred on Greentree Lane. The same thing is true of family members and other people who love Rod, Scott, Dana and Charity. They have suffered and will continue to suffer.

So, who is to blame? Was it merely bad karma at work? Or was one individual so cruelly warped and twisted from early childhood by forces beyond his control that nothing could have altered the destructive path his life was fated to take?

There are strong indications that Dana and Charity, and very possibly Scott, could have played out their lives without ever getting into serious trouble with the law if they hadn't come under Rod's noxious influence. Could it have been bad chemistry at work? Could it be that if 1930s-era desperadoes Bonnie and Clyde had paired off with other sweethearts, they both would have married, raised children and lived fruitful and peaceful lives? If there had been a Bonnie and Clarence, or a Beverly and Clyde, would they have teamed up to kill cops and rob grocery stores, gas stations and small-town banks until they were finally ambushed by Texas lawmen and blasted into history? Perhaps some people should never meet.

Rod was trouble, and like the seductive vampires of legend and literature, the evil he projected was contagious. Whoever developed or already had close emotional ties and friendships with him took the chance of polluting their lives with the sinister virus he carried and of sharing the malevolence and rot. The morbid, belligerent boy who called himself "Vassago" has shown character traits linked with words in medical textbooks like "psychopath," "sociopath" and "anti-social personality." Some of the traits that might apply to Rod are lack of conscience, a low tolerance for frustration and an inability to look ahead and consider the consequences of his behavior. His actions are indicative of someone who is irrational and filled with rage, and that makes him a very dangerous person.

HE STOLE THEIR HEARTS—THEN TOOK THEIR LIVES...

SMOOTH OPERATOR

THE TRUE STORY OF SEDUCTIVE SERIAL KILLER
GLEN ROGERS

Clifford L. Linedecker

Strikingly handsome Glen Rogers used his dangerous charms to lure women into the night—and on a cruel date with destiny. For when he got them alone, Rogers would turn from a sweet-talking Romeo into a psychopathic killer, murdering four innocent women during a six-week killing spree that would land him on the FBI's "Ten Most Wanted" list. Finally, after a twenty-mile high speed police chase, authorities caught the man now known as one of history's most notorious serial killers.